Statutes Revised

on

Commercial Law
1695 - 1913

Seán ó Cuinn

Sean E. Quinn
B. A. (Hons), H. Dip. in Ed.,
of King's Inns,
Barrister-at-Law,
Lecturer in Law.

Irish Law Publishing

Seo linn sa bhearna baoil

For

Anne

Ena

and

Niall

Published in 1992 by Irish Law Publishing
15 Rathclaren, Killarney, Bray, Co. Wicklow, Ireland

Quinn, Sean Eugene

Statutes Revised on Commercial Law
1695-1913

ISBN 1 871509 07 6 Hbk.

Printed by Colour Books Ltd., Baldoyle, Co. Dublin and
bound by Duffy Bookbinders Ltd., 106 Seville Place, Dublin.

Foreword

A large body of the law that applies in Ireland is based on statutes passed by the parliaments of Ireland from earliest times, together with certain statutes passed by the parliaments of England and Great Britain and by the parliaments of the United Kingdom from the Act of Union. Many of these statutes are not easily obtained, and when found, account has to be taken of any amendments since their passing. As a lawyer, and particularly as a law teacher, it is often necessary to consult and to refer students to these statutes.

This present work will I hope, make some of these statutes readily available. It gathers together a selection of statutes in the area of commercial law. It is to be hoped that practitioners, law teachers and students will find it useful.

A first edition of the Statues Revised for another jurisdiction in Ireland was first published in 1956. There has been no similar work made available in this jurisdiction. There is no easily accessible record of the law that applies in this part of Ireland. The absence of recent volumes of both the Statutes and Statutory Instruments, and of a comprehensive index to either contributes to the problem. The failure of the Executive to rectify the situation is a gross dereliction of duty.

This book is not published by authority and should not be treated as such. The greatest care has been taken to ensure that the text of each statute, as amended, is accurate, however no liability legal or otherwise is accepted for any defect or omission.

I have endeavoured to take account of any enactments up to and including the 16th April 1992.

Sean E. Quinn

Bray
18th May 1992

Contents

Statutes

A short legislative history

There have been a number of distinct legislative periods in Ireland. A basic knowledge of them is useful in understanding the development of Statutory law. What follows is an outline of the parliaments that have promulgated, statutes affecting Ireland.

Establishment of the Parliament of Ireland

By the Treaty of Windsor in 1175, Ard Rí Ruaidrí Ua Conchobair recognised Henry II as his overlord. Thus was established the Lordship of Ireland. In 1210 King John came to Ireland, before his departure he compelled the barons to swear that they would observe the laws and customs of England in Ireland. When King John accepted *Magna Carta* on 15th June 1215, this established the principle that the King could not overrule the law and thus led to the rise of Parliament as a law making body. A Statute of 1236 passed by the Parliament of Ireland was repealed only in 1983. By an Act of 1468 the Irish parliament asserted that it must ratify English statutes in order for them to be valid in Ireland.

Poynings' Law

On the 13th October 1494 Edward Poynings arrived in Ireland, with instructions from King Henry VII to reduce the Lordship of Ireland to "whole and perfect obedience". A Parliament meet in Drogheda on the 1st December 1494, and lasted into 1495. It was this assembly that passed "Poynings Law" which states that: no parliament shall be held in Ireland "till the Lieutenant and council of Ireland shall first certify the King under the Great seal of such causes and acts as them seemeth should pass; then the King and his Council, after affirming such causes and acts to be good and expedient for the said land, shall send his license thereupon, as well in affirmation of the said causes and acts as to summon the said parliament under his Great seal of England: that done, a parliament shall be holden after the form and effect afore rehearsed, any parliament holden hereafter contrary to these forms to be void and of no effect." The freedom of the Irish Parliament to legislate was greatly fettered by Poynings' Law.

The Kingdom of Ireland was established in June 1541, when a parliament specially summoned for the purpose conferred upon Henry VIII the title "King of Ireland".

In its original form Poynings' Law required all proposed bills to be submitted before a licence was issued. During the reign of Philip and Mary, an amendment made possible the introduction of new bills after Parliament had met.

"Sixth of George I"

In 1707 the Parliaments of England and Scotland were united and the Parliament of Great Britain was established. The Parliament of England had asserted a right to legislate for Ireland, but this had been resisted by the Irish Parliament. In 1719 a dispute arose as to the appellate jurisdiction of the Irish House of Lords and the British Parliament in March 1720 passed the Dependancy of Ireland Act, 1719, an "Act for the better securing the dependency of the Kingdom of Ireland on the crown of Great Britain".

Legislative Independence

The legislative curbs on the Parliament of Ireland gave rise to opposition amongst the ascendancy classes throughout the eighteenth century. The establishment of the Volunteers following the American War of Independence eventually led to the successful assertion by Henry Grattan of the independence of the Irish Parliament on the 16th April 1782.

Act of Union

The independent Irish Parliament did not last long after the French Revolution and the United Irishmen. The Government bought itself a majority in the Parliament and on the 28th March 1800, an Act of Union between Great Britain and Ireland was finally accepted. On 2nd August the Parliament of Ireland met for the last time.

United Kingdom of Great Britain and Ireland

The Parliaments of the United Kingdom sitting from 1801 to 1922, passed a great body of law that still applies in Ireland and it is with such legislation that the bulk of this text deals.

Irish Free State

The Constitution of Saorstát Éireann was enacted by Dáil Éireann on 25th October 1922 sitting as a Constituent Assembly. It provided that the laws in force at the date of the coming into operation of the Constitution would continue to be in force and effect until the same, be repealed or amended by the Oireachtas.

Constitution of Ireland

The Constitution of Ireland came into effect on 29th December 1937. Article 50.1 states "Subject to this Constitution and to the extent to which they are not inconsistent therewith, the laws in force in Saorstát Éireann ... shall continue to be of full force and effect until the same or any of them shall have been repealed or amended by enactment of the Oireachtas."

Statutory revision to date

A revised edition of the Statutes passed by the Irish Parliament from the year 1310 to the Act of Union was published under authority in 1885.

A Statute Law Committee for the United Kingdom was established in 1868. The first edition of the Statutes Revised to the year 1878 was published in 1885. The second edition to the year 1920 was published between 1888 and 1929.

Acts of a local or personal nature are not contained in the editions of the Statutes Revised and must be sought elsewhere.

The Interpretation Act, 1889, 52 & 53 Vict. c. 63, at section 35(2) provides that references in any Act passed after the end of that year are, unless the contrary intention appears, to "be read as referring, in the case of statutes included in any revised edition of the statutes purporting to be printed by authority, to that edition"

A first edition of the Statues Revised for another jurisdiction in Ireland was first published in 1954. As stated in the Foreword no similar work has been made available in this jurisdiction.

Accordingly the statute law of Ireland is to be found in the single volume of the Irish Statutes Revised, the twenty-four volumes of the Second Edition of the United Kingdom Statutes, the annual volumes containing legislation passed by the Oireachtas, published since 1922, together with the individual unbound statutes to date.

The thirty-seventh edition of the Chronological Table and Index of Statutes in force for the United Kingdom is the last edition to include Ireland, it refers to all legislation to December 31st 1921.

An Index to the Statutes 1922 to 1982 with Tables and Supplement for 1983 to 1985, has been published by the Stationary Office. An Index to the Statutes for the year 1986 also been published. From 1986 to date it is necessary to peruse the individual statutes to check their effect.

The statutes are not only affected by subsequent statutes, they are also affected by way of subordinate legislation.

Subordinate leglislation

There are two aspects to the effect of subordinate leglislation on the statutes in this text: the making of regulations as required by such statutes and the modification of such statutes by a power to amend contained in subsequent amending leglislation.

The statutory rules and orders were not systematically published or made available to the public in a single series prior to 1890. Those statutory rules and orders which had been made under statutory powers before 1890 and which remained operative were collected and published in eight official volumes in the year 1896.

Between 1890 and 1893 inclusive, annual volumes of Statutory Rules and Orders were published by the Treasury; from 1894 "Statutory rules" as defined by the Rules Publication Act, 1893, 56 & 57 Vict. c. 66, were numbered and printed.

A revised edition of the Statutory Rules and Orders was published in 1903. From 1903 onwards there are annual volumes of the Statutory Rules and Orders. These regulations made prior to 1923 are valid unless they have been subsequently repealed or amended.

The ninth edition of "The Index to the Statutory Rules and Orders" for the United Kingdom, giving reference to every statutory provision authorising the making of Rules or Orders and to the "Statutory Rules and Orders" in force under such authorities on December 31st 1919, was published in 1920. This was the last edition to include Ireland.

Since 1922 any changes by way of subordinate legislation were affected by: Executive Council Orders from 1922 to 1925, Statutory Rules and Orders from 1925 to 1948, and by Statutory Instruments from 1948.

The Statutory Instruments Act, 1947 (No. 44), contains the present leglislation dealing with subordinate leglislation. The Act provides for the making of Statutory Instruments.

There are annual volumes of Statutory Instruments to 1984. The Statutory Instruments have been indexed to December 31st 1986.

A number of Statutes in the text have been amended by means of Statutory Instrument, the power to modify being contained in amending legislation passed by the Oireachtas. Examples of such amending legislation are:

Banker's Books Evidence Act (Amendment) Act., 1959;

Friendly Societies (Amendment) Act, 1977;

Industrial and Provident Societies (Amendment) Act, 1978

Accordingly amendments to statutes passed prior to 1922 must also be sought amongst the Statutory Instruments, such being made under a power contained in a statute passed since 1922.

Guide to the use of this book

Title
Each Act is given its short title in bold, with the session and chapter in plain text. The session and chapter is most useful when seeking to locate the enactment in the official publications.

List of Sections
The text of the Act is preceded by a list of sections (except where there are very few sections). This list is made up of the section headings, except where the section is repealed (which fact is stated). The page number of each section is given for the longer statutes.

Text
The text of each statute consists of the original text with the additions and omissions rendered necessary by subsequent legislation. That is: as amended by the parliament of the United Kingdom prior to 1923 and as amended by the Oireachtas since 1922.

Repealed sections
The section headings of those sections that are repealed are noted in plain text rather than in bold, stating the statutory basis of their repeal. Any repeal within sections of an Act are indicated by dots and a footnote number.

Marginal notes
In the text of the statutes the section headings, together with section numbers, are in bold and are to the head of the section. In some earlier statutes the section headings are spread throughout the section where this is considered appropriate.

The Interpretation Act, 1937 (No. 38), at section 11(g) provides that " No Marginal Notes placed at the side of any section or provision to indicate the subject, contents, or effect of such section ......shall be taken to be part of the Act or instrument or be considered or judicially noted in relation to the construction or interpretation of the Act..."

Footnotes
The affecting provision and in most cases an abbreviation of its effect is stated in the footnotes. The footnote number is repeated in

many of the statutes rather than creating a new footnote.

Citation

The citation of Acts is given as "Credit Union Act, 1966 (No. 21)," rather than as "Credit Union Act, (No. 21 of 1966)", the citation of subordinate legislation is given as "S. I. 385/1985" rather than as "Statutory Instrument No. 385 of 1985"

Expressions

A number of expressions used in the statutes have been officially adapted, where this is the case it is indicated in the text. In addition certain expressions are to be construed or to have effect in a certain way, this too is indicated in the footnotes. Accordingly expressions used in one section of a statute are changed, while in other sections this has not happened in respect of the same expression.

The Constitution (Consequential Provisions) Act, 1937 (No. 40), at section 4(1) with regard to the general adaptation of references to officials and authorities provides: "Every mention in any statute or statutory instrument in force immediately prior to the date of the coming into operation of the Constitution and continued in force thereafter .... of or to any official person or body or any governmental authority, whether legislative, judicial, or executive, established by or under or functioning .(under the Constitution).. shall (b) in relation to anything done or to be done or an event occurring after the coming into force of the Constitution be construed and have effect (unless the context otherwise requires) as a mention of or a reference to the official person or body or the governmental authority (as the case may be) established .. who or which correspondends to or has been or has the like function as ..."

Where it has been considered apppropriate a construction has been incorporated into the text of a statute, there is a footnote to indicate where this has happened.

It may be helpful to read the "United Kingdom" as "the State" or "Ireland", the "Treasury" as "Minister for Finance" and the "Board of Trade" as the "Minister for Industry and Commerce".

Construction

It will be noted from the text that sections or parts of sections rather than having been amended, are by later Acts to be construed, or take effect, in a certain way. A subsequent repeal of the later Act, in the absence of a textual change, restores the original wording. Accordingly constructions must be treated with caution, in the light of possible future amending leglislation.

England, Scotland, etc.

Some material relating exclusively to England, Scotland, the Isle of Man and the Channel Islands is omitted. This will be clear from the text.

Table of amendments

A table of amendments preceeds the text of the statutes. It may be used as a quick reference to find out whether a statute has been amended in any way.

Blank pages

There are a number of blank pages at the end of the book, these will facilitate the inclusion of information on any subsequent amendments to the statutes.

Correspondence

Correspondence about this book is welcome.

S.E.Q.

Table

of

Amendments

Note

All statutes in the text, are listed.

The short title with session and chapter is given

A change in any preamble, sections, or schedule is noted.

A change having general effect is listed at the beginning.

Where there is no listing below a statute, it has not been amended.

Reference is made to the affecting provision, preceded by an abbreviation of how affected.

pre. indicates a preamble, **1.** section 1, **Sch.** a schedule.

Statutes Revised on Commercial Law

Statute of Parliaments of Ireland

Statute of Frauds, 1695
7 William III, chapter 12

1. r. Statute Law Revision (Pre-Union Irish Statutes) Act, 1962 (No. 29), s. 1, sch.
2. r. in pt. Statute Law Revision (Pre-Union Irish Statutes) Act, 1962 (No. 29), s. 1, sch.
3. r. with savings Wills Act, 1837, ss. 2, 34.
4. r. in pt. Statute Law Revision (Pre-Union Irish Statutes) Act, 1962 (No. 29), s. 1, sch.
7. r. in pt. Statute Law Revision (Pre-Union Irish Statutes) Act, 1962 (No. 29), s. 1, sch.
    r. in pt. Succession Act, 1965 (No. 27), ss. 8, 9, sch. 2, pt. II.
8. r. Succession Act, 1965 (No. 27), ss. 8, 9, sch. 2, pt. II.
9. r. with savings Wills Act, 1837, s. 2.
10. r. in pt. Statute Law Revision (Pre-Union Irish Statutes) Act, 1962 (No. 29), s. 1, sch.
12. r. in pt. Statute Law Revision (Pre-Union Irish Statutes) Act, 1962 (No. 29), s. 1, sch.
13. r. Statute Law Revision (Pre-Union Irish Statutes) Act, 1962 (No. 29), s. 1, sch.
14. r. in pt. Statute Law Revision (Pre-Union Irish Statutes) Act, 1962 (No. 29), s. 1, sch.
15 to 18.
    r. with savings Wills Act, 1837, s. 2.
19 & 20.
    r. Succession Act, 1965 (No. 27), ss. 8, 9, sch. 2, pt. II.

Statute of Parliaments of Great Britain

Life Assurance Act, 1774
14 George 3, chapter 48

ext. I. Life Insurance (Ireland) Act, 1866, s. 1.
rstrct. Insurance Act, 1936 (No. 45), s. 51(1).

2. r. in pt. Statute Law Revision Act, 1888.
    ref. Insurance Act, 1989 (No. 3), s. 26(1).
3. r. in pt. Statute Law Revision Act, 1888.

Statutes Revised on Commercial Law

Statutes of Parliaments of the United Kingdom of Great Britain and Ireland

Statute of Frauds Amendment Act, 1828
9 George 4, chapter 14

Pre.   r. Statute Law Revision Act, 1890.
1.   *am. Common Law Procedure Amendment (Ireland) Act, 1853, s. 3.*
           r. Statute of Limitations, 1957 (No. 6), s. 9, sch., pt. 2.
2.   r. Statute Law Revision Act 1890.
3.   *am. Common Law Procedure Amendment (Ireland) Act, 1853, s. 3.*
           r. Statute of Limitations, 1957 (No. 6), s. 9, sch., pt. 2.
4.   *am. Common Law Procedure Amendment (Ireland) Act, 1853, s. 3.*
           r. Statute of Limitations, 1957 (No. 6), s. 9, sch., pt. 2.
5.   r. Statute Law Revision Act, 1875.
6.   r. in pt. Statute Law Revision (No. 2) Act, 1888.
7.   r. Sale of Goods Act, 1893, s. 60, sch.
8.   r. Statute of Limitations, 1957 (No. 6), s. 9, sch., pt. 2.
9.   r. in pt. Statute Law Revision (No. 2), Act, 1888 / Scotland.
10.   r. Statute Law Revision Act, 1873.

Bills of Exchange (Ireland) Act, 1828
9 George 4, chapter 24

r. in pt. Statute Law Revision (No. 2), Act,1888.

Pre.   r. Statute Law Revision Act,1890.
1.   r. Statute Law Revision Act,1873.
2.   r. Bills of Exchange Act, 1882, s. 96, sch. 2.
3.   r. Statute Law Revision Act,1891.
4.   r. Bills of Exchange Act, 1882, s. 96 sch. 2.
5.   r. Statute Law Revision Act,1891.
6.   am. Statute Law Revision (No. 2), Act,1888.
7 to 11.
           r. Bills of Exchange Act, 1882, s. 96 sch. 2.
12.   r. Statute Law Revision Act,1873.
15.   r. in pt. Bills of Exchange (Ireland) Act, 1864.
           r. in pt. Statute Law Revision (No. 2), Act,1888.
16.   r. in pt. Statute Law Revision (No. 2), Act,1888.

Infants' Property Act, 1830
11 George 4 & William 4, chapter 65

ext. I.   Infants' Property (Ireland) Act, 1835, ss. 1, 2.
r. in pt. Statute Law Revision (No. 2), Act,1888.
constr. Age of Majority Act, 1985 (No. 2), s. 2(2).

Pre.   r. Statute Law Revision (No. 2), Act,1888.
1.   r. Statute Law Revision Act,1873.
2.   r. in pt. Statute Law Revision, 1983 (No. 11), s. 1, sch., pt. IV.
3 to 10.
   r. Statute Law Revision, 1983 (No. 11), s. 1, sch., pt. IV.
11.   r. Statute Law Revision Act,1874.
12.   r. in pt. Statute Law Revision Act,1874.
13.   r. Statute Law Revision Act,1873.
14.   r. in pt. Statute Law Revision, 1983 (No. 11), s. 1, sch., pt. IV.
16.   r. Statute Law Revision, 1983 (No. 11), s. 1, sch., pt. IV.
19.   r. Statute Law Revision Act,1873.
21.   r. in pt. Statute Law Revision Act,1873.
22.   r. Statute Law Revision Act,1874.
23 to 25.
   r. Statute Law Revision Act,1873.
26.   r. in pt. Statute Law Revision Act,1873.
27 to 30.
   r. Statute Law Revision Act,1873.
33 to 34.
   r. Statute Law Revision Act,1873.
37.   r. Statute Law Revision Act,1874.
38.   r. in pt. Statute Law Revision Act,1874.
39.   r. Statute Law Revision Act,1874.
40 to 42.
   r. Statute Law Revision Act,1873.
43.   r. Statute Law Revision Act,1874.

Carriers Act, 1830
11 George 4 & William 4, chapter 68

non applic.
   International Carriage of Goods by Road Act, 1990 (No. 13), s. 3(3)

Pre.   r. Statute Law Revision (No. 2) Act,1890.

1.   am. Carriers Act Amendment Act, 1865.
              applic. Railways Act, 1924 (No. 29), s. 51(1), sch. 9;
              Transport Act, 1944 (No. 21), s. 87(1), sch 9.
2.   applic. Railways Act, 1924 (No. 29), s. 51(1), sch. 9;
              Transport Act, 1944 (No. 21), s. 87(1), sch 9.
2 to 10.
              r. in pt. Statute Law Revision (No. 2) Act,1888.
11.   r. Statute Law Revision Act,1888 (No. 2).
              applic. Railways Act, 1924 (No. 29), s. 51(1), sch. 9;
              Transport Act, 1944 (No. 21), s. 87(1), sch. 9

Railway and Canal Traffic Act, 1854
17 & 18 Victoria, chapter 31

ext.   ․ Tramways (Ireland) Act, 1860, s. 46.
ext.   Railway Clauses Act, 1863, s. 31(b).

1.   am. Canals Act, 1986 (No. 3), ss. 2, 18, sch. 3.
2.   *am. Regulation of Railways Act, 1873, s. 11.*
            am. & ext. Railway and Canal Traffic Act, 1888, ss. 25, 28, 59.
            ext. Railways (Private Sidings) Act, 1904, s. 2.
            r. Transport Act, 1958 (No. 19), s. 6, sch. 1.
4. & 5.
            r. Railway and Canal Traffic Act, 1888, s. 59, sch.
6.   am. Canals Act, 1986 (No. 3), ss. 2, 18, sch. 3.
7.   applic. Railways Act, 1924 (No. 29), s. 51(1), sch. 9;
            Transport Act, (No. 21) 1944, s. 87(1), sch. 9;
            Transport Act, 1950, (No. 12) s. 51.
            rstrct.:
            International Carriage of Goods by Road Act, 1990 (No. 13), s. 3(3).

Bills of Lading Act, 1855
18 & 19 Victoria, chapter 111

Bills of Exchange (Ireland) Act, 1864
27 & 28 Victoria, chapter 7

Pre.   r. Statute Law Revision Act, 1893.
1.   r. Statute Law Revision Act, 1875.

2.   am. Statute Law Revision Act, 1893.

Promissory Notes (Ireland) Act, 1864
27 & 28 Victoria, chapter 20

perm.   Expiring Laws Act, 1924 (No. 60), s. 1, sch. 1 pt. 1.

Pre.   Statute Law Revision Act, 1893.
1.   r. in pt. Statute Law Revision Act, 1893.
2.   r. Statute Law Revision Act, 1893.

Life Insurance (Ireland) Act, 1866
29 & 30 Victoria, chapter 42

Pre.   r. Statute Law Revision Act, 1893.
1.   r. in pt. Statute Law Revision Act, 1893.

Policies of Assurance Act, 1867
30 & 31 Victoria, chapter 144

Pre.   r. Statute Law Revision Act, 1893.
4 & 6. rstrct. Finance Act, 1958 (No. 25), s. 40(11);
Income Tax Act, 1967 (No. 6), s. 235(10).

Infants Relief Act, 1874
37 & 38 Victoria, chapter 62

appl.   Age of Majority Act, 1985 (No. 2), s. 2

Pre.   r. Statute Law Revision Act, 1893 (No. 2)

Bankers' Books Evidence Act, 1879
42 & 43 Victoria, chapter 11

applic.   Central Bank Act, 1971, (No. 24), s. 40(1);
Postal & Telecommunications Services Act, 1983 (No. 24),
s. 67(1) & (3)

2.   r. Statute Law Revision Act, 1894.
5.   sub. Central Bank Act, 1989 (No. 16), s. 131(a).
6.   appl. Solicitors (Amendment) Act, 1960 (No. 37), s. 18.
          r. in pt. Central Bank Act, 1989 (No. 16), s. 131(b).
7A.   ins. Central Bank Act, 1989 (No. 16), s. 131(c).
9.   sub. Banker's Books Evidence Act (Amendment) Act, 1959 (No. 21),
          s. 2, sch.
9.1(a). *am. National Bank Transfer Act, 1966 (No. 8), s. 8.*
          constr. S. I. : 20/1972, 21/1972, 22/1972, 23/1972, 24/1972, arts.
          4(a), 9, in all cases.
9.1(d). ins. Trustee Savings Bank Act, 1989 (No. 21), s. 59.
9.1(e). ins. Building Societies Act, 1989 (No. 17), s. 126(1).
9.1(f). ins. ACC Bank Act, 1992 (No. 6).
9.2(a). sub. Central Bank Act, 1989 (No. 16), s. 131(d).
9.4.   ins. Central Bank Act, 1971, (No. 24), ss. 1(3), 56.
9.5.   ins. Trustee Savings Bank Act, 1989 (No. 21), s. 59.
10.   r. in pt. Statute Law Revision Act, 1898.
11.   sub. Central Bank Act, 1989 (No. 16), s. 131(e).

Bills of Sale (Ireland) Act, 1879
42 & 43 Victoria, chapter 50

mod.   Central Bank Act, 1971 (No. 24), s. 36(b).
rstrct. Agricultural Credit Act, 1978 (No. 2), ss. 2, 36.

Pre. r. Statute Law Revision Act, 1894.
2.   r. in pt. Statute Law Revision Act, 1894
8.   r. Bills of Sale (Ireland) Act (1879) Amendment Act, 1883, s. 15.
13, 14, 16 & 17.
          am. Statute Law Revision Act, 1898.
20.   r. Bills of Sale (Ireland) Act (1879) Amendment Act, 1883, s. 15.
23.   am. Statute Law Revision Act, 1894.

Bills of Exchange Act, 1882
45 & 46 Victoria, chapter 61

mod.   Decimal Currency Act, 1970 (No. 21), s. 3.

2.   *ins. Building Societies Act, 1989 (No. 17), s. 126(2).*
          am. ACC Bank Act,1992 (No. 6);

      Central Bank Act, 1989 (No. 16), s. 132(1)(a)(i), (ii), (iii).
3.   appl. Payment of Wages Act, 1991 (No. 25), s. 2(1)(a).
14(1). sub. Central Bank Act, 1989 (No. 16), s. 132(b).
45A.   ins. Central Bank Act, 1989 (No. 16), s. 132(c).
51(4). ins. Bills of Exchange (Time of Noting) Act, 1917, s. 1.
64.   mod. Decimal Currency Act, 1970 (No. 21), s. 4(1) & (2).
76 to 82.
      appl. in pt. Cheques Act, 1959 (No. 19), s. 5.
82.   *ext. Revenue Act, 1883, s. 17.*
      am. Bills of Exchange (Crossed Cheques) Act, 1906, s. 1.
      r. Cheque Act, 1959 (No. 19), s. 6(3), sch.
96.   r. Statute Law Revision Act, 1898.
97(3)(a).
      r. in pt. Statute Law Revision Act, 1898.
Sch.2 r. Statute Law Revision Act, 1898.

Bills of Sale (Ireland) Act (1879) Amendment Act, 1883
46 & 47 Victoria, chapter 7

mod.   Central Bank Act, 1971 (No. 24), s. 36(b).
rstrct.   Agricultural Credit Act, 1978 (No. 2), s. 36(1).

Pre.   r. Statute Law Revision Act, 1898.
10.   r. in pt. Statute Law Revision Act, 1898.
13, 15, & 16.
      r. in pt. Statute Law Revision Act, 1898.

Merchandise Marks Act, 1887
50 & 51 Victoria, chapter 28

rstrct.   Consumer Information Act, 1978 (No. 1), s. 23.
applic.   S.I. 128/1985, reg. 3(g).

2(1)(d) saved, Industrial Research and Standards Act, 1961 (No. 20), s. 23(3).
          am. Consumer Information Act, 1978 (No. 1), s. 4.
2(1)(f) defences, Consumer Information Act, 1978 (No. 1) s. 3(1).
2(2).   am. Consumer Information Act, 1978 (No. 1). s. 4(2).
          constr. Merchandise Marks Act, 1931 (No. 48), s. 29(2).
2(2).   ext. Hallmarking Act, 1981 (No. 18), ss. 5, 18(2).
3(1).   pt. sub. Consumer Information Act, 1978 (No. 1), s. 2(1).

3(1). constr. Consumer Information Act, 1978 (No. 1) s. 2(2)(a).
 appl. Merchandise Marks Act,1891.
 appl. Agricultural Produce (Fresh Meat) Act, 1930 (No 10), s. 27(4).
 appl. Agricultural Produce (Potatoes) Act, 1931 (No. 26), s. 19(4).
 pw. to appl. Spanish Trade Agreement Act, 1936 (No. 6), s. 2.
 appl. Agricultural Produce(Eggs) Act, 1939 (No.2), ss. 38(8)(9), 40(4)
 appl. Seed Production Act, 1955 (No. 14) s. 22(3).
 ext. Road Traffic Act, 1968 (No. 25), ss. 4, 14(2).
 rstrct. Packaged Good (Quality Control) Act, 1980 (No. 11),
 ss. 1(2), 12(1).
5. am. Consumer Information Act, 1978 (No. 1), s. 4(3).
8. r. Hallmarking Act, 1981 (No. 18), ss. 15, 18(2), sch.
8(2). *declarations, S.R. & O. 256/1935.*
9. appl. Merchandise Marks Act, 1931 (No. 48), s. 20(7).
15. pt. r. Restrictive Practices (Amendment) Act, (No. 31), 1987, s. 3,
 sch. 2, pt. 1.
16. ref. Merchandise Marks Act, 1911, s. 1.
 appl. Merchandise Marks Act, 1931 (No. 48), s. 17(1).
 constr. Merchandise Marks Act, 1931 (No. 48), s. 29(1), (4), (5), (6).
16(1). r. in pt. S.I. 238/1985, reg. 2(1).
16(6). r. in pt. Statute Law Revision Act, 1908.
16(8) r. in pt. Merchandise Marks Act, 1931 (No. 48), s. 29(7).
16(10).r. Statute Law Revision Act, 1908.
23. r. in pt. Statute Law Revision Act, 1908.

Factors Act, 1889
52 & 53 Victoria, chapter 45

12(2). sub. Bankruptcy Act, 1988 (No. 27), s. 77.
14. r. Statute Law Revision Act, 1908.
15 r. Statute Law Revision Act, 1908.
16. Virtually r. Factors (Scotland) Act,1890.
Sch. r. Statute Law Revision Act, 1908.

Partnership Act, 1890
53 & 54 Victoria, chapter 39

appl. Limited Partnership Act, 1907.

23(1). r. in pt. Statute Law Revision Act, 1908.

33(1). applic. Bankruptcy Act, 1988 (No. 27), ss. 30 to 37, 138.
48. r. Statute Law Revision Act, 1908.
49. r. Statute Law Revision Act, 1908.
Sch. r. Statute Law Revision Act, 1908.

Merchandise Marks Act, 1891
54 & 55 Victoria, chapter 15

2. r. Merchandise Marks Act, 1931 (No. 48). s. 35, sch.

Industrial and Provident Societies Act, 1893
56 & 57 Victoria, chapter 39

shareholding:
  Creamery Act, 1928 (No. 26), s. 11.
pw. of regd. co-oper. socy. ext.
  Agricultural Credit Act, 1929 (No. 30), s. 29.
rstrct. Creamery Act, 1928 (No. 26), ss. 6, 7, 8;
  Credit Union Act, 1966 (No.19), s. 3(2).
ext. Credit Union Act, 1966 (No.19), ss. 2(1), 39(2).
applic. Credit Union Act, 1966 (No.19), ss. 3(1), 39(2).
applic. rstrct.
  Mergers, Take-overs and Monopolys (Control) Act, 1978 (No. 17),
  s. 14(1).

Pre. r. Statute Law Revision Act, 1908.
2. r. in pt. Statute Law Revision Act, 1908, s. 80, sch.
3. rstrct. Credit Union Act, 1966 (No.19), s. 3(2).
4. ext. Credit Union Act, 1966 (No.19), s. 2(1).
  am. S.I. 392/1985, reg. 3.
  constr. S.I. 246/1990.
4(a). excl. Housing (Ireland) Act, 1919, s. 14(2).
4(b). non applic. Credit Union Act, 1966 (No.19), ss. 36(1), 39(2).
5. mod. Industrial & Provident Societies (Amendment) Act, 1913, s. 11.
5(1). am. Credit Union Act, 1966 (No.19), ss. 37, 39(2), sch. pt. 1.
6 to 8. non applic. Credit Union Act, 1966 (No.19), ss. 36(1), 39(2).
7(1). sub. Industrial & Provident Societies (Amendment) Act, 1895, ss. 3,4.
9(1)(bb) & (bc).
  ins. Industrial and Providend Societies (Amendment) Act, 1978 (No.
  23), s. 34..

10(1) & (6).
non applic. Credit Union Act, 1966 (No.19), ss. 36(1), 39(2).

13(1). r. Industrial and Provident Societies (Amendment) Act, 1913, ss. 3(1), 12(3), sch.

14(2)(c).
sub. Industrial and Provident Societies (Amendment) Act, 1913, ss. 3(1), 12(3), sch.;
am. Credit Union Act, 1966 (No.19), ss. 7(4), 39(2).

14(2)(d)r. Industrial and Provident Societies (Amendment) Act, 1913, s. 12(3).

19. non applic. Credit Union Act, 1966 (No.19), ss. 36(1), 39(2).

23(2). am. Credit Union Act, 1966 (No.19), ss. 37, 39(2), sch. pt. 1.

24. r. Income Tax Act, 1918, s. 238, sch. 7.

25. sub. Industrial and Provident Societies (Amendment) Act, 1913, ss. 5(1), 12(3), sch.

25(1) & (3).
constr. Credit Union Act, 1966 (No.19), ss. 37, 39(2), sch. pt. 1.
constr. S.I. 392/1985, reg. 4.

26. sub. Industrial and Provident Societies (Amendment) Act, 1913, ss. 5(2), 12(3), sch.

26(1) constr. S.I. 392/1985, reg. 5.

27(1). r. in pt. Industrial and Provident Societies (Amendment) Act, 1913, s. 12(3), sch.
constr. S. I. 392/1985, reg. 6.

28. *sub. Industrial and Provident Societies (Amendment) Act, 1913, ss. 6, 12(3), sch.*
r. Credit Union Act, 1966 (No.19) ss. 37, sch. pt. 1.

29. r. in pt. Industrial and Provident Societies (Amendment) Act, 1913, ss. 7, 12(3), sch.

49. applic. Credit Union Act, 1966 (No.19) ss. 36(2).

50(4). ins. Industrial and Provident Societies (Amendment) Act, 1913, s. 9.

51(a) am. Industrial and Provident Societies (Amendment) Act, 1971 (No. 31), s. 1.

53. mod. Industrial and Provident Societies (Amendment) Act, 1913, s. 8.

53(3). ins. Credit Union Act, 1966 (No.19), ss. 37, sch. pt. 1.

54 & 55.
non applic. Credit Union Act, 1966 (No.19), ss. 36(1), 39(2).

56. mod. Mergers, Take-overs and Monopolys (Control) Act, 1978 (No.17), s. 14(3)(a).

58. mod. Industrial and Provident Societies (Amendment) Act, 1913, s: 8.

61(e). adapt. Courts (Supplemental Provisions) Act, 1961 (No. 39), 22(4)(a), sch. 5.

62.   sub. Industrial and Provident Societies (Amendment) Act, 1913, ss. 10, 12(3), sch.
69(3) & (4).
      ins. Industrial and Provident Societies (Amendment) Act, 1913, s. 11.
72.   r. in pt. Industrial and Provident Societies (Amendment) Act, 1913, s. 12(3), sch.
73.   am. S.I. 291/1983.
74.   regs. S.R. & O. 731/1894 & 1551/1914.
      am. S.I. 351/1986.
79.   non appl. Credit Union Act, 1966 (No.19), ss. 36(1), 39(2).
80.   r. Statute Law Revision Act, 1908.
Sch.1   r. Statute Law Revision Act, 1908.
Sch.2   non appl. Credit Union Act, 1966 (No.19), s. 36(1).

Trustee Act, 1893
56 & 57 Victoria, chapter 53

1.   *ext. Colonial Stock Act, 1900, s. 2;*
      Metropolis Water Act, 1902, s. 17(4);
      Housing (Additional Powers) Act, 1919, s. 9;
      Government of Ireland Act, 1920, ss. 33, 73.
      sub. Trustee (Authorised Investments) Act, 1958 (No. 8), s. 1
      pw. to vary, Trustee (Authorised Investments) Act, 1958 (No. 8), s. 2(1)
      add.: S.I. 285/1967, 241/1969, 377/1974, 41/1977, 344/1977, 407/1979, 366/1983, 372/1986, 327/1990, 75/1992
      am. S.I. 58/1983, art. 2, 224/1985, art. 2.
1(a)(ii)ins. Central Bank Act, 1989 (No.16), s. 137(1), s. 137(2).
1(j).   ref. Educational Exchange (Ireland/U S A) Act, 1991 (No. 12), s. 7(e).
1(j)(v).am. 20/1972, 21/1972,22/1972, 23/1972, 24/1972, art 4(b), 9.
2(2).   *appl. Colonial Stock Act, 1900, s. 2.*
      r. Trustee (Authorised Investments) Act, 1958 (No. 8), s. 6, sch.
16.   r. Married Women's Status Act, 1957 (No. 5), s. 19, sch.
21.   r. in pt. Succession Act, 1965 (No. 27), ss. 8, 9, sch. 2, pt. 3.
25.   ext. Trustee Act, 1931 (No. 20), ss. 3, 4.
30.   r. in pt. Trustee Act, 1893, Amendment Act, 1894, ss. 1, 2, 3.
42.   appl. Dublin and Blessington Steam Tramway (Abandonment) Act, 1932 (No. 13), s. 15.
44.   ins. Trustee Act, 1893, Amendment Act, 1894, s. 3.
      rstrct. Conveyancing Act, 1911, s. 4(4).
45(1).   r. in pt. Married Women's Status Act, 1957 (No. 5), s. 19, sch.

51.   r. Statute Law Revision Act, 1908.
54.   r. Statute Law Revision Act, 1908.
Sch.   r. Statute Law Revision Act, 1908.

Sale of Goods Act 1893
56 & 57 Victoria chapter 71

"dealing as consumer":
    Sale of Goods and Supply of Services Act, 1980 (No. 16), ss. 1(2).

3(1).   appl.Trading Stamps Act, 1980 (No. 23), s. 8.
    non applic. International Carriage of Goods by Road Act, 1990 (No. 13), s. 3(3).

11 to 15.
    sub. Sale of Goods and Supply of Services Act, 1980 (No. 16), ss. 1(2), 10.

34 & 35.
    sub. Sale of Goods and Supply of Services Act, 1980 (No. 16), s. 20.

53.   sub. Sale of Goods and Supply of Services Act, 1980 (No. 16), s. 21.

55.   sub. Sale of Goods and Supply of Services Act, 1980 (No. 16), s. 22.
    application of criteria to Sale of Goods and Supply of Services Act, 1980 (No. 16), s. 2(3).
    ref. Sale of Goods and Supply of Services Act, 1980 (No. 16), s. 11

55(1).   rstrct. Sale of Goods and Supply of Services Act, 1980 (No. 16), ss. 12(3), 13(9).

55A.   ins. Sale of Goods and Supply of Services Act, 1980 (No. 16), s. 23.

60.   r. Statute Law Revision Act, 1908.

61(6)   ins. Sale of Goods and Supply of Services Act, 1980 (No. 16), s. 24.

63.   r. Statute Law Revision Act, 1908.

Sch.   r. Statute Law Revision Act, 1908.

Trustee Act, 1893 (Amendent) Act, 1894
57 & 58 Victoria, chapter 10

Industrial and Provident Societies (Amendment) Act, 1895
58 & 59 Victoria, chapter 30

Statutes Revised on Commercial Law
Life Assurance Companies (Payments into Court) Act, 1896
59 & 60 Victoria, chapter 8

Friendly Societies Act, 1896
59 & 60 Victoria, chapter 25

rstrct. re reg.   Credit Union Act 1966 (No. 19), ss. 3(2), 39(2).
Applic. rstrt. Friendly Societies (Amendment) Act, 1977 (No. 17), s. 3(3).
Mergers, Take-overs and Monopolies (Control) Act, 1978 (No.17), s. 14(1).

1.   mod. S. R. & O. 43/1926, par. 4.
         r. in pt. Statute Law Revision Act, 1908.
         constr. Friendly Societies (Amendment) Act, 1977 (No. 17), s. 5(5)
1(4).   r. Registry of Friendly Societies Act, 1936 (No. 51), s. 4(2).
2.   r. in pt. Statute Law Revision Act, 1908.
4.   r. in pt. Statute Law Revision Act, 1908.
5.   constr. Friendly Societies (Amendment) Act, 1977 (No. 17), s. 5(5).
6.   ins. Credit Union Act 1966 (No. 19) ss. 37, 39, sch. pt. 2.
8.   pw. am. Friendly Societies (Amendment) Act, 1977 (No. 17), s. 8.
8(1).   ins. Friendly Societies Act 1908.
         rstrct. Workmen's Compensations Act, 1906, sch. 1;
         Workmen's Compensations Act, 1934 (No. 9), s. 62(8).
         pt. sub. Friendly Societies (Amendment) Act, 1953 (No. 28), s. 2.
         pt. sub. Credit Union Act 1966 (No. 19), ss. 37, 39, sch. pt. 2;
         S.I. 74/1988,
         pt. sub. S.I. 59/1992, reg. 4, sch.
16.   *rstrct. Workmen's Compensations Act, 1906, sch. 1;*
         Workmen's Compensations Act, 1934 (No. 9), s. 62(8).
         pw. am. Friendly Societies (Amendment) Act, 1977 (No. 17), s. 8
36.   r. in pt. Friendly Societies Act 1908, s. 2.
41.   *rstrct. Workmen's Compensations Act, 1906, sch. 1;*
         rstrct. Workmen's Compensations Act, 1934 (No. 9), s. 62(8).
         pw. am. Friendly Societies (Amendment) Act, 1977 (No. 17), s. 8.
41(1). pt. sub. Friendly Societies Act, 1908, s. 3.
         pt. sub. Credit Union Act, 1966 (No. 19), s. 37, 39, sch. pt. 2;
         S.I. 74/1988.
         pt. sub. S.I. 59/1992, reg. 4, sch.
43(1) *am. Territorial Army and Militia Act, 1920, s. 4(1), sch. 2.*
44(1)(f).
         ins. Friendly Societies Act, 1908, s. 4

46(a) to (d).
pw. alter rstrct. Friendly Societies (Am.) Act, 1977 (No. 17), s. 2.

46(b) & (c).
pt. sub. S.I. 74/1988, reg. 3;
S.I. 59/1992, reg. 3.

56 to 61.
appl. National Insurance Act, 1911, s. 42(f);
S.R. & O. 1093/1913

56. pw. am. Friendly Societies (Amendment) Act, 1977 (No. 17), s. 8.

56(1). *pt. sub. Credit Union Act 1966 (No. 19) s. 37, sch. pt. 2.*
pt. sub. S.I. 74/1988.

56(6). ins. Friendly Societies Act, 1908, s. 5.
Friendly Societies (Amendment) Act, 1953 (No. 28), s. 3.

57(1). pt. sub. Friendly Societies Act, 1908, s. 5.
am. Friendly Societies (Amendment) Act, 1953 (No. 28), s. 4(a).
pt. sub. Credit Union Act 1966 (No. 19) s. 37, 39, sch. pt. 2.

57(3) & (4).
r. Friendly Societies (Amendment) Act, 1953, s. 4(b).

58. pw. am. Friendly Societies (Amendment) Act, 1977 (No. 17), s. 8

58(1). *pt. sub. Credit Union Act 1966 (No. 19) s. 37, 39, sch. pt. 2;*
S.I. 74/1988.
r. in pt. Friendly Societies (Amendment) Act, 1953, s. 5.

59. r. Credit Union Act 1966 (No. 19) s. 37, 39(2), sch. pt. 2.

62. pw. am. Friendly Societies (Amendment) Act, 1977 (No. 17), s. 8.
pt. sub. Credit Union Act 1966 (No. 19) s. 37, sch. pt. 2;
S.I. 74/1988.

65. pw. am. Friendly Societies (Amendment) Act, 1977 (No. 17), s. 8.

65(1). *pt. sub. Credit Union Act 1966 (No. 19), s. 37, sch. pt. 2;*
S.I. 74/1988.

68(1)(b).
r. in pt. Friendly Societies Act, 1908, s. 6.

68(8). ins. Friendly Societies Act, 1908, s. 6.

75. ins. Friendly Societies Act, 1908, s. 6.
rstrct. on reg. Mergers, Take-overs & Monopolies (Control) Act, 1978 (No. 17), s. 14(4).

76(4). ins. Friendly Societies Act, 1908, s. 7.

77(1)(b).
am. Friendly Societies (Amendment) Act, 1977 (No. 17), s. 6.

80(1)(c).
am. Friendly Societies Act, 1908, s. 8.

84(a) & (b).
ins. Friendly Societies (Amendment) Act, 1977 (No. 17), s. 7.

87(3). pt. ins. Friendly Societies Act, 1908, s. 9.

am. Friendly Societies (Amendment) Act, 1977 (No. 17), s. 9(1).

88. am. Friendly Societies (Amendment) Act, 1977 (No. 17), s. 9(2).

89. am. Friendly Societies (Amendment) Act, 1977 (No. 17), s. 9(3).

ins. Friendly Societies Act, 1908, s. 10.

91(3). ins. Friendly Societies Act, 1908, s. 10.

94(6) & (7).

ins. Friendly Societies Act, 1908, s. 11.

96. fees, S.I. 290/1983.

97. reduced fees alt. S. I. 46/1982, 148/1983, 359/1984.

99. regs. S.R. & O. 6/1897, 428/1897, 1/1903.

106. ins. Friendly Societies Act, 1908, s. 13.

107. r. Statute Law Revision Act, 1908.

108. r. in pt. Statute Law Revision Act, 1908.

Sch.3 r. Statute Law Revision Act, 1908.

Money-lenders Act, 1900
63 & 64 Victoria, chapter 51

non applic.

Credit Union Act 1966 (No. 19), s. 28.

rstrct. Central Bank Act, 1971 (No. 24), s. 52(1).

non applic.

Postal and Telecommunications Services Act, 1983 (No. 24), s. 67(1)&(3).

1. am. Moneylenders Act., 1933 (No. 36), s. 17(1).

2 & 3. r. Moneylenders Act, 1933 (No. 36), s. 24(1), sch. 2.

6(d). *am. Central Bank Act, 1971 (No. 24), s.52(2).*

as now am. Central Bank Act, 1989 (No. 16), s. 136(a)(i).

6(dd). ins. Central Bank Act, 1989 (No. 16), s. 136(a)(ii).

6(e). *r. in pt. Moneylenders Act., 1933 (No. 36), s. 24(1), sch. 2.*

exempt. S.R. & O. 11/1934.

as now sub. Central Bank Act, 1989 (No. 16), s. 136(a)(iii).

6(f). ins. Industrial & Provident Societies (Amendment) Act, 1978 (No. 23), s. 37.

non applic. S.I. 344/1983, 169/1988.

6A. ins. Central Bank Act, 1989 (No.16), s. 136(b).

7(2). r. Statute Law Revision Act, 1908.

Limited Partnership Act, 1907
7 Edward 7, chapter 24

4(2). non applic. Companies (Am.) Act, 1982 (No. 10), s. 13(5), 24(3).
5. req. Finance Act, 1973 (No. 19), s. 69.
6(2). Bankruptcy Act, 1988 (No. 27), ss. 30 to 37, 138.
6(4). r. Companies (Consolidation) Act, 1908, s. 286, sch. 6 pt. 1.
11. *am. Finance Act, 1920, s. 39(1)(c).*
  r. Finance Act, 1973 (No. 19), s. 96 sch. 11.
17. regs. S.R.& O. 1020/1907.

Friendly Societies Act, 1908
8 Edward 7, chapter 32

Assurance Companies Act, 1909
9 Edward 7, chapter 49

rstrct. Insurance (Amendment) Act, 1938 (No. 31), ss. 3(b), 12, 19(2)(b)
appl. S.I.(EEC): 115/1976; 276/1976; 401/1977; 178/1978; 382/1978;
  65/1983; 57/1984; 296/1985; 297/1985; 437/1986; 143/1988;
  144/1988; 150/1990; 211/1990; 212/1990.

1. adapt. S.R. & O. 7/1928, par. 3.
  non appl. Insurance (Amendment) Act, 1978 (No. 30), s. 1.
  appl. with mods. Insurance Act, 1936 (No. 45), ss. 54, 104.
1(f). ins. Road Traffic Act, 1961 (No. 24), s. 74(1).
2. adapt. E.C.O. 5/1923, pt. 2, par. 1.
  rstrct. Local Authorities (Mutual Assurance) Act, 1926 (No. 34), s. 4.
  appl. Insurance Act, 1936 (No. 45), s. 22(2).
  regs. S.R. & O. 140/1943; 78/1940.
2(5) & (6).
  appl. Insurance Act, 1936 (No. 45), s. 23(4).
2(6). *regs. S.R. & O. 63/1928.*
3(1). r. in pt. Insurance Act, 1936 (No. 45), s. 7(3).
4. am. as to accounts Insurance Act, 1936 (No. 45), ss. 97, 99.
5. rstrct. Insurance Act, 1936 (No. 45), s. 58.
6. ext. Insurance Act, 1936 (No. 45), s. 102(1).
7. add. Insurance Act, 1936 (No. 45), s. 100, 101.
  appl. Insurance Act, 1936 (No. 45), s. 102(2).

7(1).   appl. Insurance Act, 1936 (No. 45), s. 103(2).
13.   rstrct. Insurance (Amendment) Act, 1938 (No. 31), ss. 7(3), 14(3).
19.   adapt. S.R. & O. 7/1928 par. 3
23.   r. Insurance Act, 1989 (No. 3), s. 9, sch. 1.
31(b) to (d).
          r. Insurance Act, 1936 (No. 45), s. 7(1).
31(f).   r. Insurance Act, 1989 (No. 3), s. 9, sch. 1.
32(d), (f) & (g).
          appl. with mods. Road Traffic Act, 1961 (No. 24), s. 74(2).
32(b) & (c).
          r. Insurance Act, 1936 (No. 45), s. 7(1).
32(e).   r. Insurance Act, 1989 (No. 3), s. 9, sch. 1.
33(1)(a).
          r. Insurance Act, 1936 (No. 45), s. 7(1).
(d) & (e).
          r. Insurance Act, 1936 (No. 45), s. 7(1).
(i).   r. Insurance Act, 1989 (No. 3), s. 9, sch. 1.
34(b) & (c).
          r. Insurance Act, 1936 (No. 45), s. 7(1).
35.   r. in pt. Insurance Act, 1936 (No. 45), s. 7.
36.   r. Insurance Act, 1936 (No. 45), s. 7(2).
Sch. 1 to 7
          pw. alt. Insurance Act, 1936 (No. 45), s. 96(1).
Sch.1   Forms C to E, r. Insurance Act, 1989 (No. 3), s. 9, sch.
Sch.1(A) & *(D) 3.*
          adapt. S.R. & O. 7/1928, par. 3, 5.
Sch.3   adapt. E.C.O. 5/1923, pt. 2, par. 1.
          am. Insurance Act, 1936 (No. 45), s. 101.
Sch.4   adapt. S.R. & O. 7/1928, par. 6.
          pw. to mod. Insurance Act, 1936 (No. 45), s. 91(2)(c).
          Forms C to E, r. Insurance Act, 1989 (No. 3), s. 9, sch.
Sch.5   pw. to mod. Insurance Act, 1936 (No. 45), s. 91(2)(c).
Sch.5   am. Insurance Act, 1936 (No. 45), s. 95(a).
          Note 7, r. in pt. Insurance Act, 1936 (No. 45), s. 95(b).
          Form E, r. Insurance Act, 1989 (No. 3), s. 9, sch.
Sch.6   pw. to mod. Insurance Act, 1936 (No. 45), s. 91(2)(c).
Sch.8   pw. to alt. Insurance Act, 1936 (No. 45), s. 96(2).

Merchandise Marks Act, 1911
1 & 2 George 5, chapter 31

1 .   adapt. Merchandise Marks Act, 1931(No. 48), s. 29(1) & (8)

Industrial and Provident Societies (Amendment) Act, 1913
3 & 4 George 5, chapter 31

List of Abbreviations

adapt.	- - -	adapted
add.	- - -	addition, additional
appl.	- - -	applied, applys
applic.	- - -	applicable, application
alt.	- - -	alter, altered
am.	- - -	amend, amended
art.	- - -	article
c.	- - -	chapter
constr.	- - -	construction
del.	- - -	deleted
E.C.O.	- - -	Executive Council Orders
Edw.	- - -	Edward
excl.	- - -	excluded
exempt.	- - -	exemption
ext.	- - -	extended, extension
Geo.	- - -	George
I.	- - -	Ireland
ins.	- - -	inserted
mod.	- - -	modification, modified, modify
No.	- - -	number
p.	- - -	page
par.	- - -	paragraph
perm.	- - -	permanent
pre.	- - -	preamble
pt.	- - -	part, partial
pw.	- - -	power
r.	- - -	repealed
ref.	- - -	reference
reg.	- - -	regulation
regs.	- - -	regulations
req.	- - -	requirements
rstrct.	- - -	restricted
S.I.	- - -	Statutory Instrument
S.R. & O.	- -	Statutory Rules and Orders
s.	- - -	section
sch.	- - -	schedule
sp.	- - -	special
ss.	- - -	sections
sub.	- - -	substituted
s-s.	- - -	subsection
Will.	- - -	William

Statute of Frauds, 1695
7 William III, chapter 12[1]

List of Sections

---

[1] Short Titles Act, 1962 (No. 5), s. 1(1), sch.

An Act for prevention of frauds and perjuries

For prevention of many fraudulent practices which are commonly endeavoured to be upheld by perjury, and subornation of perjury; be it enacted ...

I. Repealed by Statute Law Revision (Pre-Union Irish Statutes) Act, 1962 (No. 29), s. 1, sch.

II. Executor or administrator not to be charged upon special promise out of his own estate, or defendant upon special promise for debt, &c of another, or upon agreement on consideration of marriage, or contract or sale of lands, or any agreement not to be performed in a year, unless in writing and signed.
And be it further enacted by the authority aforesaid,
That ....² .... no action shall be brought whereby to charge any executor or administrator upon any special promise, to answer damages out of his own estate, or whereby to charge the defendant upon any special promise to answer for the debt, default, or miscarriage of another person, or to charge any person upon any agreement made upon consideration of marriage, or upon any contract or sale of lands, tenements, or hereditaments, or any interest in or concerning them, or upon any agreement that is not to be performed within the space of one year from the making thereof, unless the agreement upon which such action shall be brought, or some memorandum or note thereof, shall be in writing, and signed by the party to be charged therewith, or some other person thereunto by him lawfully authorised.

III. Repealed by Wills Act, 1837³ ss. 2, 34, save as to wills made before 1st January 1838

IV. Declarations or creations of trusts of lands shall be in writing and signed, or by last will in writing.
And be it further enacted by the authority aforesaid, That ...².. all declarations or creations of any trusts or confidences of any lands, tenements, or hereditaments, shall be manifested and proved by some writing signed by the party who is by law enabled to declare such trust, or by his last will in writing, or else they shall be utterly void and of none effect.

---

² Repealed by Statute Law Revision (Pre-Union Irish Statutes) Act 1962 (No, 29), s. 1, sch.
³ 7 Will 4 & 1 Vict. c. 26

V. Not to extend to trusts arising by implication, or transferred or extinguished by act of law.

Provided always, that where any conveyance shall be made of any lands or tenements, by which a trust or confidence shall or may arise by implication or construction of law, or to be transferred or extinguished by act or operation of law, then, and in every such case, such trust or confidence shall be of the like force and effect as the same would have been if this statute had not been made; any thing herein before contained to the contrary notwithstanding.

VI. Grants and assignments of trusts shall be in writing signed, or by such last will.

And be it further enacted, That all grants and assignments of any trust or confidence shall likewise be in writing, signed by the party granting or assigning the same, or by such last will and devise, or else shall likewise be utterly void and of none effect.

VII. Lands, &c. in trust, may be delivered in execution upon judgments, &c. as if *cestuy q' trust* in possession,

And be it further enacted by the authority aforesaid, That ..².. it shall and may be lawful for every sheriff, or other officer, to whom any precept or writ is or shall be directed at the suite of any person or persons of, for, and upon any judgment, statute or recognisance hereafter to be made, or had, to do, make, and deliver execution on to the party in that behalf sueing, of all such lands, tenements, rectories, tyths, rents, and hereditaments, as any other person or persons be in any manner of wise seized or possessed in trust for him, against whom execution is so sued, like as the sheriff or other officer might or ought to have done, if the said party against whom execution hereafter shall be so sued had been seized of such lands, tenements, rectories, tyths, rents, or other hereditaments of such estate as they be seized of in trust for him at the time of the said execution sued;

and held free from incumbrances of those seised in trust. ...

which lands, tenements, rectories, tyths, rents, or other hereditaments, by force and vertue of such executions shall accordingly be held and enjoyed, freed, and discharged from all incumbrances of such person or persons, as shall be so seized or possessed in trust for the person against whom such execution shall be sued .....⁴ ..

VIII. Repealed: Succession Act, 1965 (No. 27), ss. 8, 9, sch. 2, pt. II.

IX. Repealed with savings by Wills Act, 1837³, s. 2

---

⁴ Repealed: Succession Act, 1965 (No. 27), ss. 8, 9, sch. 2, pt. II.

X. Mischievous to purchasers that judgments signed in vacation should relate to first day of term, &c.

And whereas it hath been found mischievous, that judgments in the King's courts at Dublin do many times relate to the first day of the term whereof they are entered, or to the day of the return of the original, or fileing the bail, and bind the defendants lands from that time, although in truth they were acknowledged, or suffered, or signed in the vacation-time after the said term, whereby many times purchasers find themselves aggrieved be it further enacted by the authority aforesaid,

Day of signing judgment shall without fee be set down upon the record and entered upon the margent of the roll,

That .² .. any judge or office in his Majesty's courts at Dublin, that shall sign any judgment, shall at the signing of the same, without fee for so doing of the same, set down the day of the month and year of his so doing, upon the paper, book, docket, or record, which he shall sign; which day of the month and year shall be also entered upon the margent of the roll of the record where the said judgment shall be entered.

XI. And as against purchasers shall be judgments from time of signing only.

And such judgments as against purchasers, *bona fide*, for valuable considerations of lands, tenements, or hereditaments, to be charged thereby, shall, in consideration of law, be judgments only from such time as they shall be so signed, and shall not relate to the first day of the term whereof they are entred, or the day of the return of the original, or fileing the bail; any law, or usage, or course of any court, to the contrary notwithstanding.

XII. Writs of execution shall bind property of goods but from the time of delivery of the writ to officer, who shall endorse the day of receiving it.

And be it further enacted by the authority aforesaid, That ..² .. no writ of *fier. fac.* or other writ of execution shall bind the property of the goods of the party against whom such writ of execution is sued forth, but from the time such writ shall be delivered to the sheriff, under-sheriff, or coroner to be executed: and for the better manifestation of the said time, the sheriff, under-sheriff, and coroners, their deputies and agents, shall upon the receipt of any such writ, without fee for doing the same, endorse upon the backside thereof the day of the month and year whereon he or they received the same.

4

XIII. Repealed by Statute Law Revision (Pre-Union Irish Statutes) Act, 1962 (No. 29), s. 1, sch.

XIV. Day of inrolment of recognisances shall be set down in margent of the roll, and lands in hands of purchasers bound from that time only.

And be it further enacted by the authority aforesaid, That the day of the month and year of the inrolment of the recognizances, shall be set down in the margent of the roll where the said recognizances are inrolled; and that ..² . no recognizances shall bind any lands, tenements, or hereditaments, in the hands of any purchaser *bona fide*, and for valuable consideration, but from the time of such inrolment; any law, usage, or course of any court, to the contrary notwithstanding.

XV. to XVIII. Repealed with savings by Wills Act, 1837³, s. 2

XIX. & XX. Repealed by Succession Act, 1965 (No. 27), ss. 8, 9, sch. 2, pt. II.

The Life Assurance Act, 1774
14 George 3, chapter 48[1,2,3]

1. No insurance to be made on lives, etc, by persons having no interest, etc.

2. No policies on lives without inserting the names of persons interested, etc.

3. How much may be recovered where the insured hath interest in lives.

4. Not to extend to insurances on ships, goods etc.

An Act for regulating Insurances upon lives, and for prohibiting all such Insurances except in cases where the persons insuring shall have an interest in the life or death of the persons insured.

Preamble

Whereas it had been found by experience that the making of insurances on lives or other events wherein the assured shall have no interest hath introduced a mischievous kind of gaming:

---

[1] This Act of the Parliament of Great Britain was extended to Ireland by Section 1 of the Life Insurance (Ireland) Act 1866, 29 & 30 Vict. c. 42.

[2] Short Titles Act, 1896, 59 & 60 Vict. c. 14

[3] The Insurance Act, 1936 (No. 45), at section 51(1) Assurances on the lives of children under the age of ten years, provides :

(i) Notwithstanding anything contained in the Life Assurance Act, 1774, as extended by the Life Insurance (Ireland) Act, 1866, it shall be lawful for an industrial assurance company to issue policies of industrial assurance on the life of a child under the age of ten years if, but only if, such policies are issued to a parent, grandparent, step-parent, brother or sister of such child or to an uncle or aunt of such child if such child resides with such uncle or aunt at the time when the policy is effected.

Life Assurance Act, 1774

1. No insurance to be made on lives, etc, by persons having no interest, etc.

From and after the passing of this Act no insurance shall be made by any person or persons, bodies politick or corporate, on the life or lives of any person or persons, or on any other event or events whatsoever, wherein the person or persons for whose use, benefit, or on whose account such policy or policies shall be made, shall have no interest, or by the way of gaming or wagering; and that every assurance made contrary to the true intent and meaning hereof shall be null and void to all intents and purposes whatsoever

2. No policies on lives without inserting the names of persons interested, etc.[4]

And ..[5] .. it shall not be lawful to make any policy or policies on the life or lives of any person or persons, or other event or events, without inserting in such policy or policies the person or persons name or names interested therein, or for whose use, benefit, or on whose account such policy is so made or underwrote.

3. How much may be recovered where the insured hath interest in lives.

And ..[5] .. in all cases where the insured hath interest in such life or lives, event or events, no greater sum shall be recovered or received from the insurer or insurers than the amount of value of the interest of the insured in such life or lives, or other event or events.

4. Not to extend to insurances on ships, goods etc.

Provided always, that nothing herein contained shall extend or be construed to extend to insurances *bona fide* made by any person or persons on ships, goods, or merchandises, but every such insurance shall be as valid and effectual in the law as if this Act had not been made.

---

[4] The Insurance Act, 1989 (No. 3), at section 26(1) provides that this section shall not invalidate a policy of insurance for the benefit of unnamed persons from time to time falling within a specified class or description if the class or description is stated in the policy with sufficient particularity to make it possible to establish the identity of all persons who, at any given time, are entitled to benefit under the policy.

[5] Repealed: Statute Law Revision Act, 1888, 51 & 52 Vict. c. 3

The Statute of Frauds Amendment Act, 1828
9 George 4, chapter 14[1]

An Act for rendering a written Memorandum necessary to the Validity of certain Promises and Engagements
9th May 1828

Preamble repealed by Statute Law Revision Act, 1890[2]

1. Repealed by Common Law Procedure Amendment (Ireland) Act, 1853[3], section 3, and by Statute of Limitations, 1957 (No. 6), section 9, sch., pt. II.

2. Repealed by Statute Law Revision Act, 1890.

3. Repealed by Common Law Procedure Amendment (Ireland) Act, 1853[2], section 3 and by Statute of Limitations, 1957 (No. 6), section 9, sch., pt. II.

4. Repealed by Common Law Procedure Amendment (Ireland) Act, 1853[2] section 3 and by Statute of Limitations, 1957 (No. 6), section 9, sch., pt. II.

5. Repealed by Statute Law Revision Act, 1875[4]

6. Action not maintainable on representations of character, &c. unless they be in writing signed by the party chargeable.
.[6] .. No action shall be brought whereby to charge any person upon or by reason of any representation or assurance made or given concerning or relating to the character, conduct, credit, ability, trade, or dealings of any other person, to the intent or purpose that such other person may obtain credit, money, or goods upon, unless such representation or assurance be made in writing, signed by the party to be charged therewith.

7. Repealed by Sale of Goods Act, 1893[5] s. 60, sch.

8. Repealed by Statute of Limitations, 1957 (No. 6), s. 9, sch., pt. II.

9. ...[6] nothing in this Act contained shall extend to Scotland.

10. Repealed by Statute Law Revision Act, 1873[7]

9

[1] Short Titles Act, 1896, 59 & 60 Vict. c. 14

[2] 53 & 54 Vict. c. 33

[3] 16 &17 Vict. c. 113

[4] 38 & 39 Vict. c. 66

[5] 56 & 57 Vict. c. 71

[6] Deletion: Statute Law Revision (No. 2) Act, 1888, 51 & 52 Vict. c. 57

[7] 36 & 37 Vict. c 91

The Bills of Exchange (Ireland) Act, 1828[1]
9 George 4, chapter 24[2]

List of Sections

---

[1] Short Titles Act, 1896, 69 & 60 Vict. c. 14

[2] Minor am.: Statute Law Revision (No. 2) Act, 1888, 51 & 52 Vict. c. 57

11

An Act ..[3] ..to consolidate and amend the Laws relating to Bills of Exchange and Promissory Notes in Ireland.
19th June 1828

Preamble repealed by Statute Law Revision Act, 1890[4]

1. Repealed by Statute Law Revision Act, 1873[5]

2. Repealed by Bills of Exchange Act, 1882[6], s. 96 sch. 2.

3. Repealed by Statute Law Revision Act, 1891

4. Repealed by Bills of Exchange Act, 1882, s. 96 sch. 2.

5. Repealed by Statute Law Revision Act, 1891

6. Bills accepted in satisfaction of any former debt to be deemed a full payment; but shall not discharge any other security for the debt.

If any person doth or shall receive any such bill or note, for and in satisfaction of any former debt, or of any sum of money formerly due unto such person, the same shall be accounted and esteemed, at law and in equity, a full and complete payment of such debt, if such person so receiving any such bill or note for his debt shall not use due diligence to obtain payment thereof by endeavouring to get such bill accepted and paid, or such note paid, and also make his protest as aforesaid, either for non-acceptance or non-payment thereof, or otherwise give due notice of the dishonour thereof as aforesaid; provided that nothing herein contained shall extend to satisfy or discharge any other and different security or remedy that any person using such due diligence as aforesaid may have for the same debt against the drawer, acceptor, or indorser of such bill, or the maker or indorser of such note.

7. to 11. Repealed by Bills of Exchange Act, 1882, s. 96, sch. 2.

12. Repealed by Statute Law Revision Act, 1873

---

[3] Deletion by Statute Law Revision (No. 2) Act, 1888
[4] 53 & 54 Vict. c. 33
[5] 36 & 37 Vict. c. 91
[6] 45 & 46 Vict. c. 61

13. Notaries public, upon receiving bills to be presented and if necessary noted for non-payment or non-acceptance shall enter and register the same in a book.

And whereas it would be productive of great benefit to the holders of foreign and inland bills of exchange and promissory notes to cause the same to be presented by a notary public and (if necessary) noted for non-acceptance or non-payment, either with a view to a future protest or otherwise, or whether such bills or notes may have been previously presented for acceptance or payment by such holders thereof, or otherwise; and also that such notary shall fairly and truly register and copy such bill of exchange or promissory note as he may so present; and it is therefore expedient to regulate the charges which such notary public may lawfully make in relation to such noting, presentment, registering, and copying: Whenever any bill of exchange or promissory note shall be sent or delivered to any notary public in Ireland, for any of the purposes aforesaid, the same shall be by him forthwith registered and copied in a book to be kept by him for that purpose; and for which registering and copying he shall be entitled and is hereby authorized to make a charge of one shilling, whether such bill shall be afterwards noted or protested or not;

Charges for registering.
presenting.
noting;

and such notary shall be further entitled to make an additional charge of one shilling and sixpence for presenting or causing to be presented any such bill or note for payment or acceptance (as the case may be); and such notary shall be further entitled to make an additional charge of one shilling and sixpence for noting every such bill or note, when the same shall be dishonoured for non-acceptance or non-payment, as the case may be; provided the place where such presentment shall be made shall be within the limits or within the bounds of any city or town in Ireland:

charges to be paid by holders;

Provided always, that every such charge as such notary public shall be so entitled to make as aforesaid shall in all cases be paid and payable to such notary by the holder or holders of such bills or notes;

who may in certain cases recover the amount of such charges from the acceptors or makers.

and every such holder shall be entitled and is hereby authorized to recover over, from the acceptor of any such bill of exchange, or maker of any such promissory note, or other party or parties liable to such holder upon such bill or note, the full amount of such notary's charge as aforesaid, for registering and copying the same in his

13

books as aforesaid, in case such bill or note shall, previously to its being sent or delivered to such notary for the purpose aforesaid, have been duly presented for acceptance or payment, and, if same be payable, shall not have been paid, or the amount thereof duly and legally tendered, or in case the same, though it may not have been so previously presented and dishonoured, shall not, upon being duly presented by such notary, be duly honoured by acceptance or payment thereof, as the case may be; and every such holder shall be further entitled and is hereby authorized to recover over, from such acceptor or maker of such bill or note, or other party or parties thereto, being liable thereon to such holder as aforesaid, the full amount of such notary's said charge for presenting or noting the same, in case the same shall not, upon being so duly presented by such notary as aforesaid, be duly honoured by acceptance or payment thereof, as the case may be: Provided also, that such holder shall be entitled and is hereby authorized to recover over, in like manner, from such acceptor or maker of such bill or note, or other party or parties thereto, as last aforesaid, the full amount of such notary's charge for presenting the same, in case (notwithstanding such acceptance or payment thereof, upon such presentment by such notary as aforesaid) the same had been previously thereto duly presented to such acceptor or maker for acceptance or payment thereof, and such acceptance or payment had not been made:

Where the holder is entitled to recover the notary's charges from the acceptor or maker, the notary may demand the amount of such charges from the acceptor or maker, and if they are not paid may refuse to receive payment of the bill, which shall thereby be dishonoured.

Provided also, that in all cases where the holder of such bill or note shall be entitled, under the aforesaid provisions of this Act, to recover from the acceptor or maker of such bill or note, or other party or parties thereto, such notary's charge for registering and copying in his books, or presenting the same for payment, or noting the same as aforesaid, it shall be lawful for such notary, at the time of presenting such bill or note for the payment thereof, to demand from the acceptor or maker thereof, or the person paying the same, the full amount of such charge or charges, over and above the sum specified in such bill or note; and in case such acceptor or maker shall, on such demand, refused to pay such notary the full amount of such charge or charges, it shall and may be lawful for such notary to refuse to receive payment of the sum specified in such bill or note, or the acceptor of such bill, notwithstanding that the same may be tendered; but every such bill or note shall, by reason of such refusal to pay such charge or charges as aforesaid, be deemed to be and shall be dishonoured to all intents and purposes whatsoever.

14. Sums allowed for protesting and registering foreign bills.

Every such notary public or other person as aforesaid shall be entitled to a sum of four shillings for protesting any foreign bill of exchange, over and above all stamp duty payable upon such protest, and also over and besides the sum of one shilling for registering and copying such bill, as herein-before provided

15. Notaries practising in Dublin to keep a public office

...[3] ...all public notaries practising in the City of Dublin shall keep a public office in some known and convenient street or place in the said city, on which the name of such notary and his profession shall be set forth in legible characters; ..[7] ..

16. Limits of Dublin for the purposes of this Act.

...[3] ., . all places within the City or County of Dublin over which the jurisdiction of the Commissioners for paving, cleaning and lighting the City of Dublin, commonly called the Paving Board, extends, pursuant to an Act passed in the forty-seventh year of his late Majesty George the Third, intituled An Act for the more effectual improvement of the City of Dublin or the environs thereof, shall be deemed and taken to be for the purposes of this Act within the bounds and limits of the said City of Dublin.

17. Act not to repeal former Acts, except so far as is herein provided.

Provided always, that nothing in this Act contained shall be construed to repeal or alter the provisions of any Act relating to bills of exchange or promissory notes now in force in Ireland, saving so far as the same are repealed or altered by the express provisions of this Act.

---

[7] Repealed: Bills of Exchange (Ireland) Act, 1864, *post p. 41*

The Infants' Property Act, 1830[1]
11 George 4 & 1 William 4, chapter 65[2,3]

List of Sections

---

[1] Short Titles Act, 1896, 59 & 60 Vict. c. 14

[2] See generally: Age of Majority Act, 1985 (No. 2), which at section 2(2) provides: Subsection (1) (of that Act) applies for the purposes of any rule of law and, in the absence of a definition or of any indication of a contrary intention, for the construction of "age of majority", "full age", "infancy", "infant", "minor", "minority" and of other cognate words and expressions in-
(a) any statutory provision passed or made before, on or after the commencement of this Act, ...

[3] This Act was extended to Ireland by the Infants' Property (Ireland) Act, 1835, 5 & 6 Will. 4, c. 17, ss. 1, 2.

Infants' Property Act, 1830

An Act for consolidating and amending the laws relating to property belonging to infants, *Feme Covert*, Idiots, Lunatics, and persons of unsound mind
    23rd July 1830

Preamble repealed by Statute Law Revision Act, 1888 (No. 2)[4]

1. Repealed by Statute Law Revision Act, 1873[5]

2. Rules for the interpretation of this Act.

And inasmuch as, in order to avoid unnecessary repetition, certain words are used in this Act as describing subjects some of which, according to their usual sense, such words would not embrace: For the understanding of the sense attached to them in this Act, be it further enacted, that the provisions of this Act shall extend and be understood to extend to and include the several other estates, persons, matters, and things herein-after mentioned; (that is to say,) those relating to land, to any manor, messuage, tenement, hereditament, or real property of whatsoever tenure, and to property of every description transferable otherwise than in books kept by any company or society, or any share thereof or charge thereon, or estate or interest therein; those relating to stock, to any fund, annuity, or security transferable in books kept by any company or society, or to any money payable for the discharge or redemption thereof, or any share or interest therein; those relating to dividends, to interest or other annual produce; those relating to the Bank of England, to the East India Company, South Sea Company, or any other company or society established or to be established; those relating to a conveyance, to any release, surrender, assignment, or other assurance, including all acts, deeds, and things necessary for making and perfecting the same; those relating to a transfer, to any assignment, payment, or other disposition; ....[6] .... unless there be something in the subject or context repugnant to such construction; and whenever this Act, in describing or referring to any person, or any land, stock, conveyance, lease, recovery, matter, or thing, uses the work importing the singular number or the masculine gender only, the same shall be understood to include, and shall be applied to several persons as well as one person, and females as well as males, and bodies corporate as well as individuals, and several lands, stocks, conveyances, leases, recoveries, matters, or things, as well as one land, stock, conveyance,

---

[4] 51 & 52 Vict. c. 57

[5] 36 & 37 Vict. c. 91

[6] Repealed: Statute Law Revision Act, 1983 (No. 11), s. 1, sch. pt. IV

19

lease, recovery, matter, or thing respectively, unless there be something in the subject or context repugnant to such construction.

3 to 10. Repealed by Statute Law Revision Act, 1983 (No. 11)[6]

11. Repealed by Statute Law Revision Act, 1874[7]

12.[8] Guardians of minors, &c. in order to the surrender and renewal of leases, may apply to the Court of Chancery, &c. and by order may surrender such leases, and accept renewals of the same, &c.

In all cases where any person, being under the age of twenty-one years[2], or a *feme covert*, is or shall become entitled to any lease or leases made or granted or to be made or granted for the life or lives of one or more person or persons, or for any term of years, either absolute or determinable upon the death of one or more person or persons, or otherwise, it shall be lawful for such person under the age of twenty-one years[2], or for his or her guardian or other person on his behalf, and for such *feme covert*, or any person on her behalf, to apply to the Court of Chancery in England, the courts of equity of the counties palatine of Lancaster, and Durham, respectively, as to land within their respective jurisdiction, by petition or motion in a summary way; and by the order and direction of the said courts respectively such infant or *feme covert*, or his guardian, or any person appointed in the place of such infant or *feme covert* by the said courts respectively, shall and may be enabled from time to time, by deed or deeds, to surrender such lease or leases, and accept and take, in the place and for the benefit of such person under the age of twenty-one years[2], or *feme covert*, one or more new lease or leases of the premises comprised in such lease surrendered by virtue of this Act, for and during such number of lives, or for such term or terms of years determinable upon such number of lives, or for such term or terms of years absolute, as was or were mentioned or contained in the lease or leases so surrender at the making thereof respectively, or otherwise as the said courts shall respectively direct.

13. Repealed by Statute Law Revision Act, 1873[9].

[7] 37 & 38 Vict. c. 35
[8] Repealed in part by Statute Law Revision Act, 1874
[9] 36 & 37 Vict. c. 91

14. Charges attending renewal to be charged on the estates as the court shall direct.

Every sum of money and other consideration paid by any guardian, trustee, ...⁶ ...... or other person as a fine, premium, or income, or in the nature of a fine, premium, or income, for the renewal of any such lease, and all reasonable charges incident thereto, shall be paid out of the estate or effects of the infant .....² ..... for whose benefit the lease shall be renewed, or shall be a charge upon the leasehold premises, together with interest for the same, as the said courts, and lord chancellor intrusted as aforesaid, respectively shall direct and determine; and as to leases to be made upon surrenders by *femes covert*, unless the fine or consideration of such lease and the reasonable charges shall be otherwise paid or secured, the same, together with interest; shall be a charge upon such leasehold premises, for the benefit of the person who shall advance the same.

15. New leases shall be to the same uses as the leases surrendered.

Every lease to be renewed as aforesaid shall operate and be to the same uses, and be liable to the same trusts, charges, incumbrances, dispositions, devices, and conditions, as the lease to be from time to time surrendered as aforesaid was or would have been subject to in case such surrender had not been made.

16. Repealed by Statute Law Revision Act, 1983 (No. 11)⁶

17. Court of Chancery may authorize leases to be made of lands belonging to infants when it is for the benefit of the estate.

Where any person, being an infant under the age of twenty-one years², is or shall be seised or possessed of or entitled to any land in fee or in tail, or to any leasehold land for an absolute interest, and it shall appear to the Court of Chancery to be for the benefit of such person that a lease or under-lease should be made of such estates for terms of years, for encouraging the erection of buildings thereon, or for repairing buildings actually being thereon, or the working of mines, or otherwise improving the same, or for farming or other purposes, it shall be lawful for such infant or his guardian in the name of such infant, by the direction of the Court of Chancery, to be signified by an order to be made in a summary way upon the petition of such infant or his guardian, to make such lease of the land of such persons respectively, or any part thereof, according to his or her interest therein respectively, and to the nature of the tenure of such estates respectively for such term or terms of years, and subject to such rents and covenants, as the said Court of Chancery shall direct; but in no such case shall any fine or premium be taken, and in every such case the best rent that can be obtained, regard being had to the nature of the lease, shall be reserved upon such lease; and the leases, and covenants and provisions therein, shall be settled and approved of by a master of the said court, and a counterpart of every such lease shall be executed by the lessee or lessees therein to be named, and such counterparts shall be deposited for safe custody in the master's office until such infants shall attain twenty-one, but with liberty to proper parties to have the use thereof, if required, in the meantime, for the purpose of enforcing any of the covenants therein contained; provided that no lease be made of the capital mansion house and the park and grounds respectively held therewith for any period exceeding the minority of any such infant.

18. If persons bound to renew are out of the jurisdiction of the court, the renewals may be made by a person appointed by the Court of Chancery, in the name of the person who ought to have renewed.

Where any person who, in pursuance of any covenant or agreement in writing, might, if within the jurisdiction and amenable to the process of the Court of Chancery, be compelled to execute any lease by way of renewal, shall not be within the jurisdiction or not amenable to the process of the said court, it shall be lawful to and for the said Court of Chancery, by an order to be made upon the petition of any person or any of the persons entitled to such renewal, (whether such person be or be not under any disability,) to direct such person as the said court shall think proper to appoint for that purpose to accept a surrender of the subsisting lease, and make and execute a new lease in the name of the person who ought to have renewed the same; and such deed, executed by the person to be appointed as aforesaid, shall be as valid as if the person in whose name and the same shall be made had executed the same, and had been alive and not under any disability;

Court may direct the party claiming renewal to file a bill to establish his right.

but in every such case it shall be in the discretion of the said Court of Chancery, if under the circumstances it shall seem requisite, to direct a bill to be filed to establish the right of the party seeking renewal, and not to make the order for such new lease unless by the decree to be made in such cause, or until after such decree shall have been made.

19. Repealed by Statute Law Revision Act, 1873[5]

20. Fines to be paid before renewals, and counterparts executed.
Providing always, that no renewed lease shall be executed by virtue of this Act, in pursuance of any covenant or agreement, unless the fine (if any), or such other sum or sums of money (if any), as ought to be paid on such renewal, and such things (if any) as ought to be performed in pursuance of such covenant or agreement by the lessee or tenant, be first paid and performed; and counterparts of every renewed lease to be executed by virtue of this Act shall be duly executed by the lessee.

21. Fines, how to be applied.
All fines, premiums, and sums of money which shall be had, received, or paid, for or on account of the renewal of any lease, after a deduction of all necessary incidental charges and expenses, shall be paid, if such renewal shall be made by or in the name of an infant, to his guardian, and be applied and disposed of for the benefit of such infant, in such manner as the said court shall direct; if such renewal shall be made by a *feme covert*, to such person or in such manner as the court shall direct for her benefit; if such renewal shall be made in the name of any person out of jurisdiction or not amenable as aforesaid, to such person or in such manner, or into the Court of Chancery to such account, and to be applied and disposed of as the said court shall direct; ......[10] ....

22. Repealed by Statute Law Revision Act, 1874,

23, 24, and 25. Repealed by Statute Law Revision Act, 1873.

26. Agreements under recited Act may be made by guardians of infants with the approbation of the court on petition.
The guardian of any infant, with the approbation of the Court of Chancery, to be signified by an order to be made on the petition of such guardian in a summary way, may enter into any agreement for or on behalf of such infant which such guardian might have entered into by virtue of the said last-recited Act, if the same had not been repealed; ......[10].....

27 to 30. Repealed by Statute Law Revision Act, 1873.

31. Surrenders, leased, &c. made under this Act deemed valid.
Every surrender and lease, agreement, conveyance, mortgage, or other disposition respectively, granted and accepted, executed and made, by virtue of this Act, shall be and be deemed as valid and legal to all intents and purposes as if the person by whom, or in whose

---

[10] Repealed by Statute Law Revision Act, 1873, 36 & 37 Vict. c. 91

place, or on whose behalf the same respectively shall be granted or accepted, executed, and made, had been of full age[2], unmarried, or of sane mind, and had granted, accepted, made, and executed the same; and every such surrender and lease respectively made and accepted by or on the behalf of a *feme covert* shall be valid, without any fine being levied by her.

32. Court of Chancery may, on petition order dividends of stock belonging to infants to be applied for their maintenance.

It shall be lawful for the Court of Chancery, by an order to be made on the petition of the guardian of any infant in whose name any stock shall be standing, or any sum of money, by virtue of any Act for paying off any stock, and who shall be beneficially entitled thereto, or if there shall be no guardian, by an order to be made in any cause depending in the said court, to direct all or any part of the dividends due or to become due in respect of such stocks, or any such sum of money, to be paid to any guardian of such infant, or to any other person, according to the discretion of such court, for the maintenance and education or otherwise for the benefit of such infant, such guardian or other person to whom such payment shall be directed to be made being named in the order directing such payment; and the receipt of such guardian or other person for such dividends of sum of money, or any part thereof, shall be as effectual as if such infant had attained the age of twenty-one years[2], and had signed and given the same.

33 and 34. Repealed by Statute Law Revision Act, 1873.

35. Costs may be directed to be paid.

The Court of Chancery, or lord chancellor intrusted as aforesaid, may order the costs and expenses of and relating to the petitions, orders, directions, conveyances, and transfers to be made in pursuance of this Act, or any of them, to be paid and raised out of or from the lands or stock or the rents or dividends in respect of which the same respectively shall be made, in such manner as the said court or lord chancellor shall think proper.

36. Extent of powers given to the court of Chancery in England.

The powers and authorities given by this Act to the Court of Chancery in England shall extend to all land and stock within any of the dominions, plantations, and colonies belonging to his Majesty, except Scotland.

37. Repealed by Statute Law Revision Act, 1874.

38.[11] **Powers given to courts in England may be exercised by courts in Ireland.**

The powers and authorities given by this Act to the courts of Chancery and Exchequer in England shall and may be exercised in like manner, and are hereby given, to the courts of Chancery and Exchequer in Ireland, with respect to land and stock in Ireland.

39. Repealed by Statute Law Revision Act, 1874.

40 to 42. Repealed by Statute Law Revision Act, 1873.

43. Repealed by Statute Law Revision Act, 1874.

44. Act to be an indemnity to the Bank of England and other companies.

This Act shall be and is hereby declared to be a full and complete indemnity and discharge to the Bank of England, and all other companies and societies, and their officers and servants, for all acts and things done or permitted to be done pursuant thereto; and such acts and things shall not be questioned or impeached in any court of law or equity to their prejudice or detriment.

---

[11] Repealed so far as relates to Court of Exchequer in Ireland, Statute Law Revision Act, 1874

25

The Carriers Act, 1830[1,2]
11 George 4 & William 4, chapter 68[3]

---

[1] Short Titles Act, 1896, 59 & 60 Vict. c. 14

[2] The International Carriage of Goods by Road Act, 1990 (No. 13), at section 3(3) provides that this Act, shall not apply in relation to contracts for the carriage of goods if the carriage is carriage in relation to which C M R (the Convention on the Contract for the International Carriage of Goods by Road, done at Geneva on the 19th day of May, 1956, and the Protocol thereto done at Geneva on the 5th day of July, 1978) applies.

[3] Minor amendment to all sections by Statute Law Revision (No. 2) Act, 1888, 51 & 52 Vict. c. 57

An Act for the more effectual Protection of Mail Contractors, Stage Coach Proprietors, and other Common Carriers for Hire, against the Loss of or Injury to Parcels or Packages delivered to them for Conveyance or Custody, the Value and Contents of which shall not be declared to them by the Owners thereof.

23rd July 1830

Preamble repealed by Statute Law Revision (No. 2) Act, 1890[4]

1. Mail contractors, coach proprietors and carriers not to be liable for loss of certain goods above the value of £10 unless they are delivered as such, and an increased charge accepted.

No mail contractor, stage coach proprietor, or other common carrier by land for hire shall be liable for the loss of or injury to any article or articles or property of the descriptions following; (that is to say,) gold or silver coin of this realm or of any foreign state, or any gold or silver in a manufactured or unmanufactured state, or any precious stones, jewellery, watches, clocks, or time-pieces of any description, trinkets, bills, notes of the governor and company of the Banks of England, Scotland, and Ireland respectively, or of any other bank in Great Britain or Ireland, orders, notes, or securities for payment of money, English or foreign, stamps, maps, writings, title deeds, paintings, engravings, pictures, gold or silver plate or plated articles, glass, china,[5] silks in a manufactured or unmanufactured state, and whether wrought up or not wrought up with other materials, furs, or lace,[6] or any of them, contained in any parcel or package which shall have been delivered, either to be carried for hire or to accompany the person of any passenger in any mail or stage coach or other public conveyance, when the value of such article or articles of property aforesaid contained in such parcel or package shall exceed the sum of ten[7] pounds, unless at the time of the delivery thereof at the office, warehouse, or receiving house of such mail contractor, stage coach proprietor, or other common carrier, or to his, her, or their book-keeper, coachman, or other servant, for the purpose of being carried or of accompanying the person of any

---

[4] 53 & 54 Vict. c. 51, also s. 1 in part

[5] In application to Railways Act, 1924 (No. 29), s. 51(1), sch. 7 and Transport Act, 1944 (No. 21), s. 87(1), sch. 9 to read as follows: "glass, china, ...furs, or lace, or any of them,"

[6] The Carriers Act Amendment Act, 1865 (28 & 29 Vict. c.94) at section 1 provides: ..., the term "Lace" shall, with respect to any Parcel or Package delivered after the commencement of this Act (30/9/1865), be construed as not including Machine-made Lace.

passenger as aforesaid, the value and nature of such article or articles or property shall have been declared by the person or persons sending or delivering the same, and such increased charge as hereinafter mentioned, or an engagement to pay the same, be accepted by the person receiving such parcel or package.

2. When any parcel shall be so delivered an increased rate of charge may be demanded.
Notice of such charge be affixed in offices or warehouses.

When any parcel or package containing any of the articles above specified shall be so delivered, and its value and contents declared as aforesaid, and such value shall exceed the sum of ten[7] pounds, it shall be lawful for such mail contractors, stage coach proprietors, and other common carriers to demand and receive an increased rate of charge, to be notified by some notice affixed in legible characters in some public and conspicuous part of the office, warehouse, or other receiving house where such parcels or packages are received by them for the purpose of conveyance, stating the increased rates of charge required to be paid over and above the ordinary rate of carriage as a compensation for the greater risk and care to be taken for the safe conveyance of such valuable articles; and all persons sending or delivering parcels or packages containing such valuable articles as aforesaid at such office shall be bound by such notice, without further proof of the same having come to their knowledge.

3. Carriers to give receipts for increased charges.

Provided always, that when the value shall have been so declared, and the increased rate of charge paid, or an engagement to pay the same shall have been accepted as herein-before mentioned, the person receiving such increased rate of charge or accepting such agreement shall, if thereto required, sign a receipt for the package or parcel, acknowledging the same to have been insured, which receipt shall not be liable to any stamp duty;

In case of neglect to give receipt or affix notice.
Carriers shall not be entitled to benefit of this Act.

and if such receipt shall not be given when required, or such notice as aforesaid shall not have been affixed, the mail contractor, stage coach proprietor, or other common carrier as aforesaid, shall not have or be entitled to any benefit or advantage under this Act, but shall be liable and responsible as at the common law, and be liable to refund the increased rate of charge.

---

[7] Application: Railways Act, 1924 (No. 29), s. 51(1), sch. 7 and Transport Act, 1944 (No. 21), s. 87(1), sch. 9 to read twenty-five pounds.

4. Public notices or declarations by carriers not to limit their liability, but they shall remain liable for all losses from which they are not protected by this Act.

Provided always, that no public notice or declaration heretofore made or hereafter to be made shall be deemed or construed to limit or in anywise affect the liability at common law of any such mail contractors, stage coach proprietors, or other public common carriers as aforesaid, for or in respect of any articles or goods to be carried and conveyed by them; but that all and every such mail contractors, stage coach proprietors, and other common carriers as aforesaid shall be liable, as at the common law, to answer for the loss of any injury to any articles and goods in respect whereof they may not be entitled to the benefit of this Act, any public notice or declaration by them made and given contrary thereto, or in anywise limiting such liability, notwithstanding.

5. Every office used to be deemed a receiving house;

For the purposes of this Act every office, warehouse, or receiving house, which shall be used or appointed by any mail contractor or stage coach proprietor or other such common carrier as aforesaid for the receiving of parcels to be conveyed as aforesaid, shall be deemed and taken to be the receiving house, warehouse, or office of such mail contractor, stage coach proprietor, or other common carrier;

and any one coach proprietor &c. may be sued.

and any one or more of such mail contractors, stage coach proprietors, or common carrier shall be liable to be sued by his, her, or their name or names only;

Action not to abate for non-joinder of co-proprietors. and no action or suit commenced to recover damages for loss or injury to any parcel, package, or person shall abate for the want of joining any co-proprietor or co-partner in such mail, stage coach, or other public conveyance by land for hire as aforesaid.

6. Special contractors not affected.

Provided always, that nothing in this Act contained shall extend or be construed to annul or in anywise affect any special contract between such mail contractor, stage coach proprietor, or common carrier, and any other parties, for the conveyance of goods and merchandises.

7. Parties entitled to damages for loss may also recover the increased charges.

Provided also, that where any parcel or package shall have been delivered at any such office, and the value and contents declared as aforesaid, and the increased rate of charges been paid, and such parcels or packages shall have been lost or damaged, the party entitled to recover damages in respect of such loss or damage shall also be entitled to recover back such increased charges so paid as aforesaid, in addition to the value of such parcel or package.

8. Nothing herein to protect felonious acts.

Provided also, that nothing in this Act shall be deemed to protect any mail contractor, stage coach proprietor, or other common carrier for hire from liability to answer for loss or injury to any goods or articles whatsoever arising from the felonious acts of any coachman, guard, book-keeper, porter, or other servant in his or their employ, nor to protect any such coachman, guard, book-keeper, or other servant from liability for any loss or injury occasioned by his or their own personal neglect or misconduct.

9. Coach proprietors and carriers liable only to such damages as are proved.

Provided also, that such mail contractors, stage coach proprietors, or other common carriers for hire shall not be concluded as to the value of any such parcel or package by the value so declared as aforesaid, but that he or they shall in all cases be entitled to require, from the party suing in respect of any loss or injury, proof of the actual value of the contents by the ordinary legal evidence, and that the mail contractors, stage coach proprietors, or other common carriers as aforesaid shall be liable to such damages only as shall be so proved as aforesaid, not exceeding the declared value, together with the increased charges as before mentioned.

10. Money may be paid into court in all actions for loss of goods.

In all actions to be brought against any such mail contractor, stage coach proprietor, or other common carrier as aforesaid for the loss of or injury to any goods delivered to be carried, whether the value of such goods shall have been declared or not, it shall be lawful for the defendant or defendants to pay money into court in the same manner and with the same effect as money may be paid into court in any other action.

11.[8] In this act the expression 'common carrier by land' shall include a common carrier by land who is also a carrier by water, and as regards every such common carrier this act shall apply to carriage by water in the same manner as it applies to carriage by land.

---

[8] Insertion; original section 11 repealed by Statute Law Revision (No. 2) Act, 1888, 51 & 52 Vict. c. 57, insert applys for the Railways Act, 1924 (No. 29), s. 51(1), sch. 7 and for the Transport Act, 1944 (No. 21), s. 87(1), sch. 9

Statutes Revised on Commercial Law

The Railway and Canal Traffic Act, 1854
17 & 18 Victoria, chapter 31[1,2]

List of Sections

---

[1] Extended to tramways in Ireland, Tramways (Ireland) Act, 1860, 23 & 24 Vict. c. 152, s. 46

[2] Extended to steam vessels, Railway Clauses Act, 1863, 26 & 27 Vict. c. 92, s. 31(b)

An Act for the better regulation of the Traffic on Railways and Canals
10th July 1854

Preamble
Whereas it is expedient to make better provision for regulating the traffic on railways and canals : Be it enacted ...

1. In the construction of this Act....

"Board of Trade"
In the construction of this Act the "Board of Trade" shall mean the Lords of the committee of her Majesty's Privy Council for Trade and Foreign Plantations

"Traffic"[3]
The word "traffic" shall include not only passengers, and their luggage, and goods, animals, and other things conveyed by railway company,.but also carriages, wagons, trucks, and vehicles of every description adapted for running or passing on the railway of any such company:

"Railway"
The word "railway" shall include every station of or belonging to such railway used for the purposes of public traffic: and

"Company"[3]
The expression "railway company," shall include any person being the owner or lessee of or any contractor working any railway constructed or carried on under the powers of any Act of Parliament:

When stations, &c. shall be deemed near one another[3]
A station, terminus, shall be deemed to be near another station, terminus, when the distance between such stations, termini, shall not exceed one mile, such stations not being situate within five miles from St. Paul's Church in London.

2. Repealed by Transport Act, 1958 (No. 19), s. 6, sch 1.

3. Parties complaining that reasonable facilities for forwarding Traffic, &c. are withheld, may apply by Motion or Summons to the Superior Courts.

It shall be lawful for any company or person complaining against any such companies or company of anything done or of any omission made in violation or contravention of this Act to apply in a summary way, by motion or summons,.... in Ireland to any of her Majesty's Superior Courts in Dublin,.... or to any judge of any such

---

[3] R. in pt. Canals Act, 1986 (No. 3), ss. 2, 18, sch. 3

Railway and Canal Traffic Act, 1854

court; and, upon the certificate to her Majesty's Attorney General in.... Ireland or.... of the Board of Trade alleging any such violation or contravention of this act by any such companies or company, it shall also be lawful for the said Attorney General.... to apply in like manner to any such court or judge; and in either of such cases it shall be lawful for such court or judge to hear and determine the matter of such complaint; and for that purpose, if such Court or Judge shall think fit, to direct and prosecute, in such mode and by such Engineer, Barrister, or other Person as they shall think proper, all such inquiries as may be deemed necessary to enable such Court or Judge to form a just judgment on the matter of such complaint; and if it be made to appear to such court or judge on such hearing, or on the report of any such person, that anything has been done or omission made in violation or contravention of this Act by such company or companies, it shall be lawful for such court or judge to issue a writ of injunction or interdict, restraining such company or companies from further continuing such violation or contravention of this Act, and enjoining obedience to the same; and in case of disobedience of any such writ of injunction or interdict, it shall be lawful for such court or judge to order that a writ or writs of attachment, or any other process of such court incident or applicable to writs of injunction or interdict, shall issue against any one or more of the directors of any company, or against any owner, lessee, contractor, or other person failing to obey such writ of injunction or interdict; and such court or judge may also, if they or he shall think fit, make and order directing the payment by any one or more of such companies of such sum of money as such court or judge shall determine, not exceeding for each company the sum of two hundred pounds, for every day after a day to be named in the order that such company or companies shall fail to obey such injunction or interdict; and such monies shall be payable as the court or judge may direct, either to the party complaining, or into court to abide the ultimate decision of the court, or to her Majesty, and payment thereof may, without prejudice to any other mode of recovering the same, be enforced by attachment or order in the nature of a writ of execution, in like manner as if the same had been recovered by decree or judgment in any Superior Court at.... Dublin, in.... Ireland, ...; and in any such proceeding as aforesaid, such Court or Judge may order and determine that all or any costs thereof or thereon incurred shall and may be paid by or to the one party or the other, as such Court or Judge shall think fit; and it shall be lawful for any such Engineer, Barrister, or other Person, if directed so to do by such Court or Judge, to receive evidence on oath relating to the matter of any such inquiry, and to administer such oath.

Railway and Canal Traffic Act, 1854

4. & 5. Repealed by Railway and Canal Traffic Act, 1888[4].

6. Mode of proceedings under this Act.[5]

No proceeding shall be taken for any violation or contravention of the above enactments, except in the manner herein provided; but nothing herein contained shall take away or diminish any rights, remedies, or privileges of any person or company against any railway under the existing law.

7.[6] Company to be liable for neglect or default in the carriage of goods, notwithstanding notice to the contrary.

Every such company as aforesaid shall be liable for the loss of or for any injury done to any horses, cattle, or other animals, or to any articles, goods, or things, in the receiving, forwarding, or delivering thereof, occasioned by the neglect or default of such company or its servants, notwithstanding any notice, condition, or declaration made and given by such company contrary thereto, or in any wise limiting such liability, every such notice, condition, or declaration being hereby declare to be null and void: Provided always, that nothing herein contained shall be construed to prevent the said companies from making such conditions with respect to the receiving, forwarding, and delivering of any of the said animals, articles, goods, or things as shall be adjudged by the court or judge before whom any question relating thereto shall be tried to be just and reasonable:

Company not to be liable beyond a limited amount in certain cases, unless the value declared and extra payment made.

Provided always, that no greater damages shall be recovered for the loss of or for any injury done to any of such animals, beyond the sums herein-after mentioned; (that is to say),[7] for any horse fifty pounds; for any neat cattle, per head, fifteen pounds; for any sheep

---

[4] 51 & 52 Vict. c. 25, s. 59, sch.

[5] As amended by Canals Act, 1986 (No. 3), s. 18, sch 3.

[6] The International Carriage of Goods by Road Act, 1990 (No. 13), at section 3(3) provides that this section, shall not apply in relation to contracts for the carriage of goods if the carriage is carriage in relation to which C M R (the Convention on the Contract for the International Carriage of Goods by Road, done at Geneva on the 19th day of May, 1956, and the Protocol thereto done at Geneva on the 5th day of July, 1978) applies.

[7] In its application as it relates to: Railways Act, 1924 (No. 29), s. 51, sch. 7, Transport Act, 1944 (No. 21), s. 87(1), sch. 9 and Transport Act, 1950 (No. 12), s. 51, shall have effect as follows: "(that is to say), for any horse one hundred pounds, for neat cattle per head fifty pounds, for any other animal five pounds unless the person"

36

or pigs, per head, two pounds unless; the person sending or delivering the same to such company shall, at the time of such delivery, have declared them to be respectively of higher value than as above mentioned; in which case it shall be lawful for such company to demand and receive by way of compensation for the increased risk and care thereby occasioned a reasonable per-centage upon the excess of the value so declared above the respective sums so limited as aforesaid, and which shall be paid in addition to the ordinary rate of charge; and such per-centage or increased rate of charge shall be notified in the manner prescribed in the Carriers Act, 1830, and shall be binding upon such company in the manner therein mentioned:

Proof of value to be on the person claiming compensation

Provided also, that the proof of the value of such animals, articles, goods, and things, and the amount of the injury done thereto, shall in all cases lie upon the person claiming compensation for such loss or injury:

No special contract to be binding unless signed

Provided also, that no special contract between such company and any other parties respecting the receiving, forwarding, or delivering of any animals, articles, goods, or things as aforesaid shall be binding upon or affect any such party unless the same be signed by him, or by the person delivering such animals, articles, goods, or things respectively for carriage:

Saving of Carriers Act.

Provided also, that nothing herein contained shall alter or affect the rights, privileges, or liabilities of any such company under the Carriers Act, 1830[8], with respect to articles of the description mentioned in the said Act.

8. Short title

This Act may be cited for all purposes as "The Railway and Canal Traffic Act, 1854."

---

[8] 11 Geo. 4 & 1 Will. 4, c. 68, *ante, p. 27*

The Bills of Lading Act, 1855[1]
18 & 19 Victoria, chapter 111

An Act to amend the law relating to Bills of Lading.
14th August 1855

WHEREAS, by the custom of merchants, a bill of lading of goods being transferable by endorsement, the property in the goods may thereby pass to the endorsee, but nevertheless all rights in respect of the contract contained in the bill of lading continue in the original shipper or owner; and it is expedient that such rights should pass with the property: And whereas it frequently happens that the goods in respect of which bills of lading purport to be signed have not been laden on board, and it is proper that such bills of lading in the hands of a *bona fide* holder for value should not be questioned by the master or other person signing the same on the ground of the goods not having been laden as aforesaid:

1. Consignees, and endorsees of bills of lading empowered to sue.
Every consignee of goods named in a bill of lading, and every endorsee of a bill of lading, to whom the property in the goods therein mentioned shall pass upon or by reason of such consignment or endorsement, shall have transferred to and vested in him all rights of suit, and be subject to the same liabilities in respect of such goods as if the contract contained in the bill of lading had been made with himself.

2. Saving as to stoppage in transitu, and claims for freight, &c.
Nothing herein contained shall prejudice or affect any right of stoppage in transitu, or any right to claim freight against the original shipper or owner, or any liability of the consignee or endorsee by reason or in consequence of his being such consignee or endorsee, or of his receipt of the goods by reason or in consequence of such consignment or endorsement.

3. Bill of lading in hands of consignee, &c.
Conclusive evidence of shipment as against master, &c.
Every bill of lading in the hands of a consignee or endorsee for valuable consideration, representing goods to have been shipped on board a vessel, shall be conclusive evidence of such shipment as against the master or other person signing the same, notwithstanding that such goods or some part thereof may not have been so shipped,

---

[1] Short Titles Act, 1896, 59 & 60 Vict. c. 14.

unless such holder of the bill of lading shall have had actual notice at the time of receiving the same that the goods had not been in fact laden on board: Provided, that the master or other person so signing may exonerate himself in respect of such misrepresentation by showing that it was caused without any default on his part, and wholly by the fraud of the shipper, or of the holder, or some person under whom the holder claims.

The Bills of Exchange (Ireland) Act, 1864
27 & 28 Victoria, chapter 7

An Act to amend the law relating to Bills of Exchange and Promissory Notes in Ireland
28th April 1864

Preamble repealed by Statute Law Revision Act, 1893[1]

1. Repealed by Statute Law Revision Act, 1875[2]

2. Notaries in Ireland not required to attend after 6 o'clock in the afternoon to receive payment of any bill or note.

....[3] ...It shall not be necessary for any notary public in Ireland, or any person for him, at his house or office, to be in attendance after the hour of six of the clock in the afternoon of any day, in order to receive payment of any bill or note; but every such bill or note whereof payment shall not be made or duly or legally tendered at or before such hour of six of the clock in the afternoon shall be considered to be and shall be dishonoured to all intents and purposes; and thereupon such notary public shall and may note or protest the same for nonpayment, any law, statute, or usage to the contrary notwithstanding.

---

[1] 56 & 57 Vict. c. 14

[2] 38 & 39 Vict. c. 66

[3] Repealed by Statute Law Revision Act, 1893, 56 & 57 Vict. c. 14

The Promissory Notes (Ireland) Act, 1864[1]
27 & 28 Victoria, chapter 20

An Act to remove certain restrictions on the negotiation of Promissory Notes and Bills of Exchange under a limited sum in Ireland.
13th May 1864

Preamble repealed by Statute Law Revision Act, 1893[2]

1. So much of 8 & 9 Vict. c. 37 as restrains the negotiations in Ireland of notes and bills under £5 repealed.
..[3] .. So much and such parts of the Bankers (Ireland) Act, 1845, as prohibits the drawing, making, and issuing or restrains or imposes any penalty for or on account of the publishing, uttering, or negotiating, in Ireland, of any promissory or other note (not being a note payable to bearer on demand), bill of exchange, draft, or undertaking in writing, being negotiable or transferable, for the payment of twenty shillings, or above that sum and less than five pounds, or on which twenty shillings, or above that sum and less than five pounds, shall remain undischarged, made, drawn, or endorsed in any other manner than is directed by the said Act, or which requires or directs that all such notes, bills, drafts, or undertakings as aforesaid which shall be issued in Ireland shall be made, drawn, or endorsed according to the forms contained in the schedules to the said Act, shall be and the same is and are hereby repealed.

2. Repealed by Statute Law Revision Act, 1893[2]

---

[1] Made permanent: Expiring Laws Act, 1924 (No. 60) s. 1, sch. 1, pt. I
[2] 56 & 57 Vict. c. 14
[3] Repealed by 56 & 57 Vict. c. 14

The Life Insurance (Ireland) Act, 1866
29 & 30 Victoria, chapter 42[1]

An Act to amend the law relating to life insurance in Ireland
28th June 1866

Preamble which recites Life Assurance Act, 1774, repealed by Statute
Law Revision Act, 1893[2]

1. Recited Act extended to Ireland.
......[3] ....the provisions of the said recited Act shall extend to
Ireland.

2. Commencement of Act.
This Act shall commence and takes effect from and after the first
day of November in the year one thousand eight hundred and sixty-
six, and shall apply to all policies of insurance upon lives entered into
upon and after that date.

---

[1] Short Titles Act, 1896, 59 & 60 Vict. c. 14

[2] 56 & 57 Vict. c. 14

[3] Repealed by 56 & 57 Vict. c. 14

Statutes Revised on Commercial Law

The Policies of Assurance Act, 1867
30 & 31 Victoria, chapter 144

List of Sections

An Act to enable Assignees of Policies of Life Assurance to sue thereon in their own names
20th August 1867

Preamble repealed by Statute Law Revision Act, 1893[1]

1. Assignees of life policies, empowered to sue
Any person or corporation now being or hereafter becoming entitled, by assignment or other derivative title, to a policy of life assurance, and possessing at the time of action brought the right in equity to receive and the right to give an effectual discharge to the assurance company liable under such policy for monies thereby assured or secured, shall be at liberty to sue at law in the name of such person or corporation to recover such monies.

2. Defence or reply on equitable grounds
In any action on a policy of life assurance, a defence on equitable grounds, or a reply to such defence on similar grounds, may be respectively pleaded and relied upon in the same manner and to the same extent as in any other personal action.

---

[1] 56 & 57 Vict. c. 14

47

3. Notice of assignment

No assignment made after the passing of this Act of a policy of life assurance shall confer on the assignee therein named, his executors, administrators, or assigns, any right to sue for the amount of such policy, or the monies assured or secured thereby, until a written notice of the date and purport of such assignment shall have been given to the assurance company liable under such policy at their principal place of business for the time being, or in case they have two or more principal places of business, then at some one of such principal places of business, either in England or Scotland or Ireland: and the date on which such notice shall be received shall regulate the priority of all claims under any assignment; and a payment bona fide made in respect of any policy by any assurance company before the date on which such notice shall have been received shall be as valid against the assignee giving such notice as if this Act had not been passed.

4.[2] Principal place of business to be specified on policies

Every assurance company shall, on every policy issued by them after the thirtieth day of September one thousand eight hundred and sixty-seven, specify their principal place or principal places of business at which notices of assignment may be given in pursuance of this Act.

5. Mode of assignment

Any such assignment may be made either by endorsement on the policy or by a separate instrument in the words or the effect set forth in the schedule hereto, such endorsement of separate instrument being duly stamped.

6.[2] Receipt of notices of assignment

Every assurance company to whom notice shall have been duly given of the assignment of any policy under which they are liable shall, upon the request in writing of any person by whom any such notice was given or signed, or of his executors, or administrators, and upon payment in each case of a fee not exceeding five shillings, deliver an acknowledgement in writing, under the hand of the manager, secretary, treasurer or other principal officer of the assurance company, of their receipt of such notice; and every such written acknowledgement, if signed by a person being *de jure* or *de facto* the manager, secretary, treasurer or other principal officer of the assurance company whose acknowledgement the same purports to be, shall be conclusive evidence as against such assurance

---

[2] Does not apply to Finance Act, 1958 (No. 25), s. 40(11) or, Income Tax Act, 1967 (No. 6), s. 235(10), regarding retirement annuities.

Policies of Assurance Act, 1867

company of their having duly received the notice to which such acknowledgement relates.

7. Interpretation of terms

In the construction and for the purposes of this Act the expression "policy of life assurance" or "policy" shall mean any instrument by which the payment of monies by or out of the funds of an assurance company, on the happening of any contingency depending on the duration of human life, is assured or secured; and the expression "assurance company" shall mean and include every corporation, association, society, or company now or hereafter carrying on the business of assuring lives, or survivorships, either alone or in conjunction with any other object or objects.

8. Saving of contracts under 16 & 17 Vict. c. 45 or 27 & 28 Vict. c. 43 and of engagements by friendly societies

Provided always, that this Act shall not apply to any policy of assurance granted or to be granted or to any contract for a payment on death entered into or to be entered into in pursuance of the provisions of the Acts sixteenth and seventeenth Victoria chapter forty-five[3], and twenty-seventh and twenty-eight Victoria chapter forty-three[4], or either of those Acts, or to any engagement for payment on death by any friendly society.

9. Short title

For all purposes this Act may be cited as "The Policies of Assurance Act, 1867".

Schedule

Section 5

I, A.B. of, &c., in consideration of, &c., do hereby assign unto C.D., of, &c., his executors, administrators, and assigns, the [within] policy of assurance granted, &c. [here describe the policy].

In witness, &c.

---

[3] Government Annuities Act, 1853
[4] Government Annuities Act, 1864

49

Statutes Revised on Commercial Law

The Infants Relief Act, 1874
37 & 38 Victoria, chapter 62

An Act to amend the Law as to the Contracts of Infants[1]
7th August 1874

Preamble repealed by Statute Law Revision Act, 1893 (No. 2)[2]

1. Contracts by infants, except for necessaries to be void.
All contracts, whether by specialty or by simple contract, henceforth entered into by infants for the repayment of money lent or to be lent, or for goods supplied or to be supplied (other than contracts for necessaries), and all accounts stated with infants, shall be absolutely void: Provided always, that this enactment shall not invalidate any contract into which an infant may, by any existing or future statute, or by the rules of common law or equity, enter, except such as now by law are voidable.

2. No action to be brought on ratification of infants contract.
No action shall be brought whereby to charge any person upon any promise made after full age to pay any debt contracted during infancy, or upon any ratification made after full age of any promise or contract made during infancy, whether there shall or shall not be any new consideration for such promise or ratification after full age.

3. Short title
This Act may be cited as "The Infants Relief Act, 1874."

---

[1] Note the Age of Majority Act, 1985 (No. 2), which at section 2(2) provides: Subsection (1) (of that Act) applies for the purposes of any rule of law and, in the absence of a definition or of any indication of a contrary intention, for the construction of "age of majority", "full age", "infancy", "infant", "minor", "minority" and of other cognate words and expressions in-
   (a) any statutory provision passed or made before, on or after the commencement of this Act, ...

[2] 56 & 57 Vict. c. 54

51

Statutes Revised on Commercial Law

The Bankers' Books Evidence Act, 1879
42 & 43 Victoria, chapter 11[1]

An Act to amend the Law of Evidence with respect to Bankers' Books.
23rd May 1879

List of Sections

1. Short title
This Act may be cited as the Bankers' Books Evidence Act, 1879.

2. Repealed by Statute Law Revision Act, 1894[2]

3. Mode of proof of entries in bankers' books.
Subject to the provisions of this Act, a copy of any entry in a banker's book shall in all legal proceedings be received as *prima facie* evidence of such entry, and of the matters, transactions, and accounts therein recorded.

---

[1] Application: Central Bank Act, 1971 (No. 24), s. 40(1) & Postal and Telecommunications Services Act, 1983 (No. 24), s. 67(1)&(3).

[2] 57 & 58 Vict. c. 56

4. Proof that book is a banker's book.

A copy of an entry in a banker's book shall not be received in evidence under this Act unless it be first proved that the book was at the time of the making of the entry one of the ordinary books of the bank, and that the entry was made in the usual and ordinary course of business, and that the book is in the custody or control of the bank.

Such proof may be given by a partner or officer of the bank, and may be given orally or by an affidavit sworn before any commissioner or person authorised to take affidavits.

5. Verification of copy[3]

(1) A copy of an entry in a banker's book shall not be received in evidence under this Act unless it is further proved that-

    (a) in the case where the copy sought to be received in evidence has been reproduced in a legible form directly by either or both mechanical and electronic means from a banker's book maintained in a non-legible form, it has been so reproduced;

    (b) in the case where the copy sought to be received in evidence has been made (either directly or indirectly) from a copy to which paragraph (a) of this section would apply:

        (i) the copy sought to be so received has been examined with a copy so reproduced and is a correct copy, and

        (ii) the copy so reproduced is a copy to which the said paragraph (a) would apply if it were sought to have it received in evidence;

    (c) in any other case, the copy has been examined with the original entry and is correct.

(2) Proof to which subsection (1) of this section relates shall be given-

    (a) in respect of paragraph (a) or (b)(ii) of that subsection, by some person who has been in charge of the reproduction concerned,

    (b) in respect of paragraph(b)(i) of that subsection, by some person who has examined the copy with the reproduction concerned,

    (c) in respect of paragraph (c) of that subsection, by some person who has examined the copy with the original entry concerned,

and may be given either orally or by an affidavit sworn before any commissioner or person authorised to take affidavits.

---

[3] Substituted by Central Bank Act, 1989 (No. 16), s. 131(a).

6. Case in which banker, &c. not compellable to produce books, &c.

A banker or officer of a bank shall not, in any [4] legal proceeding, ...[5] be compellable to produce any banker's book the contents of which can be proved under this Act, or to appear as a witness to prove the matters, transactions, and accounts therein recorded, unless by order of a judge made for special cause.

7. Court or judge may order inspection, &c.

On the application of any party to a legal proceeding a court or judge may order that such party be at liberty to inspect and take copies of any entries in a banker's book for any of the purposes of such proceedings. An order under this section may be made either with or without summoning the bank or any other party, and shall be served on the bank three clear days before the same is to be obeyed, unless the court or judge otherwise directs.

7A. Extension of section 7[6]

If, on application made by a member of the Garda Síochána not below the rank of Superintendent, a court or a judge is satisfied that there are reasonable grounds for believing-

(a) that an indictable offence has been committed; and

(b) that there is material in the possession of a bank specified in the application which is likely to be of substantial value (whether by itself or together with other material) to the investigation of the offence;

a court or judge may make an order that the applicant or another member of the Garda Síochána designated by him be at liberty to inspect and take copies of any entries in a banker's book for the purposes of investigation of the offence.

8. Costs.

The costs of any application to a court or judge under or for the purposes of this Act, and the costs of anything done or to be done under order of a court or judge made under or for the purposes of this Act shall be in the discretion of the court or judge, who may order the same or any part thereof to be paid to any party by the bank where the same have been occasioned by any default or delay on the part of the bank. Any such order against a bank may be enforced as if the bank was a party to the proceeding

---

[4] Applied; Solicitors (Amendment) Act, 1960 (No. 37), s. 18

[5] As amended by the Central Bank Act, 1989 (No. 16), s. 131(b)

[6] Inserted by the Central Bank Act, 1989 (No. 16), s. 131(c)

9. Interpretation of "bank," "banker," and "bankers' books."[7]

(1) In this Act the expression "bank" and "banker" means any of the following -

  (a) the Bank of Ireland[8], the Allied Irish Banks Limited[9], the National City Bank, Limited, the Northern Bank, Limited, and the Ulster Bank, Limited;

  (b) any other person who is the holder of a licence issued under section 47 of the Central Bank Act, 1942;

  (c) the Post Office Savings Bank;

  (d) a Trustee Savings Bank within the meaning of the Trustee Savings Banks Act, 1989[10] ;

  (e)[11]a building society (within the meaning of the Building Societies Act, 1989).

  (f)[12] ACC Bank public limited company.

(2) Expressions in this Act relating to "bankers' books" -

  (a)[13]includes any records used in the ordinary business of a bank, or used in the transfer department of a bank acting as registrar of securities, whether-

    (i) comprised in bound volume, loose-leaf binders or other loose-leaf filing systems, loose-leaf ledger sheets, pages, folios or cards, or

    (ii) kept on microfilm, magnetic tape or in any non-legible form (by the use of electronic or otherwise) which is capable of being reproduced in a permanent legible form, and

  (b) cover documents in manuscript, documents which are typed, printed, stencilled or created by any other mechanical or partly mechanical process in use from time to time and documents which are produced by any photographic or photostatic process.

(3) A certificate which -

  (a) purports to be signed by an officer of the Revenue

---

[7] Sub: Banker's Books Evidence Act (Amendment) Act, 1959 (No. 21), s. 2 sch.

[8] By Statutory Instrument the Hibernian Bank, Ltd.(21/1972, art 4(a), 9) and the National Bank of Ireland Limited (20/1972, art 4(a), 9) are to be known as the Bank of Ireland.

[9] By Statutory Instrument the Munster and Leinster Bank, Ltd.,(22/1972), the Provincial Bank of Ireland, Ltd. (23/1972), and the Royal Bank of Ireland, Ltd. (24/1972) are to be known as Allied Irish Banks Limited (now AIB Bank).

[10] Inserted: Trustee Savings Bank Act, 1989 (No. 21), s. 59, (see S.I. 55/1992)

[11] Inserted by the Building Societies Act, 1989 (No. 17), s. 126(1)

[12] Inserted by ACC Bank Act, 1992 (No. 6)

[13] Substituted by the Central Bank Act, 1989 (No. 16), s. 131(d)

Bankers' Books Evidence Act, 1879

Commissioners, and

(b) certifies that a licence was issued under section 47 of the Central Bank Act, 1942, to a specified person and authorised him to carry on banking business from a specified day until the next following 31st day of December,

shall be *prima facie* evidence of the licence for the purposes of this Act, and it shall not be necessary to prove the signature of the officer or that he was in fact an officer of the Revenue Commissioners.

(4)[14] A certificate which -

(a) purports to be signed by an officer of the Bank, and
(b) certifies that a licence was granted under section 9 of the Central Bank Act, 1971, to a specified person,

shall be *prima facie* evidence of the licence for the purposes of this Act, and it shall not be necessary to prove the signature of the officer or that he was in fact an officer of the Bank.

(5)[15] A certificate that-

(a) purports to be signed by an officer of the Central Bank, and
(b) certifies that a licence was granted under section 10 of the Trustee Savings Banks Act, 1989, in respect of a specified Trustee Savings Bank (within the meaning of that Act),

shall be *prima facie* evidence of the licence for the purposes of this Act, and it shall not be necessary to prove the signature of the officer or that he was in fact an officer of the Central Bank.

10. Interpretation of "legal proceedings," "court," "judge."[16]

The expression "legal proceedings" means any civil or criminal proceedings or inquiry in which evidence is or may be given, and includes an arbitration ;

The expression "the court" means the court, judge, arbitrator, persons or person before whom a legal proceeding is held or taken ;

The expression "a judge" means with respect to England a judge of the High Court .., and with respect to Scotland a lord ordinary of the Outer House of the Court of Session, and with respect to Ireland a judge of the High Court .. in Ireland ;

The judge of a county court may with respect to any action in such court exercise the powers of a judge under this Act.

---

[14] Inserted by Central Bank Act, 1971 (No. 24), ss. 1(3), 56

[15] Inserted by Trustee Savings Bank Act, 1989 (No. 21), s. 59

[16] As amended by Statute Law Revision Act, 1898, 61 & 62 Vict. c. 22

57

11. Computation of time[17]

Days which are non-business days for the purposes of, and to the extent provided by the Bills of Exchange Act, 1882, shall be excluded from the computation of time under this Act.

---

[17] Substituted by the Central Bank Act, 1989 (No. 16), s. 131(e)

The Bills of Sale (Ireland) Act, 1879
42 & 43 Victoria, chapter 50

List of Sections

An Act to amend the Law relating to Bills of Sale in Ireland[1,2]
11th August 1879

Preamble repealed by Statute Law Revision Act, 1894[3]

1. Short title
This Act may be cited for all purposes as the Bills of Sale (Ireland) Act, 1879.

2. Commencement of Act
.[4] ..the first day of November one thousand eight hundred and seventy-nine,.. is in this Act referred to as the commencement of this Act.

3. Application of Act
This Act shall apply to every bill of sale executed on or after the first day of November one thousand eight hundred and seventy nine (whether the same be absolute, or subject or not subject to any trust) whereby the holder or grantee has power, either with or without notice, and either immediately or at any future time, to seize or take possession of any personal chattels comprised in or made subject to such bill of sale.

4. Interpretation of terms
In this Act the following words and expressions shall have the meanings in this section assigned to them respectively, unless there be something in the subject or context repugnant to such

---

[1] Modification : The Central Bank Act, 1971 (No. 24), at s. 36(b) provides : where s. 35 of this Act effects an extension of or in relation to any such security so as to include future advances by or future liabilities to the transferee, such extension shall not require registration under or in pursuance of the ..., the Bills of Sale (Ireland) Acts, 1879 and 1883, ... but shall operate for the purposes of those Acts as if it were made by deed duly registered on the transfer date under or in pursuance of whichever of those Acts may be applicable thereto.

[2] Rstrct. ; The Agricultural Credit Act, 1978 (No.2) at s. 36(1) provides : A bill of sale of stock (whether including or not including any other chattels) made after the commencement of this Act shall, notwithstanding anything contained in the Bills of Sale (Ireland) Acts, 1879 and 1883, be void and be incapable of being registered under those Acts.

[3] 57 & 58 Vict. c. 56

[4] Repealed by Statute Law Revision Act, 1894, 42 & 43 Vict. c. 50

construction; (that is to say,)

bill of sale

The expression "bill of sale" shall include bills of sale, assignments, transfers, declarations of trust without transfer, inventories of goods with receipt thereto attached, or receipts for purchase moneys of goods, and other assurances of personal chattels, and also powers of attorney, authorities, or licences to take possession of personal chattels as security for any debt, and also any agreement, whether intended or not to be followed by the execution of any other instrument, by which a right in equity to any personal chattels, or to any charge or security thereon, shall be conferred, but shall not include the following documents; that is to say, assignments for the benefit of the creditors of the person making or giving the same, marriage settlements, transfers or assignments of any ship or vessel or any share thereof, transfers of goods in the ordinary course of business of any trade or calling, bills of sale of goods in foreign parts or at sea, bills of lading, India warrants, warehouse-keepers certificates, warrants or orders for the delivery of goods, or any other documents used in the ordinary course of business as proof of the possession or control of goods, or authorising or purporting to authorise, either by indorsement or by delivery, the possessor of such document to transfer or receive goods thereby represented:

personal chattels

The expression "personal chattels" shall mean goods, furniture, and other articles capable of complete transfer by delivery, and (when separately assigned or charged) fixtures and growing crops, but shall not include chattel interests in real estate, nor fixtures (except trade machinery as hereinafter defined), when assigned together with a freehold or leasehold interest in any land or building to which they are affixed, nor growing crops when assigned together with any interest in the land on which they grow, nor shares or interests in the stock, funds, or securities of any government, or in the capital or property of incorporated or joint stock companies, nor choses in action, nor any stock or produce upon any farm or lands which by virtue of any covenant or agreement or of the custom of the country ought not to be removed from any farm where the same are at the time of making or giving of such bill of sale:

apparent possession

Personal chattels shall be deemed to be in the "apparent possession" of the person making or giving a bill of sale, so long as they remain or are in or upon any house, mill, warehouse, building, works, yard, land, or other premises occupied by him, or are used and enjoyed by him in any place whatsoever, notwithstanding that formal possession thereof may have been taken by or given to any other person:

Prescribed

"Prescribed" means prescribed by rules made under the provisions of this Act.

5. Application of Act to trade machinery

From and after the commencement of this Act trade machinery shall for the purposes of this Act, be deemed to be personal chattels, and any mode of disposition of trade machinery by the owner thereof which would be a bill of sale as to any other personal chattels shall be deemed to be a bill of sale within the meaning of this Act.

For the purposes of this Act-

Trade machinery

"Trade machinery" means the machinery used in or attached to any factory or workshop;

1st. Exclusive of the fixed motive-powers, such as the water-wheels and steam-engines, and the steam-boilers, donkey engines, and other fixed appurtenances of the said motive-powers; and

2nd. Exclusive of the fixed power machinery, such as the shafts, wheels, drums, and their fixed appurtenances, which transmit the action of the motive-powers to the other machinery fixed and loose; and

3rd Exclusive of the pipes for steam, gas and water in the factory or workshop.

The machinery or effects excluded by this section from the definition of trade machinery shall not be deemed to be personal chattels within the meaning of this Act.

Factory or workshop

"Factory or workshop" means any premises on which any manual labour is exercised by way of trade, or for purposes of gain, in or incidental to the following purposes or any of them; that is to say,

(a) In or incidental to the making any article or part of an article; or

(b) In or incidental to the altering, repairing, ornamenting, finishing, of any article; or

(c) In or incidental to the adapting for sale any article.

6. Certain instruments giving powers of distress to be subject to this Act

Every attornment, instrument, or agreement, not being a mining lease, whereby a power of distress is given or agreed to be given by any person to any other person by way of security for any present, future, or contingent debt or advance, and whereby any rent is reserved or made payable as a mode of providing for the payment of interest on such debt or advance, or otherwise for the purpose of such security only, shall be deemed to be a bill of sale, within the meaning of this Act, of any personal chattels which may be seized or taken under such power of distress.

Provided, that nothing in this section shall extend to any mortgage of any estate or interest in any land, tenement, or hereditament which the mortgagee, being in possession, shall have demised to the mortgagor as his tenant at a fair and reasonable rent.

7. Fixtures or growing crops not to be deemed separately assigned when the land passes by the same instrument

No fixtures or growing crops shall be deemed, under this Act, to be separately assigned or charged by reason only that they are assigned by separate words, or that power is given to sever them from the land or building to which they are affixed, or from the land on which they grow, without otherwise taking possession of or dealing with such land or building, or land, if by the same instrument any freehold or leasehold interest in the land or building to which such fixtures are affixed, or in the land on which such crops grow, is also conveyed or assigned to the same persons or person.

The same rule of construction shall be applied to all deeds or instruments, including fixtures or growing crops, executed before the commencement of this Act and then subsisting and in force, in all questions arising under any bankruptcy, arrangement with creditors, liquidation, assignment for the benefit of creditors, or execution of any process of any court, which shall take place or be issued after the commencement of this Act.

8. Repealed by Bills of Sale (Ireland) Act (1879) Amendment Act, 1883[5]

9. Avoidance of certain duplicate bills of sale

Where a subsequent bill of sale is executed within or on the expiration of seven days after the execution of a prior unregistered bill of sale, and comprises all or any part of the personal chattels comprised in such prior bill of sale, then, if such subsequent bill of sale is given as a security for the same debt as is secured by the prior bill of sale, or for any part of such debt, it shall, to the extent to which it is a security for the same debt or part thereof, and so far as respects the personal chattels or part thereof comprised in the prior bill, be absolutely void unless it is proved to the satisfaction of the court having cognizance of the case that the subsequent bill of sale was *bona fide* given for the purpose of correcting some material error in the prior bill of sale, and not for the purpose of evading this Act.

---

[5] 46 & 47 Vict. c. 7, s. 15

10. Mode of registering bills of sale
(1) The execution of every bill of sale shall be attested by a solicitor of the Court of Judicature in Ireland and the attestation shall state that before the execution of the bill of sale the effect thereof has been explained to the grantor by the attesting solicitor :

(2) Such bill, with every schedule or inventory thereto annexed or therein referred to, and also a true copy of such bill and of every such schedule or inventory, and of every attestation of the execution of such bill of sale, together with an affidavit of the time of such bill of sale being made or given, and of its due execution and attestation, and a description of the residence and occupation of the person making or giving the same (or in case the same is made or given by any person under or in the execution of any process, then a description of the residence and occupation of the person against whom such process issued), and of every attesting witness to such bill of sale, shall be presented to and the said copy and affidavit shall be filed with the registrar within seven clear days after the making or giving of such bill of sale, in like manner as a warrant of attorney in any personal action given by a trader is now by law required to be filed:

(3) If the bill of sale is made or given subject to any defeasance, condition, or declaration of trust not contained in the body thereof, such defeasance, condition, or declaration shall be deemed to be part of the bill, and shall be written on the same paper or parchment therewith before the registration, and shall be truly set forth in the copy filed under this Act therewith and as part thereof, otherwise the registration shall be void.

In case two or more bills of sale are given, comprising in whole or in part any of the same chattels, they shall have priority in the order of the date of their registration respectively as regards such chattels.

A transfer or assignment of a registered bill of sale need not be registered.

11. Renewal of registration
The registration of a bill of sale, whether executed before or after the commencement of this Act, must be renewed once at least every five years, and if a period of five years elapses from the registration or renewed registration of a bill of sale without a renewal or further renewal (as the case may be) the registration shall become void:

Provided, that where a period of five years from the original registration of any bill of sale has expired before the first day of July one thousand eight hundred and eighty, such bill of sale shall be as valid to all intents and purposes as it would have been if this Act had not been passed, if such registration be renewed in the manner prescribed by this Act before the first day of July one thousand eight hundred and eighty.

The renewal of a registration shall be effected by filing with the registrar an affidavit stating the date of the bill of sale and of the last registration thereof, and the names, residences, and occupations of the parties thereto as stated therein, and that the bill of sale is still a subsisting security.

Every such affidavit may be in the form set forth in the Schedule (A) to this Act annexed.

A renewal of registration shall not become necessary by reason only of the transfer or assignment of a bill of sale.

12. Form of register

The registrar shall keep a book (in this Act called "the register") for the purposes of this Act, and shall, upon the filing of any bill of sale or copy under this Act, enter therein in the form set forth in the second Schedule (B) to this Act annexed, or in any other prescribed form, the name, residence, and occupation of the person by whom the bill was made or given (or in case the same was made or given by any person under or in the execution of process, then the name, residence, and occupation of the person against whom such process was issued, and also the name of the person or persons to whom or in whose favour the bill was given), and the other particulars shown in the said schedule or to be prescribed under this Act, and shall number all such bills registered in each year consecutively, according to the respective dates of their registration.

Upon the registration of any affidavit of renewal the like entry shall be made, with the addition of the date and number of the last previous entry relating to the same bill, and the bill of sale or copy originally filed shall be thereupon marked with the number affixed to such affidavit of renewal.

The registrar shall also keep an index of the names of the grantors of registered bills of sale with reference to entries in the register of the bills of sale given by each such grantor.

Such index shall be arranged in divisions corresponding with the letters of the alphabet, so that all grantors whose surnames being with the same letter (and no others) shall be comprised in one division, but the arrangement within each such division need not be strictly alphabetical.

13. As to registrar

The Master of the Supreme Court .[6] .. attached to the Queen's Bench Division of the High Court .[6] .., or such other officer as may for the time being be assigned for this purpose under the provisions of the Supreme Court of Judicature Act (Ireland) 1877, shall be

[6] Amended: Statute Law Revision Act, 1898, 61 & 62 Vict. c. 22

registrar for the purposes of this Act.

14.[6] Rectification of register

Any judge of the High Court, on being satisfied that the omission to register a bill of sale or an affidavit of renewal thereof within the time prescribed by this Act, or the omission or mis-statement of the name, residence, or occupation of any person, was accidental or due to inadvertence, may in his discretion order such omission or mis-statement to be rectified by the insertion in the register of the true name, residence, or occupation, or by extending the time for such registration on such terms and conditions (if any) as to security, notice by advertisement or otherwise, or as to any other matter, as he thinks fit to direct.

15. Memorandum of satisfaction on registered copy of bill of sale

Subject to and in accordance with any rules to be made under and for the purposes of this Act, the registrar may order a memorandum of satisfaction to be written upon any registered copy of a bill of sale, upon the prescribed evidence being given that the debt (if any) for which such bill of sale was made or given has been satisfied or discharged.

16.[6] Copies may be taken, &c.

Any person shall be entitled to have an office copy or extract of any registered bill of sale and affidavit of execution filed therewith, or copy thereof, and of any affidavit filed therewith, if any, or registered affidavit of renewal, upon paying for the same at the like rate as for office copies of judgments of the High Court, and any copy of a registered bill of sale, and affidavit purporting to be an office copy thereof, shall, in all courts and before all arbitrators or other persons, be admitted as *prima facie* evidence thereof, and of the fact and date of registration as shown thereon. Any person shall be entitled at all reasonable times to search the register and every registered bill of sale, upon the payment of one shilling for every copy of a bill of sale inspected such payment shall be made by a judicature, Ireland, stamp.

17.[6] Affidavits

Every affidavit required by or for the purposes of this Act may be sworn before a master of any division of the High Court ... , or before any commissioner empowered to take affidavits in the Supreme Court .... Whoever wilfully makes or uses any false affidavit for the purposes of this Act shall be deemed guilty of wilful and corrupt perjury.

18. Fees

There shall be paid and received in stamps the following fees[7] , viz.:
On filing a bill of sale 1s. 0d
On filing the affidavit of execution of a bill of sale 1s. 0d
On the affidavit used for the purpose of re-registering a bill of sale
(to include the fee for filing) 2s. 6d

19. Collection of fees under 40 & 41 Vict. c. 57. s. 84

Section eighty-four of the Supreme Court of Judicature Act
(Ireland), 1877, and any enactments for the time being in force
amending or substituted for that section, shall apply to fees under
this Act, and an order under that section may, if need be, be made in
relation to such fees accordingly.

20. Repealed by Bills of Sale (Ireland) Act (1879) Amendment Act,
1883[8]

21. Rules 40 & 41 Vict. c 57

Rules for the purposes of this Act may be made and altered from
time to time by the like persons and in the like manner in which
rules and regulations may be made under and for the purposes of
the Supreme Court of Judicature Act (Ireland), 1877.

22. Time for registration

When the time for registering a bill of sale expires on a Sunday, or
other day on which the registrar's office is closed, the registration
shall be valid if made on the next following day on which the office
is open.

23. Repeal of 17 & 18 Vict. c. 55

..[9] .. Provided that (except as is herein expressly mentioned with
respect to construction and with respect to renewal of registration)
nothing in this Act shall affect any bill of sale executed before the
commencement of this Act, and as regards bills of sale so executed
the Act hereby repealed shall continue in force.

Any renewal after the commencement of this Act of the
registration of a bill of sale executed before the commencement of
this Act, and registered under the Act hereby repealed, shall be made
under this Act in the same manner as the renewal of a registration
made under this Act.

---

[7] See: Decimal Currency Act, 1970 (No. 21), s. 9(1)

[8] 46 & 47 Vict. c 7, s. 15

[9] Repealed : Statute Law Revision Act, 1894, 42 & 43 Vict. c. 50

Bills of Sale (Ireland) Act, 1879

24. Extent of Act

This Act shall not extend to England or Scotland.

Schedule A

Section 11

I [A.B.]   of   do swear that a bill of sale, bearing date the   day of   18 [insert the date of the bill], and made between [insert the names and descriptions of the parties in the original bill of sale], and which said bill of sale [or, and a copy of which said bill of sale, as the case may be] was registered on the day of 18 [insert date of registration], is still a subsisting security.

sworn, &c.

Schedule B

Section 12

Satisfaction entered	Number	By whom given (or against whom process issued)			To whom given	Nature of instrument	Date	Date of registration	Date of registration of affidavit of renewal
		Name	Residence	Occupation					

The Bills of Exchange Act, 1882
45 & 46 Victoria, chapter 61

69

Liabilities of Parties.

Discharge of Bill.

Acceptance and Payment for Honour.

Lost Instruments.

Bill in a Set.

Conflict of Laws.

Part 111.

Cheques on a banker.

Crossed Cheques.

An Act to codify the law relating to Bills of Exchange, Cheques, and Promissory Notes.
18th August 1882

Be it enacted ...

Part 1.
Preliminary.

1. Short title

This Act may be cited as the Bills of Exchange Act, 1882.

2. Interpretation of terms

In this Act, unless the context otherwise requires, -
"Acceptance" means an acceptance completed by delivery or notification.
"Action" includes counter claim and set off.
"Banker"[1] includes -
(a) a body of persons whether incorporated or not who carry on the business of banking,
(b) a building society (within the meaning of the Building Societies Act, 1989) and
(c) ACC Bank Public Limited Company.
"Bankrupt" includes any person whose estate is vested in a trustee or assignee under the law for the time being in force relating to bankruptcy.
"Bearer" means the person in possession of a bill or note which is payable to bearer.
"Bill" means bill of exchange, and "note" means promissory note.
"Business days" means those days which are not non-business days[2]
"Delivery" means transfer of possession, actual or constructive, from one person to another.
"Holder" means the payee or indorse of a bill or note who is in possession of it, or the bearer thereof.
"Indorsement" means an indorsement completed by delivery.
"Issue" means the first delivery of a bill or note, complete in form to a person who takes it as a holder.
"Non-business days " means-[2]
  (a) Saturday, except in a case and to the extent to which the proviso to the paragraph numbered (1) of section 14 of this Act applies,
  (b) Sunday,
  (c) such days as are public holidays, and

---

[1] As now amended: ACC Bank Act, 1992 (No. 6)

[2] Inserted: Central Bank Act, 1989 (No. 16), s. 132(1)(a)(i), (ii) & (iii)

(d) where and to the extent that any direction under section 134 of the Central Bank Act, 1989, provides, such other day or days as so provided,"

"Person" includes a body of persons whether incorporated or not.

"Public holiday" has the same meaning as it has for the purposes of the Holidays (Employees) Act, 1973[2] .

"Value" means valuable consideration.

"Written" includes printed, and "writing" includes print.

Part 11.
Bills of Exchange.

Form and Interpretation.

3. Bill of exchange defined[3]

(1) A bill of exchange is an unconditional order in writing, addressed by one person to another, signed by the person giving it, requiring the person to whom it is addressed to pay on demand or at a fixed or determinable future time a sum certain in money to or to the order of a specified person, or to bearer.

(2) An instrument which does not comply with these conditions, or which orders any act to be done in addition to the payment of money, is not a bill of exchange.

(3) An order to pay out of a particular fund is not unconditional within the meaning of this section; but an unqualified order to pay, coupled with (a) an indication of a particular fund out of which the drawee is to reimburse himself or a particular account to be debited with the amount, or (b) a statement of the transaction which gives rise to the bill, is unconditional.

(4) A bill is not invalid by reason -
  (a) That it is not dated;
  (b) That it does not specify the value given, or that any value has been given therefor;
  (c) That it does not specify the place where it is drawn or the place where it is payable.

4. Inland and foreign bills

(1) An inland bill is a bill which is or on the face of it purports to be (a) both drawn and payable within the British Islands, or (b) drawn within the British Islands upon some person resident therein. Any other bill is a foreign bill.

For the purposes of this Act "British Islands" mean any part of the United Kingdom of Great Britain and Ireland, the islands of Man,

---

[3] A mode of payment: see Payment of Wages Act, 1991 (No. 25), s. 2(1)(a)

Guernsey, Jersey, Alderney, and Sark, and the islands adjacent to any of them being part of the dominions of Her Majesty.

(2) Unless the contrary appear on the face of the bill the holder may treat it as an inland bill.

5. Effect where different parties to the bill are that same person

(1) A bill may be drawn payable to, or to the order of, the drawer; or it may be drawn payable to, or to the order of, the drawee.

(2) Where in a bill drawer and drawee are the same person, or where the drawee is a fictitious person or a person not having capacity to contract, the holder may treat the instrument, at his option, either as a bill of exchange or as a promissory note.

6. Address to drawee

(1 The drawee must be named or otherwise indicated in a bill with reasonable certainty.

(2) A bill may be addressed to two or more drawees whether they are partners or not, but an order addressed to two drawees in the alternative or to two or more drawees in the alternative or to two or more drawees in succession is not a bill of exchange.

7. Certainty required as to payee

(1) Where a bill is not payable to bearer, the payee must be named or otherwise indicated therein with reasonable certainty.

(2) A bill may be made payable to two or more payees jointly, or it may be made payable in the alternative to one of two, or one or some of several payees. A bill may also be made payable to the holder of an office for the time being.

(3) Where the payee is a fictitious or non-existing person the bill may be treated as payable to bearer.

8. What bills are negotiable

(1) When a bill contains words prohibiting transfer, or indicating an intention that it should not be transferable, it is valid as between the parties thereto, but is not negotiable.

(2) A negotiable bill may be payable either to order or to bearer.

(3) A bill is payable to bearer which is expressed to be so payable, or on which the only or last indorsement is an indorsement in blank.

(4) A bill is payable to order which is expressed to be so payable, or which is expressed to be payable to a particular person, and does not contain words prohibiting transfer or indicating an intention that it should not be transferable.

(5) Where a bill, either originally or by indorsement, is expressed to be payable to the order of a specified person, and not to him or his order, it is nevertheless payable to him or his order at his option.

9. Sum payable

(1) The sum payable by a bill is a sum certain within the meaning of this Act, although it is required to be paid-
   (a) With interest.
   (b) By stated instalments.
   (c) By stated instalments, with a provision that upon default in payment of any instalment the whole shall become due.
   (d) According to an indicated rate of exchange or according to a rate of exchange to be ascertained as directed by the bill.

(2) Where the sum payable is expressed in words and also in figures, and there is a discrepancy between the two, the sum denoted by the words is the amount payable.

(3) Where a bill is expressed to be payable with interest, unless the instrument otherwise provides interest runs from the date of the bill, and if the bill is undated from the issue thereof.

10. Bill payable on demand

(1) A bill is payable on demand-
   (a) Which is expressed to be payable on demand, or at sight, or on presentation; or
   (b) In which no time for payment is expressed.

(2) Where a bill is accepted or indorsed when it is overdue, it shall as regards the acceptor who so accepts, or any indorser who so indorses it, be deemed a bill payable on demand.

11. Bill payable at a future time

A bill is payable at a determinable future time within the meaning of this Act which is expressed to be payable-

(1) At a fixed period after date or sight.

(2) On or at a fixed period after the occurrence of a specified event which is certain to happen, though the time of happening may be uncertain.

An instrument expressed to be payable on a contingency is not a bill, and the happening of the event does not cure the defect.

12. Omission of date in bill payable after date or sight

Where a bill expressed to be payable at a fixed period after date is issued undated, or where the acceptance of a bill payable at a fixed period after sight is undated, any holder may insert therein the true date of issue or acceptance, and the bill shall be payable accordingly.

Provided that (1) where the holder in good faith and by mistake inserts a wrong date, and (2) in every case where a wrong date is inserted, if the bill subsequently comes into the hands of a holder in due course the bill shall not be avoided thereby, but shall operate and be payable as if the date so inserted had been the true date.

13. Ante-dating and post-dating

(1) Where a bill or an acceptance or any indorsement on a bill is dated, the date shall, unless the contrary be proved, be deemed to be the true date of the drawing, acceptance, or indorsement, as the case may be.

(2) A bill is not invalid by reason only that it is ante-dated or post-dated, or that it bears date on a Sunday.

14. Computation of time of payment

Where a bill is not payable on demand the day on which it falls due is determined as follows:-

(1)[4] The bill is due and payable in all cases on the last day of the time of payment as fixed by the bill or, if that is a non-business day, on the succeeding business day:

Provided that nothing in this paragraph shall operate to prevent a bill being paid by the drawee on a Saturday (other than a Saturday that is a public holiday or to which paragraph (d) of the definition of 'non-business days' in section 2 of this Act relates) or cause him to incur any liability thereby, where -

  (a) the drawee is a banker, and

  (b) the Saturday concerned is the last day fixed by the bill as the time of payment, and

  (c) the drawee is normally open for business on a Saturday at his address given in or ascertainable from the bill,

and, accordingly, presentation and payment of such bill on the Saturday shall be valid and shall discharge it as fully as if it had been presented and paid on the next succeeding business day: but this provision shall not be construed as compelling the person entitled to payment on the bill to accept such payment on the Saturday.

(2) Where a bill is payable at a fixed period after date, after sight, or after the happening of a specified event, the time of payment is determined by excluding the day from which the time is to begin to run and by including the day of payment.

(3) Where a bill is payable at a fixed period after sight, the time begins to run from the date of the acceptance if the bill be accepted, and from the date of noting or protest if the bill be noted or protested for non-acceptance, or for non-delivery.

(4) The term "month" in a bill means calendar month.

15. Case of need

The drawer of a bill and any indorser may insert therein the name of a person to whom the holder may resort in case of need, that is to say, in case the bill is dishonoured by non-acceptance or non-payment. Such person is called the referee in case of need. It is in the

---

[4] Substituted by Central Bank Act, 1989 (No. 16), s. 132(b)

option of the holder to resort to the referee in case of need or not as he may think fit.

16. Optional stipulations by drawee or indorser

The drawer of a bill, and any indorser, may insert therein an express stipulation-

(1) Negativing or limiting his own liability to the holder.

(2) Waiving as regards himself some or all of the holder's duties.

17. Definition and requisites of acceptance

(1) The acceptance of a bill is the signification by the drawee of his assent to the order of the drawer.

(2) An acceptance is invalid unless it complies with the following conditions, namely:

(a) It must be written on the bill and be signed by the drawee. The mere signature of the drawee without additional words is sufficient.

(b) It must not express that the drawee will perform his promise by any other means than the payment of money.

18. Time for acceptance

A bill may be accepted-

(1) Before it has been signed by the drawer, or while otherwise incomplete:

(2) When it is overdue, or after it has been dishonoured by a previous refusal to accept or by non-payment:

(3) When a bill payable after sight is dishonoured by non-acceptance, and the drawee subsequently accepts it, the holder, in the absence of any different agreement, is entitled to have the bill accepted as of the date of first presentment to the drawee for acceptance.

19. General and qualified acceptance

(1) An acceptance is either (a) general or (b) qualified.

(2) A general acceptance assents without qualification to the order of the drawer. A qualified acceptance in express terms varies the effect of the bill as drawn.

In particular an acceptance is qualified which is-

(a) conditional, that is to say, which makes payment by the acceptor dependent on the fulfilment of a condition therein stated:

(b) partial, that is to say, an acceptance to pay part only of the amount for which the bill is drawn.

(c) local, that is to say, an acceptance to pay only at a particular specified place:

An acceptance to pay at a particular place is a general acceptance, unless it expressly states that the bill is to be paid there only and not elsewhere:

(d) qualified as to time:

(e) the acceptance of some one or more of the drawees, but not of all.

20. Inchoate instruments

(1) Where a simple signature, on a blank stamped paper is delivered by the signer in order that it may be converted into a bill, it operates as a *prima facie* authority to fill up as a complete bill for any amount the stamp will cover, using the signature for that of the drawer, or the acceptor, or an indorser; and, in like manner, when a bill is wanting in any material particular, the person in possession of it has a *prima facie* authority to fill up the omission in any way he thinks fit.

(2) In order that any such instrument when completed may be enforceable against any person who became a party thereto prior to its completion, it must be filled up within a reasonable time, and strictly in accordance with the authority given. Reasonable time for this purpose is a question of fact.

Provided that if any such instrument after completion is negotiated to a holder in due course it shall be valid and effectual for all purposes in his hands, and he may enforce it as if it had been filled up within a reasonable time and strictly in accordance with the authority given.

21. Delivery

(1) Every contract on a bill, whether it be the drawer's, the acceptor's, or an indorser's, is incomplete and revocable, until delivery of the instrument in order to give effect thereto.

Provided that where an acceptance is written on a bill, and the drawee gives notice to or according to the directions of the person entitled to the bill that he has accepted it, the acceptance then becomes complete and irrevocable.

(2) As between immediate parties, and as regards a remote party other than a holder in due course, the delivery-

(a) in order to be effectual must be made either by or under the authority of the party drawing, accepting, or indorsing, as the case may be :

(b) may be shown to have been conditional or for a special purpose only, and not for the purpose of transferring the property in the bill.

But if the bill be in the hands of a holder in due course a valid delivery of the bill by all parties prior to him so as to make them liable to him is conclusively presumed.

(3) Where a bill is no longer in the possession of a party who has signed it as drawer, acceptor, or indorser, a valid and unconditional delivery by him is presumed until the contrary is proved.

Capacity and Authority of parties

22. Capacity of parties

(1) Capacity to incur liability as a party to a bill is co-extensive with capacity to contract.

Provided that nothing in this section shall enable a corporation to make itself liable as drawer, acceptor, or indorser of a bill unless it is competent to it so to do under the law for the time being in force relating to corporations.

(2) Where a bill is drawn or indorsed by an infant, minor, or corporation having no capacity or power to incur liability on a bill, the drawing or indorsement entitles the holder to receive payment of the bill, and to enforce it against any other party thereto.

23. Signature essential to liability

No person is liable as drawer, indorser, or acceptor of a bill who has not signed it as such.

Provided that-

(1) Where a person signs a bill in a trade or assumed name, he is liable thereon as if he had signed it in his own name:

(2) The signature of the name of a firm is equivalent to the signature by the person so signing of the names of all persons liable as partners in that firm.

24. Forged or unauthorised signature

Subject to the provisions of this Act, where a signature on a bill is forged or placed thereon without the authority of the person whose signature it purports to be, the forged or unauthorised signature is wholly inoperative, and no right to retain the bill or to give a discharge therefor or to enforce payment thereof against any party thereto can be acquired through or under that signature, unless the party against whom it is sought to retain or enforce payment of the bill is precluded from setting up the forgery or want of authority.

Provided that nothing in this section shall affect the ratification of an unauthorised signature not amounting to a forgery.

25. Procuration signatures

A signature by procuration operates as notice that the agent has but a limited authority to sign, and the principal is only bound by such signature if the agent in so signing was acting within the actual limits of his authority.

81

26. Person signing as agent or in representative capacity

(1) Where a person signs a bill as a drawer, indorser, or acceptor, and adds words to his signature, indicating that he signs for or on behalf of a principal, or in a representative character, he is not personally liable thereon; but the mere addition to his signature of words describing him as an agent, or as filling a representative character, does not exempt him from personal liability.

(2) In determining whether a signature on a bill is that of the principal or that of the agent by whose hand it is written, the construction most favourable to the validity of the instrument shall be adopted.

The Consideration for a Bill.

27. Value and holder for value

(1) Valuable consideration for a bill may be constituted by,-
   (a) Any consideration sufficient to support a simple contract;
   (b) An antecedent debt or liability. Such a debt or liability is deemed valuable consideration whether the bill is payable on demand or at a future time.

(2) Where value has at any time been given for a bill the holder is deemed to be a holder for value as regards the acceptor and all parties to the bill who became parties prior to such time,

(3) Where the holder of a bill has a lien on it arising either from contract or by implication of law, he is deemed to be a holder for value to the extent of the sum for which he has a lien.

28. Accommodation bill or party

(1) An accommodation party to a bill is a person who has signed a bill as drawer, acceptor, or indorser, without receiving value therefor, and for the purpose of lending his name to some other person.

(2) An accommodation party is liable on the bill to a holder for value; and it is immaterial whether, when such holder took the bill, he knew such party to be an accommodation party or not.

29. Holder in due course

(1) A holder in due course is a holder who has taken a bill, complete and regular on the face of it, under the following conditions; namely,
   (a) That he became the holder of it before it was overdue, and without notice that it had been previously dishonoured, if such was the fact:
   (b) That he took the bill in good faith and for value, and that at the time the bill was negotiated to him he had no notice of any defect in the title of the person who negotiated it.

(2) In particular the title of a person who negotiates a bill is defective within the meaning of this Act when he obtained the bill, or the acceptance thereof, by fraud, duress, or force and fear, or other unlawful means, or for an illegal consideration, or when he negotiates it in breach of faith, or under such circumstances as amount to a fraud.

(3) A holder (whether for value or not), who derives his title to a bill through a holder in due course, and who is not himself a party to any fraud or illegality affecting it, has all the rights of that holder in due course as regards the acceptor an all parties to the bill prior to that holder.

30. Presumption of value and good faith

(1) Every party whose signature appears on a bill is *prima facie* deemed to have become a party thereto for value.

(2) Every holder of a bill is *prima facie* deemed to be a holder in due course; but if in an action on a bill it is admitted, or proved that the acceptance, issue, or subsequent negotiation of the bill is affected with fraud, duress, or force and fear, or illegality, the burden of proof is shifted, unless and until the holder proves that, subsequent to the alleged fraud or illegality, value has in good faith been given for the bill.

Negotiation of Bills.

31. Negotiation of bill

(1) A bill is negotiated when it is transferred from one person to another in such a manner as to constitute the transferee the holder of the bill.

(2) A bill payable to bearer is negotiated by delivery.

(3) A bill payable to order is negotiated by the indorsement of the holder completed by delivery.

(4) Where the holder of a bill payable to his order transfers it for value without indorsing it, the transfer gives the transferee such title as the transferor had in the bill, and the transferee in addition acquires the right to have the indorsement of the transferor.

(5) Where any person is under obligation to indorse a bill in a representative capacity, he may indorse the bill in such terms as to negative personal liability.

32. Requisites of a valid indorsement

An indorsement in order to operate as a negotiation must comply with the following conditions, namely:-

(1) It must be written on the bill itself and be signed by the indorser. The simple signature of the indorser on the bill, without

additional words, is sufficient.

An indorsement written on an allonge, or on a "copy" of a bill issued or negotiated in a country where "copies" are recognised, is deemed to be written on the bill itself.

(2) It must be an indorsement of the entire bill. A partial indorsement, that is to say, an indorsement which purports to transfer to the indorsee a part only of the amount payable, or which purports to transfer the bill to two or more indorsees severally, does not operate as a negotiation of the bill.

(3) Where a bill is payable to the order of two or more payees or indorsees who are not partners all must indorse, unless the one indorsing has authority to indorse for the others.

(4) Where, in a bill payable to order, the payee or indorsee is wrongly designated, or his name is mis-spelt, he may indorse the bill as therein described, adding, if he think fit, his proper signature.

(5) Where there are two or more indorsements on a bill, each indorsement is deemed to have been made in the order in which it appears on the bill, until the contrary is proved.

(6) An indorsement may be made in blank or special. It may also contain terms making it restrictive.

33. Conditional indorsement

Where a bill purports to be indorsed conditionally the condition may be disregarded by the payer, and payment to the indorsee is valid whether the condition has been fulfilled or not.

34. Indorsement in blank and special indorsement

(1) An indorsement in blank specifies no indorsee, and a bill so indorsed becomes payable to bearer.

(2) A special indorsement specifies the person to whom, or to whose order, the bill is to be payable.

(3) The provisions of this Act relating to a payee apply with the necessary modifications to an indorsee under a special indorsement.

(4) When a bill has been indorsed in blank, any holder may convert the blank indorsement into a special indorsement by writing above the indorser's signature a direction to pay the bill to or to the order of himself or some other person.

35. Restrictive indorsement

(1) An indorsement is restrictive which prohibits the further negotiation of the bill or which expresses that it is a mere authority to deal with the bill as thereby directed and not a transfer of the ownership thereof, as, for example, if a bill be indorsed "Pay D only", or "Pay D for the account of "X", or "Pay D, or order for collection."

(2) A restrictive indorsement gives the indorsee the right to receive

payment of the bill and to sue any party thereto that his indorser could have sued, but gives him no power to transfer his rights as indorsee unless it expressly authorise him to do so.

(3) Where a restrictive indorsement authorises further transfer, all subsequent indorsees take the bill with the same rights and subject to the same liabilities as the first indorsee under the restrictive indorsement.

36. Negotiation of overdue or dishonoured bill

(1) Where a bill is negotiable in its origin it continues to be negotiable until it has been (a) restrictively indorsed or (b) discharged by payment or otherwise.

(2) Where an overdue bill is negotiated, it can only be negotiated subject to any defect of title affecting it at its maturity, and thenceforward no person who takes it can acquire or give a better title than that which the person from whom he took it had.

(3) A bill payable on demand is deemed to be overdue within the meaning and for the purposes of this section, when it appears on the face of it to have been in circulation for an unreasonable length of time. What is an unreasonable length of time for this purpose is a question of fact.

(4) Except where an indorsement bears date after the maturity of the bill, every negotiation is *prima facie* deemed to have been effected before the bill was overdue.

(5) Where a bill which is not overdue has been dishonoured any person who takes it with notice of the dishonour takes it subject to any defect of title attaching thereto at the time of dishonour, but nothing in this subsection shall affect the rights of a holder in due course.

37. Negotiation of bill to party already liable thereon

Where a bill is negotiated back to the drawer, or to a prior indorser or to the acceptor, such party may, subject to the provisions of this Act, re-issue and further negotiate the bill, but he is not entitled to enforce payment of the bill against any intervening party to whom he was previously liable.

38. Rights of the holder acquired by negotiation

The rights and powers of the holder of a bill are as follows:

(1) He may sue on the bill in his own name:

(2) Where he is a holder in due course, he holds the bill free from any defect of title of prior parties, as well as from mere personal defences available to prior parties among themselves, and may enforce payment against all parties liable on the bill:

(3) Where his title is defective (a) if he negotiates the bill to a

holder in due course, that holder obtains a good and complete title to the bill, and (b) if he obtains payment of the bill the person who pays him in due course gets a valid discharge for the bill.

General duties of the Holder.

39. When presentment for acceptance is necessary

(1) Where a bill is payable after sight, presentment for acceptance is necessary in order to fix the maturity of the instrument.

(2) Where a bill expressly stipulates that it shall be presented for acceptance, or where a bill is drawn payable elsewhere than at the residence or place of business of the drawee it must be presented for acceptance before it can be presented for payment.

(3) In no other case is presentment for acceptance necessary in order to render liable any party to the bill.

(4) Where the holder of a bill, drawn payable elsewhere than at the place of business or residence of the drawee has not time, with the exercise of reasonable diligence, to present the bill for acceptance before presenting it for payment on the day that it falls due, the delay caused by presenting the bill for acceptance before presenting it for payment is excused, and does not discharge the drawer and indorsers.

40. Time for presenting bill payable after sight

(1) Subject to the provisions of this Act, when a bill payable after sight is negotiated, the holder must either present it for acceptance or negotiate it within a reasonable time.

(2) If he do not do so, the drawer and all indorsers prior to that holder are discharged.

(3) In determining what is a reasonable time within the meaning of this section, regard shall be had to the nature of the bill, the usage of trade with respect to similar bills, and the facts of the particular case.

41. Rules as to presentment for acceptance and excuses for non-presentment

(1) A bill is duly presented for acceptance which is presented in accordance with the following rules:
  - (a) The presentment must be made by or on behalf of the holder to the drawee or to some person authorised to accept or refuse acceptance on his behalf at a reasonable hour on a business day and before the bill is overdue.
  - (b) When a bill is addressed to two or more drawees, who are not partners, presentment must be made to them all, unless one has authority to accept for all, then presentment may be made to him only.
  - (c) Where the drawee is dead, presentment may be made to his

personal representative.

(d) Where the drawee is bankrupt, presentment may be made to him or to his trustee.

(e) Where authorized by agreement or usage, a presentment through the post office is sufficient.

(2) Presentment in accordance with these rules is excused, and a bill may be treated as dishonoured by non-acceptance -

(a) Where the drawee is dead or bankrupt, or is a fictitious person or a person not having capacity to contract by bill:

(b) Where, after the exercise of reasonable diligence, such presentment cannot be effected:

(c) Where, although the presentment has been irregular, acceptance has been refused on some other ground.

(3) The fact that the holder has reason to believe that the bill, on presentment, will be dishonoured does not excuse presentment.

42. Non-acceptance

(1) When a bill is duly presented for acceptance and is not accepted within the customary time, the person presenting it must treat it as dishonoured, by non-acceptance. If he do not, the holder shall lose his right of recourse against the drawer and indorsers.

43. Dishonour by non-acceptance and its consequences

(1) A bill is dishonoured by non-acceptance-

(a) When it is duly presented for acceptance, and such an acceptance as is prescribed by this Act is refused or cannot be obtained; or

(b) When presentment for acceptance is excused and the bill is not accepted.

(2) Subject to the provisions of this Act when a bill is dishonoured by non-acceptance, an immediate right of recourse against the drawer and indorsers accrues to the holder, and no presentment for payment is necessary.

44. Duties as to qualified acceptances

(1) The holder of a bill may refuse to take a qualified acceptance, and if he does not obtain an unqualified acceptance may treat the bill as dishonoured by non-acceptance.

(2) Where a qualified acceptance is taken, and the drawer or an indorser has not expressly or impliedly authorised the holder to take a qualified acceptance, or does not subsequently assent thereto, such drawer or indorser is discharged from his liability on the bill.

The provisions of this sub-section do not apply to a partial acceptance, whereof due notice has been given. Where a foreign bill has been accepted as to part, it must be protested as to the balance.

Bills of Exchange Act, 1882

(3) When the drawer or indorser of a bill receives notice of a qualified acceptance, and does not within a reasonable time express his dissent to the holder he shall be deemed to have assented thereto.

45. Rules as to presentment for payment

Subject to the provisions of this Act a bill must be duly presented for payment. If it be not so presented the drawer and indorsers shall be discharged.

A bill is duly presented for payment which is presented in accordance with the following rules:-

(1) Where the bill is not payable on demand, presentment must be made on the day it falls due.

(2) Where the bill is payable on demand, then, subject to the provisions of this Act, presentment must be made within a reasonable time after its issue in order to render the drawer liable, and within a reasonable time after its indorsement, in order to render the indorser liable.

In determining what is a reasonable time, regard shall be had to the nature of the bill, the usage of trade with regard to similar bills, and the facts of the particular case.

(3) Presentment must be made by the holder or by some person authorised to receive payment on his behalf at a reasonable hour on a business day, at the proper place as hereinafter defined, either to the person designated by the bill as payer, or to some person authorised to pay or refuse payment on his behalf if with the exercise of reasonable diligence such person can there be found.

(4) A bill is presented at the proper place:-

   (a) Where a place of payment is specified in the bill and the bill is there presented:

   (b) Where no place of payment is specified, but the address of the drawee or acceptor is given in the bill, and the bill is there presented :

   (c) Where no place of payment is specified and no address given and the bill is presented at the drawee's or acceptor's place of business if known, and if not, at his ordinary residence if known:

   (d) In any other case if presented to the drawee or acceptor wherever he can be found, or if presented at his last known place of business or residence:

(5) Where a bill is presented at the proper place and after the exercise of reasonable diligence no person authorised to pay or refuse payment can be found there, no further presentment to the drawee or acceptor is required.

(6) Where a bill is drawn upon, or accepted by two or more persons who are not partners, and no place of payment is specified,

presentment must be made to them all.

(7) Where the drawee or acceptor of a bill is dead, and no place of payment is specified, presentment must be made to a personal representative, if such there be, and with the exercise of reasonable diligence he can be found.

(8) Where authorised by agreement or usage, a presentment through the post office is sufficient.

45A. Additional rules as to presentment of cheques and other documents[5]

(1) Subject to the provisions of this section, presentment for payment of a cheque may be made by a banker (in this section referred to as the "collecting banker") on his own behalf or on behalf of a customer or any other person to the banker on whom it is drawn (in this section referred to as the "drawee banker") by notification to the drawee banker of the essential features of the cheque other than by its physical presentment, whether by the transmission of an electronic message or by any other means.

(2) A drawee banker to whom a cheque is presented by notification in the manner provided for in subsection (1) of this section may, before the close of business on the next business day following receipt of such notification, request the collecting banker that the cheque be physically presented to him.

(3) A request by the drawee banker for physical presentment of a cheque in accordance with subsection (2) of this section shall not constitute dishonour of the cheque by non-payment.

(4) A cheque paid upon presentment in the manner provided for in subsection (1) of this section shall be deemed to have been paid in the ordinary course of business.

(5) Where a cheque is presented for payment by notification in the manner provided for in subsection (1) of this section, nothing in this section shall be taken to relieve the collecting banker or the drawee banker from any liability in relation to the collection or payment of the cheque to which the collecting banker or the drawee banker would have been subject if the cheque had been physically presented for payment.

(6) This section shall apply to -

    (a) any document issued by a customer of a banker which, though not a bill of exchange, is intended to enable a person to obtain payment from that banker of the sum mentioned in the document.

    (b) any document issued by a public officer which is intended to enable a person to obtain payment from the Paymaster General of the sum mentioned in the document but is not a

---

[5] Inserted by Central Bank Act, 1989 (No. 16), s. 132(c)

· bill of exchange, and
(c) any draft payable on demand drawn by a banker upon himself, whether payable at the head office or some other office of his bank,

as it applies to cheques.

(7) In this section, unless the context otherwise requires -

"the essential features of the cheque" includes -
(a) the serial number of the cheque,
(b) the identification code number of the drawee banker,
(c) the account number of the drawer of the cheque,
(d) the amount of the cheque as entered by the drawer of the cheque,

and any such particulars as may be given in the form of letters or figures or any other code which as between bankers represent those particulars;

"physical presentment" means presentment of a cheque for payment in accordance with banking practice other than as provided for in subsection (1).

46. Excuses or delay or non-presentment for payment

(1) Delay in making presentment for payment is excused when the delay is caused by circumstances beyond the control of the holder, and not imputable to his default, misconduct, or negligence. When the cause of delay ceases to operate presentment must be made with reasonable diligence.

(2) Presentment for payment is dispensed with,-
(a) Where, after the exercise of reasonable diligence presentment, as required by this Act, cannot be effected.

The fact that the holder has reason to believe that the bill will, on presentment, be dishonoured, does not dispense with the necessity of presentment.
(b) Where the drawee is a fictitious person.
(c) As regards the drawer where the drawee or acceptor is not bound, as between himself and the drawer, to accept or pay the bill, and the drawer has no reason to believe that the bill would be paid if presented.
(d) As regards an indorser, where the bill was accepted or made for the accommodation of that indorser, and he has no reason to expect that the bill would be paid if presented.
(e) By waiver of presentment, express or implied.

47. Dishonour by non-payment

(1) A bill is dishonoured by non-payment (a) when it is duly presented for payment and payment is refused or cannot be obtained, or (b) when presentment is excused and the bill is overdue and

unpaid.

(2) Subject to the provisions of this Act, when a bill is dishonoured by non-payment, an immediate right of recourse against the drawer and indorsers accrues to the holder.

48. Notice of dishonour and effect of non-notice

Subject to the provisions of this Act, when a bill has been dishonoured by non-acceptance or by non-payment, notice of dishonour must be given to the drawer and each indorser, and any drawer or indorser to whom such notice is not given is discharged;

Provided that-

(1) Where a bill is dishonoured by non-acceptance, and notice of dishonour is not given, the rights of a holder in due course subsequent to the omission, shall not be prejudiced by the omission.

(2) Where a bill is dishonoured by non-acceptance and due notice of dishonour is given, it shall not be necessary to give notice of a subsequent dishonour by non-payment unless the bill shall in the meantime have been accepted.

49. Rules as to notice of dishonour

Notice of dishonour in order to be valid and effectual must be given in accordance with the following rules-

(1) The notice must be given by or on behalf of the holder, or by or on behalf of an indorser who, at the time of giving it, is himself liable on the bill.

(2) Notice of dishonour may be given by an agent either in his own name or in the name of any party entitled to give notice whether that party be his principal or not.

(3) Where the notice is given by or on behalf of the holder it enures for the benefit of subsequent holders and all prior indorsers who have a right of recourse against the party to whom it is given.

(4) Where notice is given by or on behalf of an indorser entitled to give notice as herein-before provided, it enures for the benefit of the holder, and all indorsers subsequent to the party to whom notice is given.

(5) The notice may be given in writing or by personal communication, and may be given in any terms which sufficiently identify the bill and intimate that the bill has been dishonoured by non-acceptance or non-payment.

(6) The return of a dishonoured bill to the drawer or an indorser is, in point of form, deemed a sufficient notice of dishonour.

(7) A written notice need not be signed, and an insufficient written notice may be supplemented and validated by verbal communication. A misdescription of the bill shall not vitiate the notice unless the party to whom the notice is given is in fact misled thereby.

(8) Where notice of dishonour is required to be given to any person, it may be given either to the party himself, or to his agent in that behalf.

(9) Where the drawer or indorser is dead, and the party giving notice knows it, the notice must be given to a personal representative if such there be, and with the exercise of reasonable diligence he can be found.

(10) Where the drawer or indorser is bankrupt, notice may be given either to the party himself or to the trustee.

(11) Where there are two or more drawers or indorsers who are not partners, notice must be given to each of them, unless one of them has authority to receive such notice for the others.

(12) The notice may be given as soon as the bill is dishonoured and must be given within a reasonable time thereafter.

In the absence of special circumstances notice is not deemed to have been given within a reasonable time, unless-

    (a) where the person giving and the person to receive notice reside in the same place, the notice is given or sent off in time to reach the latter on the day after the dishonour of the bill.

    (b) where the person giving and the person to receive notice reside in different places, the notice is sent off on the day after the dishonour of the bill, if there be a post at a convenient hour on that day, and if there be no such post on that day then by the next post thereafter.

(13) Where a bill when dishonoured is in the hands of an agent, he may either himself give notice to the parties liable on the bill, or he may give notice to his principal. If he give notice to his principal, he must do so within the same time as if he were the holder, and the principal upon receipt of such notice has himself the same time for giving notice as if the agent had been an independent holder.

(14) Where a party to a bill receives due notice of dishonour, he has after the receipt of such notice the same period of time for giving notice to antecedent parties that the holder has after the dishonour.

(15) Where a notice of dishonour is duly addressed and posted, the sender is deemed to have given due notice of dishonour, notwithstanding any miscarriage by the post office.

50. Excuses for non-notice and delay

(1) Delay in giving notice of dishonour is excused where the delay is caused by circumstances beyond the control of the party giving notice, and not imputable to his default, misconduct, or negligence. When the cause of delay ceases to operate the notice must be given with reasonable diligence.

(2) Notice of dishonour is dispensed with-

    (a) When, after the exercise of reasonable diligence, notice as required by this Act cannot be given to or does not reach the drawer or indorser sought to be charged :

(b) By waiver express or implied. Notice of dishonour may be waived before the time of giving notice has arrived, or after the omission to give due notice:

(c) As regards the drawer in the following cases, namely (1) where drawer and drawee are the same person, (2) where the drawee is a fictitious person or a person not having capacity to contract, (3) where the drawer is the person to whom the bill is presented for payment, (4) where the drawee or acceptor is as between himself and the drawer under no obligation to accept or pay the bill, (5) where the drawer has countermanded payment:

(d) As regards the indorser in the following cases, namely-(1) where the drawee is a fictitious person or a person not having capacity to contract and the indorser was aware of the fact at the time he indorsed the bill, (2) where the indorser is the person to whom the bill is presented for payment, (3) where the bill was accepted or made for his accommodation.

51. Noting or protest of bill

(1) Where an inland bill has been dishonoured it may, if the holder think fit, be noted for non-acceptance or non-payment, as the case may be; but it shall not be necessary to note or protest any such bill in order to preserve the recourse against the drawer or indorser.

(2) Where a foreign bill, appearing on the face of it to be such, has been dishonoured by non-acceptance it must be duly protested for non-acceptance, and where such a bill, which has not been previously dishonoured by non-acceptance, is dishonoured by non-payment it must be duly protested for non-payment. If it be not so protested the drawer and indorsers are discharged. Where a bill does not appear on the face of it to be a foreign bill, protest thereof in case of dishonour is unnecessary.

(3) A bill which has been protested for non-acceptance may be subsequently protested for non-payment.

(4) Subject to the provisions of this Act, when a bill is noted or protested, [it may be noted on the day of its dishonour, and it must be noted not later than the next succeeding business day]. When a bill has been duly noted, the protest may be subsequently extended as of the date of the noting.[6]

(5) Where the acceptor of a bill becomes bankrupt or insolvent or suspends payment before it matures the holder may cause the bill to be protested for better security against the drawer and indorsers.

[6] The words in square brackets were substituted by the Bills of Exchange (Time of Noting) Act, 1917, 7 & 8 Geo. 5 c. 48

(6) A bill must be protested at the place where it is dishonoured: Provided that-
- (a) When a bill is presented through the post office, and returned by post dishonoured, it may be protested at the place to which it is returned and on the day of its return if received during business hours, and if not received during business hours, then not later than the next business day:
- (b) When a bill drawn payable at the place of business or residence of some person other than the drawee has been dishonoured by non-acceptance, it must be protested for non-payment at the place where it is expressed to be payable, and no further presentment for payment to, or demand on, the drawee is necessary.

(7) A protest must contain a copy of the bill, and must be signed by the notary making it, and must specify-
- (a) The person at whose request the bill is protested.
- (b) The place and date of protest, the cause or reason for protesting the bill, demand made, and the answer given, if any, or the fact that the drawee or acceptor could not be found.

(8) Where a bill is lost or destroyed, or is wrongly detained from the person entitled to hold it, protest may be made on a copy or written particulars thereof.

(9) Protest is dispensed with by any circumstance which would dispense with notice of dishonour. Delay in noting or protesting is excused when the delay is caused by circumstances beyond the control of the holder, and not imputable to his default, misconduct, or negligence. When the cause of delay ceases to operate the bill must be noted or protested with reasonable diligence.

52. Duties of holder as regards drawee or acceptor

(1) When a bill is accepted generally presentment for payment is not necessary in order to render the acceptor liable.

(2) When by the terms of a qualified acceptance presentment for payment is required, the acceptor, in the absence of an express stipulation to that effect, is not discharged by the omission to present the bill for payment on the day that it matures.

(3) In order to render the acceptor of a bill liable it is not necessary to protest it, or that notice of dishonour should be given to him.

(4) Where the holder of a bill presents it for payment, he shall exhibit the bill to the person from whom he demands payment, and when a bill is paid the holder shall forthwith deliver it up to the party paying it.

Liabilities of Parties.

53. Funds in hand of drawee
(1) A bill, of itself, does not operate as an assignment of funds in the hands of the drawee available for the payment thereof, and the drawee of a bill who does not accept as required by this Act is not liable on the instrument. This subsection shall not extend to Scotland.
(2) In Scotland where the drawee of a bill has in his hands funds available for the payment thereof, the bill operates as an assignment of the sum for which it is drawn in favour of the holder from the time when the bill is presented to the drawee.

54. Liability of acceptor
The acceptor of a bill, by accepting it:
(1) Engages that he will pay it according to the tenour of his acceptance:
(2) Is precluded from denying to a holder in due course-
  (a) The existence of the drawer, the genuineness of his signature, and his capacity and authority to draw the bill:
  (b) In the case of a bill payable to drawer's order, the then capacity of the drawer to indorse, but not the genuineness or validity of his indorsement:
  (c) In the case of a bill payable to the order of a third person, the existence of the payee and his then capacity to indorse, but not the genuineness or validity of his indorsement.

55. Liability of drawer or indorser
(1) The drawer of a bill by drawing it -
  (a) Engages that on due presentment it shall be accepted and paid according to its tenour, and that if it be dishonoured he will compensate the holder or any indorser who is compelled to pay it, provided that the requisite proceedings on dishonour be duly taken:
  (b) Is precluded from denying to a holder in due course the existence of the payee and his then capacity to indorse.
(2) The indorser of a bill by indorsing it-
  (a) Engages that on due presentment it shall be accepted and paid according to its tenour, and that if it be dishonoured he will compensate the holder or a subsequent indorser who is compelled to pay it, provided that the requisite proceedings on dishonour be duly taken;
  (b) Is precluded from denying to a holder in due course the genuineness and regularity in all respects of the drawer's signature and all previous indorsements;
  (c) Is precluded from denying to his immediate or a subsequent

indorsee that the bill was at the time of his indorsement a valid
and subsisting bill, and that he had then a good title thereto.

56. Stranger signing bill liable as indorser
Where a person signs a bill otherwise than as drawer or acceptor, he
thereby incurs the liabilities of an indorser to a holder in due course.

57. Measure of damages against parties to dishonoured bill
Where a bill is dishonoured, the measure of damages, which shall
be deemed to be liquidated damages, shall be as follows:

(1) The holder may recover from any party liable on the bill, and
the drawer who has been compelled to pay the bill may recover from
the acceptor, and an indorser who has been compelled to pay the bill
may recover from the acceptor or from the drawer, or from a prior
indorser-

(a) The amount of the bill:
(b) Interest thereon from the time of presentment for payment if
the bill is payable on demand, and from the maturity of the
bill in any other case:
(c) The expenses of noting, or, when protest is necessary, and the
protest has been extended the expenses of protest.

(2) In the case of a bill which has been dishonoured abroad, in lieu
of the above damages, the holder may recover from the drawer or an
indorser, and the drawer or an indorser who has been compelled to
pay the bill may recover from any party liable to him, the amount of
the re-exchange with interest thereon until the time of payment.

(3) Where by this Act interest may be recovered as damages, such
interest may, if justice require it, be withheld wholly or in part, and
where a bill is expressed to be payable with interest at a given rate,
interest as damages may or may not be given at the same rate as
interest proper.

58. Transferor by delivery and transferee
(1) Where the holder of a bill payable to bearer negotiates it by
delivery without indorsing it, he is called a "transferor by delivery".

(2) A transferor by delivery is not liable on the instrument.

(3) A transferor by delivery who negotiates a bill thereby warrants
to his immediate transferee being a holder for value that the bill is
what it purports to be, that he has a right to transfer it, and that at the
time of transfer he is not aware of any fact which renders it valueless.

59. Payment in due course

(1) A bill is discharged by payment in due course by or on behalf of the drawee or acceptor.

"Payment in due course" means payment made at or after the maturity of the bill to the holder thereof in good faith and without notice that his title to the bill is defective.

(2) Subject to the provisions hereinafter contained, when a bill is paid by the drawer or an indorser it is not discharged; but

(a) Where a bill payable to, or to the order of, a third party is paid by the drawer, the drawer may enforce payment thereof against the acceptor, but may not re-issue the bill.

(b) Where a bill is paid by an indorser, or where a bill payable to drawer's order is paid by the drawer, the party paying it is remitted to his former rights as regards the acceptor or antecedent parties, and he may, if he thinks fit, strike out his own and subsequent indorsements, and again negotiate the bill.

(3) Where an accommodation bill is paid in due course by the party accommodated the bill is discharged.

60. Banker paying demand draft where an indorsement is forged

When a bill payable to order on demand is drawn on a banker, and the banker on whom it is drawn pays the bill in good faith and in the ordinary course of business, it is not incumbent on the banker to show that the indorsement of the payee or any subsequent indorsement was made by or under the authority of the person whose indorsement it purports to be, and the banker is deemed to have paid the bill in due course, although such indorsement has been forged or made without authority.

61. Acceptor the holder at maturity

When the acceptor of a bill is or becomes the holder of it at or after its maturity, in his own right, the bill is discharged.

62. Express waiver

(1) When the holder of a bill at or after its maturity absolutely and unconditionally renounces his rights against the acceptor the bill is discharged.

The renunciation must be in writing, unless the bill is delivered up to the acceptor.

(2) The liabilities of any party to a bill may in like manner be renounced by the holder before, at, or after its maturity; but nothing in this section shall affect the rights of a holder in due course without

notice of the renunciation.

63. Cancellation

(1) Where a bill is intentionally cancelled by the holder or his agent, and the cancellation is apparent thereon, the bill is discharged.

(2) In like manner any party liable on a bill may be discharged by the intentional cancellation of his signature by the holder or his agent. In such case any indorser who would have had a right of recourse against the party whose signature is cancelled, is also discharged.

(3) A cancellation made unintentionally, or under a mistake, or without the authority of the holder is inoperative; but where a bill or any signature thereon appears to have been cancelled the burden of proof lies on the party who alleges that the cancellation was made unintentionally, or under a mistake, or without authority.

64. Alteration of bill [7]

(1) Where a bill or acceptance is materially altered without the assent of all parties liable on the bill, the bill is discharged except as against a party who has himself made, authorised, or assented to the alteration, and subsequent indorsers.

Provided that,

Where a bill has been materially altered, but the alteration is not apparent, and the bill is in the hands of a holder in due course, such holder may avail himself of the bill as if it had not been altered, and may enforce payment of it according to its original tenour.

(2) In particular the following alterations are material, namely, any alteration of the date, the sum payable, the time of payment, the place of payment, and where a bill has been accepted generally the addition of a place of payment without the acceptor's assent.

Acceptance and Payment for Honour.

65. Acceptance for honour *supra protest*

(1) Where a bill of exchange has been protested for dishonour by non-acceptance,or protested for better security, and is not overdue, any person, not being a party already liable thereon, may, with the consent of the holder, intervene and accept the bill supra protest, for the honour of any party liable thereon, or for the honour of the person for whose account the bill is drawn.

(2) A bill may be accepted for honour for part only of the sum for which it is drawn.

(3) An acceptance for honour *supra protest* in order to be valid must-

---

[7] Modified by Decimal Currency Act, 1970 (No. 21), s. 4(1)&(2)

(a) be written on the bill, and indicate that it is an acceptance for honour:

(b) be signed by the acceptor for honour.

(4) Where an acceptance for honour does not expressly state for whose honour it is made, it is deemed to be an acceptance for the honour of the drawer.

(5) Where a bill payable after sight is accepted for honour, its maturity is calculated from the date of the noting for non-acceptance and not from the date of the acceptance for honour.

66. Liability of acceptor for honour

(1) The acceptor for honour of a bill by accepting it engages that he will, on due presentment, pay the bill according to the tenour of his acceptance, if it is not paid by the drawee, provided it has been duly presented for payment, and protested for non-payment, and that he receives notice of these facts.

(2) The acceptor for honour is liable to the holder and to all parties to the bill subsequent to the party for whose honour he has accepted.

67. Presentment to acceptor for honour or case of need

(1) Where a dishonoured bill has been accepted for honour *supra protest*, or contains a reference in case of need, it must be protested for non-payment before it is presented for payment to the acceptor for honour, or referee in case of need.

(2) Where the address of the acceptor for honour is in the same place where the bill is protested for non-payment, the bill must be presented to him not later than the day following its maturity; and where the address of the acceptor for honour is in some place other than the place where it was protested for non-payment, the bill must be forwarded not later than the day following its maturity for presentment to him.

(3) Delay in presentment or non-presentment is excused by any circumstance which would excuse delay in presentment for payment or non-presentment for payment.

(4) When a bill of exchange is dishonoured by the acceptor for honour it must be protested for non-payment by him.

68. Payment for honour *supra protest*

(1) Where a bill has been protested for non-payment, any person may intervene and pay it *supra protest* for the honour of any party liable thereon, or for the honour of the person for whose account the bill is drawn.

(2) Where two or more persons offer to pay a bill for the honour of different parties, the person whose payment will discharge most parties to the bill shall have the preference.

(3) Payment for honour *supra protest*, in order to operate as such and not as a mere voluntary payment, must be attested by a notarial act of honour, which may be appended to the protest or form an extension of it.

(4) The notarial act of honour must be founded on a declaration made by the payer for honour, or his agent in that behalf, declaring his intention to pay the bill for honour, and for whose honour he pays.

(5) Where a bill has been paid for honour, all parties subsequent to the party for whose honour it is paid are discharged, but the payer for honour is subrogated for, and succeeds to both the rights and duties of, the holder as regards the party for whose honour he pays, and all parties liable to that party.

(6) The payer for honour on paying to the holder the amount of the bill and the notarial expenses incidental to its dishonour is entitled to receive both the bill itself and the protest. If the holder do not on demand deliver them up he shall be liable to the payer for honour in damages.

(7) Where the holder of a bill refuses to receive payment supra protest he shall lose his right of recourse against any party who would have been discharged by such payment.

Lost Instruments.

69. Holder's right to duplicate of lost bill

Where a bill has been lost before it is overdue, the person who was the holder of it may apply to the drawer to give him another bill of the same tenour, giving security to the drawer if required to indemnify him against all persons whatever in case the bill alleged to have been lost shall be found again.

If the drawer on request as aforesaid refuses to give such duplicate bill, he may be compelled to do so.

70. Action on lost bill

In any action or proceeding upon a bill, the court or a judge may order that the loss of the instrument shall not be set up, provided an indemnity be given to the satisfaction of the court or judge against the claims of any other person upon the instrument in question.

Bill in a Set.

71. Rules as to sets

(1) Where a bill is drawn in a set, each part of the set being numbered, and containing a reference to the other parts, the whole of the parts constitute one bill.

(2) Where the holder of a set indorses two or more parts to different persons, he is liable on every such part, and every indorser subsequent to him is liable on the part he has himself indorsed as if the said parts were separate bills.

(3) Where two or more parts of a set are negotiated to different holders in due course, the holder whose title first accrues is as between such holders deemed the true owner of the bill; but nothing in this subsection shall affect the rights of a person who in due course accepts or pays the part first presented to him.

(4) The acceptance may be written on any part, and it must be written on one part only.

If the drawee accepts more than one part, and such accepted parts get into the hands of different holders in due course, he is liable on every such part as if it were a separate bill.

(5) When the acceptor of a bill drawn in a set pays it without requiring the part bearing his acceptance to be delivered up to him, and that part at maturity is outstanding in the hands of a holder in due course, he is liable to the holder thereof.

(6) Subject to the preceding rules, where any one part of a bill drawn in a set is discharged by payment or otherwise, the whole bill is discharged.

Conflict of Laws.

72. Rules where laws conflict

Where a bill drawn in one country is negotiated, accepted, or payable in another, the rights, duties, and liabilities of the parties thereto are determined as follows-

(1) The validity of a bill as regards requisites in form is determined by the law of the place of issue, and the validity, as regards requisites in form, of the supervening contracts, such as acceptance, or indorsement, or acceptance *supra protest*, is determined by the law of the place where such contract was made.

Provided that-

(a) Where a bill is issued out of the United Kingdom it is not invalid by reason only that it is not stamped in accordance with the law of the place of issue :

(b) Where a bill, issued out of the United Kingdom, conforms, as regards requisites in form, to the law of the United Kingdom, it may, for the purpose of enforcing payment thereof, be treated as valid as between all persons who negotiate, hold, or become parties to it in the United Kingdom.

(2) Subject to the provisions of this Act, the interpretation of the drawing, indorsement, acceptance *supra protest* of a bill, is determined by the law of the place where such contract is made.

Provided that where an inland bill is indorsed in a foreign country the indorsement shall as regards the payer be interpreted according to the law of the United Kingdom.

(3) The duties of the holder with respect to presentment for acceptance or payment and the necessity for or sufficiency of a protest or notice of dishonour, or otherwise, are determined by the law of the place where the act is done or the bill is dishonoured.

(4) Where a bill is drawn out of, but payable in, the United Kingdom, and the sum payable is not expressed in the currency of the United Kingdom, the amount shall, in the absence of some express stipulation, be calculated according to the rate of exchange for sight drafts at the place of payment on the day the bill is payable.

(5) Where a bill is drawn in one country and is payable in another, the due date thereof is determined according to the law of the place where it is payable.

Part 111.

Cheques on a banker

73. Cheque defined

A cheque is a bill of exchange drawn on a banker payable on demand.

Except as otherwise provided in this part, the provisions of this Act applicable to a bill of exchange payable on demand apply to a cheque.

74. Presentment of cheque for payment

Subject to the provisions of this Act-

(1) Where a cheque is not presented for payment within a reasonable time of its issue, and the drawer or person on whose account it it is drawn had the right at the time of such presentment, as between him and the banker, to have the cheque paid and suffers actual damage through the delay, he is discharged to the extent of such damage, that is to say, to the extent to which such drawer or person is a creditor of such banker to a larger amount than he would have been had such cheque been paid.

(2) In determining what is a reasonable time regard shall be had to the nature of the instrument, the usage of trade and of bankers, and the facts of the particular case.

(3) The holder of such cheque as to which such drawer or person is discharged shall be a creditor in lieu of such drawer or person of such banker to the extent of such discharge, and entitled to recover the amount from him.

Bills of Exchange Act, 1882

75. Revocation of banker's authority

The duty and authority of a banker to pay a cheque drawn on him by his customer are determined by-
(1) Countermand of payment :
(2) Notice of a customer's death.

Crossed Cheques[8]

76. General and special crossings defined

(1) Where a cheque bears across its face an addition of-
  (a) The words "and company" or any abbreviation thereof between two parallel transverse lines, either with or without the words "not negotiable"; or,
  (b) Two parallel transverse lines simply, either with or without the words "not negotiable", that addition constitutes a crossing, and the cheque is crossed generally.
(2) Where a cheque bears across its face an addition of the name of a banker, either with or without the words "not negotiable", that addition constitutes a crossing, and the cheque is crossed specially and to that banker.

77. Crossing by drawer or after issue

(1) A cheque may be crossed generally or specially by the drawer.
(2) Where a cheque is uncrossed, the holder may cross it generally or specially.
(3) Where a cheque is crossed generally the holder may cross it specially.
(4) Where a cheque is crossed generally or specially, the holder may add the words "not negotiable".
(5) Where a cheque is crossed specially, the banker to whom it is crossed may again cross it specially to another banker for collection.
(6) Where an uncrossed cheque, or a cheque crossed generally, is sent to a banker for collection, he may cross it specially to himself.

78. Crossing a material part of cheque

A crossing authorised by this Act is a material part of the cheque; it shall not be lawful for any person to obliterate or, except as authorised by this Act, to add to or alter the crossing.

79. Duties of banker as to crossed cheques

(1) Where a cheque is crossed specially to more than one banker,

---

[8] Sections 76 to 82: extended to any document issued by a customer, Revenue Act, 1883, 46 & 47 Vict. c. 52, s. 17 and applied in part by Cheques Act, 1959 (No. 19), s. 5

except when crossed to an agent for collection being a banker, the banker on whom it is drawn shall refuse payment thereof.

(2) Where the banker on whom a cheque is drawn which is so crossed nevertheless pays the same, or pays a cheque crossed generally otherwise than to a banker, or if crossed specially otherwise than to the banker to whom it is crossed, or his agent for collection being a banker, he is liable to the true owner of the cheque for any loss he may sustain owing to the cheque having been so paid.

Provided that where a cheque is presented for payment which does not at the time of presentment appear to be crossed, or to have had a crossing which has been obliterated, or to have been added to or altered otherwise than as authorised by this Act, the banker paying the cheque in good faith and without negligence shall not be responsible or incur any liability, nor shall the payment be questioned by reason of the cheque having been crossed, or of the crossing having been obliterated or having been added to or altered otherwise than as authorised by this Act, and of payment having been made otherwise than to a banker or to the banker to whom the cheque is or was crossed, or to his agent for collection being a banker, as the case may be.

80. Protection to banker and drawer where cheque crossed

Where the banker, on whom a crossed cheque is drawn in good faith and without negligence pays it, if crossed generally, to a banker, and if crossed specially to the banker to whom it is crossed, or his agent for collection being a banker, the banker paying the cheque, and, if the cheque has come into the hands of the payee, the drawer, shall respectively be entitled to the same rights and be placed in the same position as if payment of the cheque had been made to the true owner thereof.

81. Effect of crossing on holder

Where a person takes a crossed cheque which bears on it the words "not negotiable", he shall not have and shall not be capable of giving a better title to the cheque than that which the person from whom he took it had.

82. Repealed by Cheque Act, 1959 (No. 19), s. 6(3), sch.

Part IV.
Promissory notes

83. Promissory note defined

(1) A promissory note is an unconditional promise in writing made by one person to another signed by the maker, engaging to pay, on

demand or at a fixed or determinable future time, a sum certain in money to, or to the order of, a specified person or to bearer.

(2) An instrument in the form of a note payable to maker's order, is not a note within the meaning of this section unless and until it is indorsed by the maker.

(3) A note is not invalid by reason only that it contains also a pledge of collateral security with authority to sell or dispose thereof.

(4) A note which is or on the face of it purports to be both made and payable within the British Islands is an inland note. Any other note is a foreign note.

84. Delivery necessary

A promissory note is inchoate and incomplete until delivery thereof to the payee or bearer.

85. Joint and several notes

(1) A promissory note may be made by two or more makers, and they may be liable thereon jointly, or jointly and severally according to its tenour.

(2) Where a note runs "I promise to pay," and is signed by two or more persons, it is deemed to be their joint and several note.

86. Note payable on demand

(1) Where a note payable on demand has been indorsed, it must be presented for payment within a reasonable time of the indorsement. If it be not so presented the indorser is discharged.

(2) In determining what is a reasonable time, regard shall be had to the nature of the instrument, the usage of trade, and the facts of the particular case.

(3) Where a note payable on demand is negotiated, it is not deemed to be overdue, for the purpose of affecting the holder with defects of title of which he had no notice, by reason that it appears that a reasonable time for presenting it for payment has elapsed since its issue.

87. Presentment of note for payment

(1) Where a promissory note is in the body of it made payable at a particular place, it must be presented for payment at that place in order to render the maker liable. In any other case, presentment for payment is not necessary in order to render the maker liable.

(2) Presentment for payment is necessary in order to render the indorser of a note liable.

(3) Where a note is in the body of it made payable at a particular place, presentment at that place is necessary in order to render an indorser liable; but when a place of payment is indicated by way of

memorandum only, presentment at that place is sufficient to render the indorser liable, but a presentment to the maker elsewhere, if sufficient in other respects, shall also suffice.

88. Liability of maker
The maker of a promissory note by making it-
(1) Engages that he will pay it according to its tenour;
(2) Is precluded from denying to a holder in due course the existence of the payee and his then capacity to indorse.

89. Application of part II to notes
(1) Subject to the provisions in this part, and except as by this section provided, the provisions of this Act relating to bills of exchange, apply, with the necessary modifications, to promissory notes.

(2) In applying those provisions the maker of a note shall be deemed to correspond with the acceptor of a bill, and the first indorser of a note shall be deemed to correspond with the drawer of an accepted bill payable to drawer's order.

(3) The following provisions as to bills do not apply to notes; namely, provisions relating to-

    (a)   Presentment for acceptance;
    (b)   Acceptance;
    (c)   Acceptance *supra protest*;
    (d)   Bills in a set.

(4) Where a foreign note is dishonoured, protest thereof is unnecessary.

Part V

Supplementary

90. Good faith
A thing is deemed to be done in good faith, within the meaning of this Act, where it is in fact done honestly; whether it is done negligently or not.

91. Signature
(1) When, by this Act, any instrument or writing is required to be signed by any person, it is not necessary that he should sign it with his own hand, but it is sufficient if his signature is written thereon by some other person by or under his authority.

(2) In the case of a corporation, where, by this Act, any instrument or writing is required to be signed, it is sufficient if the instrument or writing be sealed with the corporate seal.

But nothing in this section shall be construed as requiring the bill or note of a corporation to be under seal.

92. Computation time
Where, by this Act, the time limited for doing any act or thing is less than three days, in reckoning time, non-business days are excluded. ..[9]..

93. When noting equivalent to protest
For the purposes of this Act, where a bill or note is required to be protested within a specified time or before some further proceeding is taken, it is sufficient that the bill has been noted for protest before the expiration of the specified time or the taking of the proceeding; and the formal protest may be extended at any time thereafter as of the date of the noting.

94. Protest when notary not accessible
Where a dishonoured bill or note is authorised or required to be protested, and the services of a notary cannot be obtained at the place where the bill is dishonoured, any householder or substantial resident of the place may, in the presence of two witnesses, give a certificate, signed by them, attesting the dishonour of the bill, and the certificate shall in all respects operate as if it were a formal protest of the bill.

The form given in Schedule 1 to this Act may be used with necessary modifications, and if used shall be sufficient.

95. Dividend warrants may be crossed
The provisions of this Act as to crossed cheques shall apply to a warrant for payment of dividend.

96. Repealed by Statute Law Revision Act, 1898[10]

97. Savings
(1) The rules in bankruptcy relating to bills of exchange, promissory notes, and cheques, shall continue to apply thereto notwithstanding anything in this Act contained.

(2) The rules of common law including the law merchant, save in so far as they are inconsistent with the express provisions of this Act, shall continue to apply to bills of exchange, promissory notes, and cheques.

(3) Nothing in this Act or in any repeal effected thereby shall affect-

---

[9] Definition of "Non-business days": see s. 2 *ante p. 74*, insert by Central Bank Act, 1989 (No. 16), s. 132(1)(a)

[10] 61 & 62 Vict. c. 22

(a) ... [11]any law or enactment for the time being in force relating to the revenue:

(b) The provisions of the Companies Act, 1862, or Acts amending it, or any Act relating to joint stock banks or companies:

(c) The provisions of any Act relating to or confirming the privileges of the Bank of England or the Bank of Ireland respectively.

(d) The validity of any usage relating to dividend warrants, or the indorsement thereof.

98. Saving of summary diligence in Scotland

Nothing in this Act or in any repeal effected thereby shall extend or restrict, or in any way alter or affect the law and practice in Scotland in regard to summary diligence.

99. Construction with other Acts, &

Where an Act or document refers to any enactment repealed by this Act, the Act or document shall be construed, and shall operate, as if it referred to the corresponding provisions of this Act.

100. Parole evidence allowed in certain judicial proceedings in Scotland

In any judicial proceeding in Scotland, any fact relating to a bill of exchange, bank cheque, or promissory note, which is relevant to any question of liability thereon, may be proved by parole evidence: Provided that this enactment shall not in any way affect the existing law and practice whereby the party who is according to the tenor of any bill of exchange, bank cheque, or promissory note, debtor to the holder in the amount thereof, may be required, as a condition of obtaining a sist of diligence, or suspension of a charge, or threatened charge, to make such consignation, or to find such caution as the court or judge before whom the cause is depending may require.

This section shall not apply to any case where the bill of exchange, bank cheque, or promissory note has undergone the sesennial prescription.

---

[11] Repealed: Statute Law Revision Act, 1898, 61 & 62 Vict. c. 22

Bills of Exchange Act, 1882

First Schedule

Section 94

Form of protest which may be used when the services of a notary
cannot be obtained

Know all that I, A.B. [householder], of   in the
county of   in the United Kingdom, at the request of C.D.,
there being no notary public available, did on the   day of
188   at   demand payment [or acceptance] of the bill of exchange
hereunder written, from E.F., to which demand he made answer [state
answer, if any] wherefore I now, in the presence of G.H. and J.K. do
protest the said bill of exchange.

(Signed)   A.B.

G.H.} Witnesses.
J.K. }

N.B. - The bill itself should be annexed, or a copy of the bill and
all that is written thereon should be underwritten.

Second Schedule

Repealed by Statute Law Revision Act, 1898, 61 & 62 Vict. c. 22

Statutes Revised on Commercial Law

110

The Bills of Sale (Ireland) Act (1879) Amendment Act, 1883
46 & 47 Victoria, chapter 7[1,2]

List of Sections

---

[1] Modification, the Central Bank Act, 1971 (No. 24), s. 36(b) provides: where s. 35 of that Act effects an extension of or in relation to any such security so as to include future advances by or future liabilities to the transferee, such extension shall not require registration under or in pursuance of ..., the Bills of Sale (Ireland) Acts, 1879 and 1883, ... but shall operate for the purposes of those Acts as if it were made by deed duly registered on the transfer date under or in pursuance of whichever of those Acts may be applicable thereto.

[2] Rstrct., the Agricultural Credit Act, 1978 (No.2) s. 36(1) provides: A bill of sale of stock (whether including or not including any other chattels) made after the commencement of this Act shall, notwithstanding anything contained in the Bills of Sale (Ireland) Acts, 1879 and 1883, be void and be incapable of being registered under those Acts.

111

An Act to amend the Bills of Sale (Ireland) Act, 1879
26th April 1883

Preamble repealed by Statute Law Revision Act, 1898[3]

1. Short title

This Act may be cited for all purposes as the Bills of Sale (Ireland) Act (1879) Amendment Act, 1883; and this Act and the Bills of Sale (Ireland) Act, 1879, may be cited together as the Bills of Sale (Ireland) Acts, 1879 and 1883.

2. Commencement of Act

This Act shall come into operation on the first day of August one thousand eight hundred and eighty-three, which date is herein-after referred to as the commencement of this Act.

3. Construction of Act 42 & 43 Vict. c. 50

The Bills of Sale (Ireland) Act, 1879, is herein-after referred to as "the principal Act," and this Act shall, so far as is consistent with the tenor thereof, be construed as one with the principal Act; but unless the context otherwise requires shall not apply to any Bill of Sale registered before the commencement of this act so long as the registration thereof is not avoided by non-renewal or otherwise.

The expression "bill of sale," and other expressions in this Act, have the same meaning as in the principal Act, except as to bills of sale or other documents mentioned in section four of the principal Act, which may be given otherwise than by way of security for the payment of money, to which last-mentioned bills of sale and other documents this Act shall not apply.

4. Bill of sale to have schedule of property attached thereto

Every bill of sale shall have annexed thereto or written thereon a schedule containing an inventory of the personal chattels comprised in the bill of sale; and such bill of sale, save as herein-after mentioned, shall have effect only in respect of the personal chattels specifically described in the said schedule; and shall be void, except as against the grantor, in respect of any personal chattels not so specifically described.

5. Bill of sale not to affect after acquired property

Save as herein-after mentioned, a bill of sale shall be void, except as against the grantor, in respect of any personal chattels specifically described in the schedule thereto of which the grantor was not the

---

[3] 61 & 62 Vict. c. 22

true owner at the time of the execution of the bill of sale.

6. Exception as to certain things

Nothing contained in the foregoing sections of this Act shall render a bill of sale void in respect of any of the following things; (that is to say,)

(1) Any growing crops separately assigned or charged where such crops were actually growing at the time when the bill of sale was executed.

(2) Any fixtures separately assigned or charged, and any plant, or trade machinery where such fixtures, plant, or trade machinery are used in, attached to, or brought upon any land, farm, factory, workshop, shop, house, warehouse, or other place in substitution for any of the like fixtures, plant, or trade machinery specifically described in the schedule to such bill of sale.

7. Power to seize except in certain events to be void

Personal chattels assigned under a bill of sale shall not be liable to be seized or taken possession of by the grantee for any other than the following causes:

(1) If the grantor shall make default in payment of the sum or sums of money thereby secured at the time therein provided for payment, or in the performance of any covenant or agreement contained in the bill of sale and necessary for maintaining the security;

(2) If the grantor shall become a bankrupt, or suffer the said goods or any of them to be distrained for rent, rates, or taxes;

(3) If the grantor shall fraudulently either remove or suffer the said goods, or any of them, to be removed from the premises;

(4) If the grantor shall not, without reasonable excuse, upon demand in writing by the grantee, produce to him his last receipts for rent, rates, and taxes;

(5) If execution shall have been levied against the goods of the grantor under any judgment at law:

Provided that the grantor may within five days from the seizure or taking possession of any chattels on account of any of the above-mentioned cases, apply to the High Court, or to a judge thereof in chambers, and such court or judge, if satisfied that by payment of money or otherwise the said cause of seizure no longer exists, may restrain the grantee from removing or selling the said chattels, or may make such other order as may seem just.

8. Bill of sale to be void unless attested and registered

Every bill of sale shall be duly attested, and shall be registered under the principal Act within seven clear days after the execution thereof, or if it is executed in any place out of Ireland then within seven clear days after the time at which it would in the ordinary course of post arrive in Ireland if posted immediately after the execution thereof; and shall truly set forth the consideration for which it was given; otherwise such bill of sale shall be void in respect of the personal chattels comprised therein.

9. Form of bill of sale

A bill of sale made or given by way of security for the payment of money by the grantor thereof shall be void unless made in accordance with the form in the schedule to this Act annexed.

10. Attestation

The execution of every bill of sale by the grantor shall be attested by one or more credible witness or witnesses, not being a party or parties thereto. ..[4].

11. Local registration of contents of bills of sale

Where the affidavit (which under section ten of the principal Act is required to accompany a bill of sale when presented for registration) describes the residence of the person making or giving the same or of the person against whom the process is issued as being situated elsewhere than within the county of the city of Dublin or the county of Dublin, or where the bill of sale describes the chattels enumerated therein as being in some place or places outside the said county of the city of Dublin or the county of Dublin, the registrar under the principal Act shall forthwith and within three clear days after registration in the principal registry, and in accordance with the prescribed directions, transmit an abstract in the prescribed form of the contents of such bill of sale to the clerk of the peace in whose district such place or places is or are situate, and if such places are in the districts of different clerks of the peace, then to each such clerk of the peace.

Every abstract so transmitted shall be filed, kept, and indexed by the clerk of the peace in the prescribed manner, and any person may search, inspect, make extracts from, and obtain copies of the abstract so registered in the like manner and upon the like terms as to payment or otherwise as near as may be as in the case of bills of sale registered by the registrar under the principal Act.

12. Bill of sale under £30 to be void

Every bill of sale made or given in consideration of any sum under thirty pounds shall be void.

---

[4]Deletion; Statute Law Revision Act, 1898, 61 & 62 Vict. c. 22

13. Chattels not to be removed or sold until five days after seizure
All personal chattels seized or of which possession is taken ..⁴ .,
under or by virtue of any bill of sale (whether registered before of
after the commencement of this Act), shall remain on the premises
where they were so seized or so taken possession of, and shall not be
removed or sold until after the expiration of five clear days from the
day they were so seized or so taken possession of.

14. Bill of sale not to protect chattels against poor and other rates
A bill of sale to which this Act applies shall be no protection in
respect of personal chattels included in such bill of sale acts but for
such bill of sale would have been liable to distress under a judgment,
decree, or warrant for the recovery of taxes, poor rates, county cess,
or other rates.

15. Repeal of part of Bills of Sale (Ireland) Act, 1879
..⁴ .. and also all . enactments contained in the principal Act which
are inconsistent with this Act are repealed, ...

16. Inspection of registered bills of sale
..⁴ . any person shall be entitled at all reasonable times to search the
register, on payment of a fee of one shilling, or such other fee as
may be prescribed, and subject to such regulations as may be
prescribed, and shall be entitled at all reasonable times to inspect,
examine, and make extracts from any and every registered bill of
sale without being required to make a written application, or to
specify any particulars in reference thereto, upon payment of one
shilling for each bill of sale inspected, and such payment shall be
made by a judicature stamp: Provided that the said extracts shall be
limited to the dates of execution, registration, renewal of registration,
and satisfaction, to the names, addresses, and occupations of the
parties, to the amount of the consideration, and to any further
prescribed particulars.

17. Debentures to which Act not to apply
Nothing in this act shall apply to any debentures issued by any
mortgage, loan, or other incorporated company, and secured upon
the capital stock or goods, chattels, and effects of such company.

18. Extent of Act
This act shall not extend to England or to Scotland.

Schedule

Form of Bill of Sale.

This indenture made the   day of   , between
A.B. of   .... of the one part, and C.D. of
of the other part, witnesseth that in consideration of the sum of £
now paid to A.B. by C.D., the receipt of which the said A.B. hereby
acknowledges (or whatever else the consideration may be), he the
said A. B. doth hereby assign unto C. D.,   his executors,
administrators, and assigns, all and singular the several chattels and
things specifically described in the schedule hereto annexed by way
of security for the payment of the sum of £   , and interest
thereon at the rate of   per cent. per annum (or whatever
else may be the rate). And the said A.B. doth agree and declare that
he will duly pay to the said C. D. the principal sum aforesaid,
together with the interest then due, by equal   payments of £
on the   day of   (or whatever else may be the
stipulated times or time of payment). And the said A.B. doth also
agree with the said C.D. that he will (here insert terms as to insurance,
payment of rent, or otherwise, which the parties may agree to for the
maintenance or defeasance of the security). Provided always, that the
chattels hereby assigned shall not be liable to seizure or to be taken
possession of by the said C.D. for any cause other than those
specified in section seven of the Bills of Sale (Ireland) act (1879)
Amendment Act, 1883

In witness, &c.

Signed and sealed by the said A.B. in the
presence of me E. F. (add witness name,
address, and description).

The Merchandise Marks Act, 1887
50 & 51 Victoria, chapter 28

List of Sections

An Act to consolidate and amend the law relating to fraudulent marks on merchandise.[1]
23rd August 1887

1. Short title.
This Act may be cited as the Merchandise Marks Act, 1887.

2. Offences as to trade marks and trade descriptions
(1) Every person who-
   (a) forges any trade mark; or
   (b) falsely applies to goods any trade mark or any mark so nearly resembling a trade mark as to be calculated to deceive; or
   (c) makes any die, block, machine, or other instrument for the purpose of forging or of being used for forging a trade mark; or
   (d)[2, 3] in the course of any trade, business or profession, applies any false trade description to goods, or
   (e) disposes of or has in his possession any die, block, machine, or other instrument for the purpose of forging a trade mark; or
   (f) causes any of the things above in this section mentioned to be done, shall, subject to the provisions of this Act, and unless he proves that he acted without intent to defraud,[4] be guilty of an offence against this Act.

(2) [5]Every person who sells, or exposes for, or has in his possession for, sale, or any purpose of trade or manufacture,[6] any goods or things to which any forged trade mark or false trade description is applied, or to which any trade mark or mark so nearly resembling a trade mark as to be calculated to deceive is falsely applied, as the case may be, shall, unless he proves-
   (a) That having taken all reasonable precautions against committing an offence against this Act, he had at the time of the commission of the alleged offence no reason to suspect the genuineness of the trade mark, mark, or trade description;

---

[1] Rstrct. Consumer Information Act, 1978 (No. 1), s. 23

[2] As amended by: Consumer Information Act, 1978 (No. 1), s. 4

[3] Saved, Industrial Research and Standards Act, 1961 (No. 20), s. 23(3)

[4] For defencec see: Consumer Information Act, 1978 (No. 1), s. 3(1)

[5] Ext. Hallmarking Act, 1981 (No. 18), ss. 5, 18(2)

[6] Amended insofar as relates to trade descriptions by the substitution of "in the course of any trade, business or profession" for "or any purpose of trade or manufacture" by Consumer Information Act, 1978 (No. 1), s. 4(2)

and
(b) That on demand made by or on behalf of the prosecutor, he gave all the information in his power with respect to the persons from whom he obtained such goods or things; or
(c) That otherwise he had acted innocently;
be guilty of an offence against this Act.

(3) Every person guilty of an offence against this Act shall be liable-
   (i) on conviction on indictment, to imprisonment, with or without hard labour, for a term not exceeded two years, or to fine, or to both imprisonment and fine; and
   (ii) on summary conviction to imprisonment, with or without hard labour, for a term not exceeding four months, or to a fine not exceeding twenty pounds, and in the case of a second or subsequent conviction to imprisonment, with or without hard labour, for a term not exceeding six months, or to a fine not exceeding fifty pounds; and
   (iii) in any case, to forfeit to *the State*[7] every chattel, article, instrument, or thing by means of or in relation to which the offence has been committed.

(4) The court before whom any person is convicted under this section may order any forfeited articles to be destroyed or otherwise disposed of as the court thinks fit.

(5) If any person feels aggrieved by any conviction made by a court of summary jurisdiction, he may appeal therefrom to a court of quarter sessions.

(6) Any offence for which a person is under this Act liable to punishment on summary conviction may be prosecuted, and any articles liable to be forfeited under this Act by a court of summary jurisdiction may be forfeited, in manner provided by the Summary Jurisdiction Acts: Provided that a person charged with an offence under this section before a court of summary jurisdiction shall, on appearing before the court, and before the charge is gone into, be informed of his right to be tried on indictment, and if he requires be so tried accordingly.

3. Definitions
(1) For the purpose of this Act-
trade mark
The expression " trade mark" means a trade mark registered in the register of trade marks kept under the Patents, Designs, and Trade Marks Act, 1883, and includes any trade mark which, either with or without registration, is protected by law in any British possession or foreign State to which the provision of the one hundred and third

---

[7] Construction of Her Majesty: Merchandise Marks Act, 1931 (No. 48), s. 29(2)

119

section of the Patents, Designs, and Trade Marks Act 1883, are, under Order in Council, for the time being applicable:

trade description

The expression "trade description"[8] means any description, statement, or other indication, direct or indirect-

(a) as to the number, quantity, measure, gauge, capacity or weight of any goods, or
(b) as to the place or country in which any goods were manufactured, produced, processed, reconditioned, repaired, packed or prepared for sale, or
(c) as to the mode of manufacturing, producing, processing, reconditioning, repairing, packing or preparing for sale of any goods, or
(d) as to the person by whom and the time at which any goods were manufactured, produced, processed, reconditioned, repaired, packed or prepared for sale, or
(e) as to the material of which any goods are composed, or
(f) as to any goods being the subject of an existing patent, privilege or copyright, or
(g) as to the fitness for any purpose, strength, performance, behaviour or accuracy of any goods, or
(h) as to any physical characteristic of any goods not referred to in the preceding paragraphs of this definition, or
(i) as to the conformity of any goods with any standard or their passing of any test or their commendation by any person, or
(j) as to the identity of the supplier or distributor, or the standing, commercial importance, competence or capabilities of, the manufacturer, producer, supplier or distributor, of any goods, or
(k) as to the contents of books or as to their authors, as to the contents of cinematograph films (within the meaning of the Performers' Protection Act, 1968) or as to their producers or as to the contents of recordings (within the meaning of the Performers' Protection Act, 1968) or as to the performers on such recordings, or
(l) as to any history of any goods not referred to in the preceding paragraphs of this definition, including their previous ownership,

and the use of any figure, word, or mark which, according to the custom of the trade, is commonly taken to be an indication of any to the above matters, shall be deemed to be a trade description within the meaning of this Act;

---

[8] Substituted: Consumer Information Act, 1978 (No. 1), s. 2(1)

false trade description[9]

The expression "false trade description" means a trade description which is false in a material respect[10] as regards the goods to which it is applied, and includes every alteration of a trade description, whether by way of addition, effacement, or otherwise, where that alteration makes the description false in a material respect, and the fact that a trade description is a trade mark, or part of a trade mark, shall not prevent such trade description being a false trade description within the meaning of this Act:

goods

The expression "goods" means anything which is the subject of trade, manufacture, or merchandise:

person, manufacturer, dealer, trader, proprietor

The expressions "person", "manufacturer, dealer, or trader," and "proprietor" include any body of persons corporate or unincorporate:

name

The expression "name" includes any abbreviation of a name.

(2) The provisions of this Act respecting the application of a false trade description to goods shall extend to the application to goods of any such figures, words, or marks, or arrangement or combination thereof, whether including a trade marks or not, as are reasonably calculated to lead persons to believe that the goods are the manufacture or merchandise of some person other than the person whose manufacture or merchandise they really are.

(3) The provision of this Act respecting the application of a false trade description to goods, or respecting goods to which a false trade description is applied, shall extend to the application to goods of any false name or initials of a person, and to goods with the false name or initials of a person which-

(a) are not a trade mark, or part of a trade mark, and

(b) are identical with, or a colourable imitation of the name or initials of a person carrying on business in connexion with

---

[9] See also the following statutes:

Appl. Agricultural Produce (Fresh Meat) Act, 1930 (No 10), s. 27(4) &

Agricultural Produce (Potatoes) Act, 1931 (No. 26), s. 19(4),

Power to appl. Spanish Trade Agreement Act, 1936 (No. 6), s. 2 &

Appl. Agricultural Produce (Eggs) Act, 1939 (No.2), s. 38(8)(9) & s. 40(4) &

Seed Production Act, 1955 (No. 14), s. 22(3),

Ext. Road Traffic Act, 1968 (No. 25), ss. 4, 14(2),

Rstrct. Packaged Good (Quality Control) Act, 1980 (No. 11), ss. 1(2), 12(1)

[10] Shall be construed as if the references to false in a material respect were references to false to a material degree and included references to misleading to a material degree: Consumer Information Act, 1978 (No. 1), s. 2(2)(a)

goods of the some description, and not having authorised the use of such name or initials, and

(c) are either those of a fictitious person or of some person not *bona fide* carrying on business in connexion with such goods.

4. Forging trade marks

A person shall be deemed to forge a trade mark who either -

(a) without the assent of the proprietor of the trade mark makes that trade mark or a mark so nearly resembling that trade mark as to be calculated to deceive; or

(b) falsifies any genuine trade mark, whether by alteration, addition, effacement, or otherwise;

and any trademark or mark so made or falsified is in this Act referred to as a forged trade mark.

Provided that in any prosecution for forging a trade mark the burden of proving the assent of the proprietor shall lie on the defendant.

5. Applying marks and descriptions[11]

(1) A person shall be deemed to apply a trade mark or mark or trade description to goods who-

(a) applies it to the goods themselves; or

------

[11] The Consumer Information Act, 1978, section 4(3) provides that this subsection is amended, insofar as it relates to trade descriptions, by the substitution of the following :

(1) (a) A person shall be deemed to apply a trade description to goods -

(i) he affixes annexes it to them or in any manner marks it on or incorporates it with-

(I) the goods themselves, or

(II) anything in, on or with which the goods are sold,

(ii) he places the goods in, on or with anything to, on or with which the trade description has been affixed, annexed, marked or incorporated or places any such thing with the goods.

(b) A person shall also be deemed to have applied a trade description to goods if he uses the trade description in any manner likely to be taken as referring to the goods.

(c) Where goods are sold in pursuance of a request in which a trade description is used and the circumstances are such as to make it reasonable to infer that the goods are sold as goods corresponding to that trade description, the person selling the goods shall be deemed to have applied that trade description to the goods.

(d) An oral statement may amount to the use of a trade description.

(b) applies it to any covering, label, reel, or other thing in or with which the goods are sold or exposed or had in possession for any purpose of sale, trade, or manufacture; or

(c) places, encloses, or annexes any goods which are sold or exposed or had in possession for any purpose of sale, trade, or manufacture, in with or to any covering, label, reel, or other thing to which a trade mark or trade description has been applied; or

(d) uses a trade mark or mark or trade description in any manner calculated to lead to the belief that the goods in connexion with which it is used are designated or described by that trade mark or mark or trade description.

(2) The expression "covering" includes any stopper, cask, bottle, vessel, box, cover, capsule, case, frame, or wrapper; and the expression "label" includes any band or ticket.

A trade mark, or mark, or trade description shall be deemed to be applies whether it is woven, impresses, or otherwise worked into, or annexed, or affixed to the goods, or to any covering label, reel, or other thing.

(3) A person shall be deemed to falsely apply to goods a trade mark or mark, who without the assent to the proprietor of a trade mark applies such trade mark or a mark so nearly resembling it as to be calculated to deceive, but in any prosecution for falsely applying a trade mark or mark to goods the burden of proving the assent of the proprietor shall lie on the defendant.

6. Exemption of certain persons employed in ordinary course of business.

Where a defendant is charged with making any die, block, machine, or other instrument for the purpose of forging, or being used for forging, a trade mark, or with falsely applying to goods any trade mark or any mark so nearly resembling a trade mark as to be calculated to deceive, or with applying to goods any false trade description, or causing any of the things in this section mentioned to be done, and proves-

(a) That in the ordinary course of his business he is employed, on behalf of other persons, to make dies, blocks, machines, or other instruments for making, or being used in making, trade marks, or as the case may be, to apply marks or descriptions to goods, and that in the case which is the subject of the charge he was so employed by some person resident in the United Kingdom, and was not interested in the goods by way of profit or commission dependent on the sale of such goods; and

(b) That he took reasonable precautions against committing the offence charged; and

(c) That he had, at the time of the commission of the alleged offence, no reason to suspect the genuineness of the trade mark, mark, or trade description; and

(d) That he gave to the prosecutor all the information in his power with respect to the persons on whose behalf the trade mark, mark, or description was applied-

he shall be discharged from the prosecution, but shall be liable to pay the costs incurred by the prosecutor, unless he has given due notice to him that he will rely on the above defence.

7. Application of Act to watches.

Where a watch case has thereon any words or marks which constitute, or are by common repute considered as constituting, a description of the country in which the watch was made, and the watch bears no description of the country where it was made, those words or marks shall *prima facie* be deemed to be a description of that country within the meaning of this Act, and the provisions or this Act with respect to goods to which a false trade description has been applied, and with respect to selling or exposing for or having in possession for sale, or any purpose of trade or manufacture, goods with a false trade description, shall apply accordingly, and for the purposes of this section the expression "watch" means all that portion of a watch which is not the watch case.

8. Repealed: Hallmarking Act, 1981 (No. 18), ss.15, 18(2), sch.

9. Trade mark, how described in pleading. [12]

In any indictment, pleading, proceeding, or document, in which any trade mark or forged trade mark is intended to be mentioned, it shall be sufficient, without further description and without any copy or facsimile, to state that trade mark or forged trade mark to be a trade mark or forged trade mark.

10. Rules as to evidence.

In any prosecution for an offence against this Act,-

(1) A defendant, and his wife or her husband, as the case may be, may, if the defendant thinks fit, be called as a witness, and, if called, shall be sworn and examined, and may be cross-examined and re-examined in like manner as any other witness.

(2) In the case of imported goods, evidence of the port of shipment shall be *prima facie* evidence of the place or country in which the goods were made or produced.

---

[12] Appl.: Merchandise Marks Act, 1931 (No. 48), s. 20(7)

11. Punishment of accessories.
Any person who, being within the United Kingdom, procures, counsels, aids, abets, or is accessory to the commission, without the United Kingdom, of any act, which, if committed in the United Kingdom, would under this Act be a misdemeanour, shall be guilty of that misdemeanour as a principal, and be liable to be indicted, proceeded against, tried, and convicted in any county or place in the United Kingdom in which he may be, as if the misdemeanour had been there committed.

12. Search Warrant.
(1) Where, upon information of an offence against this Act, a justice has issued either a summons requiring the defendant charged by such information to appear to answer to the same, or a warrant for the arrest of such defendant, and either the said justice on or after issuing the summons or warrant, or any other justice, is satisfied by information on oath that there is reasonable cause to suspect that any goods or things by means of or in relation to which such offence has been committed are in any house or premises of the defendant, or otherwise in his possession or under his control in any place, such justice may issue a warrant under his hand by virtue of which it shall be lawful for any constable named or referred to in the warrant, to enter such house, premises, or place at any reasonable time by day, and to search there for and seize and take away those goods or things; and any goods or things seized under any such warrant shall be brought before a court of summary jurisdiction for the purpose of its being determined whether the same are or are not liable to forfeiture under this Act.

(2) If the owner of any goods or things which, if the owner thereof had been convicted, would be liable to forfeiture under this Act, is unknown or cannot be found, an information or complaint may be laid for the purpose only of enforcing such forfeiture, and a court of summary jurisdiction may cause notice to be advertised stating that, unless cause is shown to the contrary at the time and place named in the notice, such goods or things will be forfeited, and at such time and place the court, unless the owner or any person on his behalf, or other person interested in the goods or things, shows cause to the contrary, may order such goods or things or any of them to be forfeited.

(3) Any goods or things forfeited under this section, or under any other provision of this Act, may be destroyed or otherwise disposed of, in such manner as the court by which the same are forfeited may direct, and the court may, out of any proceeds which may be realised by the disposition of such goods (all trade marks and trade description being first obliterated), award to any innocent party any

loss he may have innocently sustained in dealing with such goods.

13. Extension of 22 & 23 Vict. c.17. to offences under this Act.

The Act of the session of the twenty-second and twenty-third years of the reign of Her present Majesty, chapter seventeen, intituled "An Act to prevent vexatious indictments for certain misdemeanours," shall apply to any offence punishable on indictment under this Act, in like manner as if such offence were one of the offences specified in section one of that Act, but this section shall not apply to Scotland.

14. Costs of defence or prosecution.

On any prosecution under this Act the court may order costs to be paid to the defendant by the prosecutor, or to the prosecutor by the defendant, having regard to the information given by and the conduct of the defendant and prosecutor respectively.

15. Limitation of prosecution. [13]

No prosecution for an offence against this Act shall be commenced after the expiration of three years next after the commission of the offence, or one year next after the first discovery thereof by the prosecutor, whichever expiration first happens.

16. Prohibition on importation. [14] [15]

Whereas it is expedient to make further provision for prohibiting the importation of goods which, if sold, would be liable to forfeiture under this Act; be it therefore enacted as follows:

(1) All such goods, .[16] .. are hereby prohibited to be imported into the *State*[17] , and, subject to the provisions of this section, shall be included among goods prohibited to be imported as if they were specified in section forty-two of the Customs Consolidation Act, 1876.

(2) Before detaining any such goods, or taking any further proceedings with a view to the forfeiture thereof under the law

---

[13] Repealed insofar as relates to summary proceedings, Restrictive Practices (Amendment) Act, 1987 (No 31), s. 3, sch. 2, pt. 1.

[14] Appl. as am. Merchandise Marks Act, 1931 (No. 48), s. 17(1)

[15] See Merchandise Marks Act, 1911, *post*

[16] Words repealed by E.C. (Repeal and Revocation of certain statutory provisions) Regulations, S.I. 238/1985, reg. 2(1)

[17] Construction of United Kingdom as reference to Saorstát Eireann, Merchandise Marks Act, 1931 (No. 48), s. 29(1)

relating to the Customs, the *Revenue Commissioners* [18] may require the regulations under this section, whether as to information, security, conditions, or other matters, to be complied with, and may satisfy themselves in accordance with those regulations that the goods are such as are prohibited by this section to be imported.

(3) The *Revenue Commissioners* may from time to time make, revoke and vary, regulations, either general or special, respecting the detention and forfeiture of goods the importation of which is prohibited by this section, and the conditions, if any, to be fulfilled before such detention and forfeiture, and may by such regulations determine the information, notices, and security to be given, and the evidence requisite for any of the purposes of this section, and the mode of verification of such evidence.

(4) Where there is on any goods a name which is identical with or a colourable imitation of the name of a place in the *State*, that name, unless accompanied by the name of the country in which such place is situate, shall be treated for the purposes of this section as if it were the name of a place in the *State*.

(5) Such regulations may apply to all goods the importation of which is prohibited by this section, or different regulations may be made respecting different classes of such goods or of offences in relation to such goods.

(6) The *Revenue Commissioners*, in making and in administering the regulations, and generally in the administration of this section, whether in the exercise of any discretion or opinion, or otherwise, shall act under the control of the ..[19] *Minister for Finance*[20] .

(7) The regulations may provide for the informant reimbursing the Commissioners of Customs all expenses and damages incurred in respect of any detention made on his information, and of any proceedings consequent on such detention.

(8) All regulations under this section shall be published in *Iris Oifigiúil*[21] and in the "Board of Trade Journal."[22]

(9) This section shall have effect as if it were part of the Customs Consolidation Act, 1876, and shall accordingly apply to the Isle of Man as if it were part of the United Kingdom.

---

[18] Construction of Commissioners of Customs, Merchandise Marks Act, 1931 (No. 48), s. 29(4)

[19] Repealed by Statute Law Revision Act, 1908

[20] Construction of Treasury, Merchandise Marks Act, 1931 (No. 48), s. 29(5)

[21] Construction of the London Gazette, Merchandise Marks Act, 1931 (No. 48), s. 29(6)

[22] Ceases to have effect, Merchandise Marks Act, 1931 (No. 48), s. 29(7)

(10) [23]

17. Implied warranty on sale of marked goods.

On the sale or in the contract for the sale of any goods to which a trade mark, or mark, or trade description has been applied, the vendor shall be deemed to warrant that the mark is a genuine trade mark and not forged or falsely applied, or that the trade description is not a false trade description within the meaning of this Act, unless the contrary is expressed in some writing signed by or on behalf of the vendor and delivered at the time of the sale or contract to and accepted by the vendee.

18. Provisions of Act as to false description not to apply in certain cases.

Where, at the passing of this Act, a trade description is law-fully and generally applied to goods of a particular class, or manufactured by a particular method, to indicate the particular class or method of manufacture of such goods, the provisions of this Act with respect to false trade description shall not apply to such trade description when so applied: Provided that where such trade description includes the name of a place or country, and is calculated to mislead as to the place or country where the goods to which it is applied were actually made or produced, and the goods are not actually made or produced in that place or country, this section shall not apply unless there is added to the trade description, immediately before or after the name of that place or country, in an equally conspicuous manner, with that name, the name of the place or country in which the goods were actually made or produced, with a statement that they were made or produced there.

19. Savings.

(1) This Act shall not exempt any person from any action, suit, or other proceeding which might, but for the provisions of this Act, be brought against him

(2) Nothing in this Act shall entitle any person to refuse to make a complete discovery, or to answer any question or interrogatory in any action, but such discovery or answer shall not be admissible in evidence against such person in any prosecution for an offence against this Act.

(3) Nothing in this Act shall be construed so as to render liable to any prosecution or punishment any servant of a master resident in the United Kingdom who *bona fide* acts in obedience to the instructions of such master, and, on demand made by or on behalf of

---

[23] Repealed by Statute Law Revision Act, 1908

the prosecutor, has given full information as to his master.

20. False representation as to Royal Warrant.

Any person who falsely represents that any goods are made by a person holding a Royal Warrant, or for the service of Her Majesty, or any of the Royal Family, or any Government department, shall be liable, on summary conviction, to a penalty not exceeding twenty pounds.

21. Application of Act to Scotland.

In the application of this Act to Scotland the following modifications shall be made:-
The expression "Summary Jurisdiction Acts" means the Summary Procedure Act, 1864, and any Acts amending the same.
The expression "justice" means sheriff.
The expression "court of summary jurisdiction" means the Sheriff Court, and all jurisdiction necessary for the purpose of this Act is hereby conferred on sheriffs.

22. Application of Act to Ireland.

In the application of this Act to Ireland the following modifications shall be made:-
The expression "Summary Jurisdiction Acts" means, so far as respects the police district of Dublin metropolis, the Acts regulating the powers and duties of justices of the peace of such district, and as regards the rest of Ireland means the Petty Sessions (Ireland) Act, 1851, and any Act amending the same.
The expression "court of summary jurisdiction" means justices acting under those Acts.

23. Repeal of 25 & 26 Vict. c. 88

.. repealed, and any unrepealed enactment referring to any enactment so repealed shall be construed to apply to the corresponding provision of this Act; provided that .[24] ..

---

[24] Repealed by Statute Law Revision Act, 1908

The Factors Act, 1889
52 & 53 Victoria, chapter 45

List of Sections

Factors Act, 1889

An Act to amend and consolidate the Factors Acts
26th August 1889

Preliminary

1. Definitions

For the purpose of this Act-

(1) The expression "mercantile agent" shall mean a mercantile agent having in the customary course of his business as such agent authority either to sell goods or to consign goods for the purpose of sale, or to buy goods, or to raise money on the security of goods:

(2) A person shall be deemed to be in possession of goods or of the documents of title to goods, where the goods or documents are in his actual custody or are held by any other person subject to his control or for him or on his behalf:

(3) The expression "goods" shall include wares and merchandise:

(4) The expression "document of title" shall include any bill of lading, dock warrant, warehouse-keeper's certificate, and warrant or order for the delivery of goods, and any other document used in the ordinary course of business as proof of the possession or control of goods, or authorising or purporting to authorise, either by endorsement or by delivery, the possessor of the document to transfer or receive goods thereby represented:

(5) The expression "pledge" shall include any contract pledging, or giving a lien or security on, goods, whether in consideration of an original advance or of any further or continuing advance or of any pecuniary liability:

(6) The expression "person" shall include any body of persons corporate or unincorporated.

Dispositions by Mercantile Agents

2. Powers of mercantile agent with respect to disposition of goods

(1) Where a mercantile agent is, with the consent of the owner, in possession of goods or of the documents of title to goods, any sale, pledge, or other disposition of the goods, made by him when acting in the ordinary course of business of a mercantile agent, shall, subject to the provisions of this Act, be as valid as if he were expressly authorised by the owner of the goods to make the same; provided that the person taking under the disposition acts in good faith, and has not at the time of the disposition notice that the person making the disposition has not authority to make the same.

(2) Where a mercantile agent has, with the consent of the owner, been in possession of goods or of the documents of title to goods,

132

any sale, pledge, or other disposition, which would have been valid if the consent had continued, shall be valid notwithstanding the determination of the consent: provided that the person taking under the disposition has not at the time thereof notice that the consent has been determined.

(3) Where a mercantile agent has obtained possession of any documents of title to goods by reason of his being or having been, with the consent of the owner, in possession of the goods represented thereby, or of any other documents of title to the goods, his possession of the first-mentioned documents shall, for the purposes of this Act, be deemed to be with the consent of the owner.

(4) For the purposes of this Act, the consent of the owner shall be presumed in the absence of evidence to the contrary.

3. Effect of pledges of documents of title
A pledge of the documents of title to goods shall be deemed to be a pledge of the goods.

4. Pledge for antecedent debt
Where a mercantile agent pledges goods as security for a debt or liability due from the pledgor to the pledgee before the time of the pledge, the pledgee shall acquire no further right to the goods than could have been enforced by the pledgor at the time of the pledge.

5. Rights acquired by exchange of goods or documents
The consideration necessary for the validity of a sale, pledge or other disposition of goods, in pursuance of this Act, may be either a payment in cash, or the delivery or transfer of other goods, or of a document of title to goods, or of a negotiable security, or any other valuable consideration; but where goods are pledged by a mercantile agent in consideration of the delivery or transfer of other goods, or of a document of title to goods, or of a negotiable security, the pledgee shall acquire no right or interest in the goods so pledged in excess of the value of the goods, documents, or security when so delivered or transferred in exchange.

6. Agreements through clerks, &c.
For the purpose of this Act an agreement made with a mercantile agent through a clerk or other person authorised in ordinary course of business to make contracts of sale or pledge on his behalf shall be deemed to be an agreement with the agent.

7. Provisions as to consignors and consignees
(1) Where the owner of goods has given possession of the goods to another person for the purpose of consignment or sale, or has

shipped the goods in the name of another person, and the consignee of the goods has not had notice that such person is not the owner of the goods, the consignee shall, in respect of advances made to or for the use of such person, have the same lien on the goods as if such person were the owner of the goods, and may transfer any such lien to another person.

(2) Nothing in this section shall limit or affect the validity of any sale, pledge, or disposition, by a mercantile agent.

Dispositions by Sellers and Buyers of Goods.

8. Disposition by seller remaining in possession

Where a person, having sold goods, continues, or is, in possession of the goods or of the documents of title to the goods, the delivery or transfer by that person, or by a mercantile agent acting for him, of the goods or documents of title under any sale, pledge, or other disposition thereof, or under any agreement for sale, pledge or other disposition thereof, to any person receiving the same in good faith and without notice of the previous sale, shall have the same effect as if the person making the delivery or transfer were expressly authorised by the owner of the goods to make the same.

9. Dispositions by buyer obtaining possession

Where a person, having bought or agreed to buy goods, obtains with the consent of the seller possession of the goods or the documents of title to the goods, the delivery or transfer, by that person or by a mercantile agent acting for him, of the goods or documents of title, under any sale, pledge, or other disposition thereof, or under any agreement for sale, pledge, or other disposition thereof, to any person receiving the same in good faith and without notice of any lien or other right of the original seller in respect of the goods, shall have the same effect as if the person making the delivery or transfer were a mercantile agent in possession of the goods or documents of title with the consent of the owner.

10. Effect of transfer of documents on vendor's lien or right of stoppage in transitu

Where a document of title to goods has been lawfully transferred to a person as a buyer or owner of the goods, and that person transfers the document to a person who takes the document in good faith and for valuable consideration, the last mentioned transfer shall have the same effect for defeating any vendor's lien or right of stoppage in transitu as the transfer of a bill of lading has for defeating the right of stoppage in transitu.

Factors Act, 1889

Supplemental.

11. Mode of transferring documents

For the purposes of this Act, the transfer of a document may be by endorsement, or, where the document is by custom or by its express terms transferable by delivery, or makes the goods deliverable to the bearer, then by delivery.

12. Saving for rights of true owner

(1) Nothing in this Act shall authorise an agent to exceed or depart from his authority as between himself and his principal, or exempt him from any liability, civil or criminal, for so doing.

(2) Nothing in this Act shall prevent the owner of goods from recovering the goods from an agent or his Official Assignee[1] at any time before the sale or pledge thereof, or shall prevent the owner of goods pledged by an agent from having the right to redeem the goods at any time before the sale thereof, on satisfying the claim for which the goods were pledged, and paying to the agent, if by him required, any money in respect of which the agent would by law be entitled to retain the goods or the documents of title thereto, or any of them, by way of lien as against the owner, or from recovering from any person with whom the goods have been pledged any balance of money remaining in his hands as the produce of the sale of the goods after deducting the amount of his lien.

(3) Nothing in this Act shall prevent the owner of goods sold by an agent from recovering from the buyer the price agreed to be paid for the same, or any part of that price, subject to any right of set off on the part of the buyer against the agent.

13. Saving for common law powers of agent

The provisions of this Act shall be construed in amplification and not in derogation of the powers exercisable by an agent independently of this Act

14 & 15. Repealed by the Statute Law Revision Act, 1908[2]

16. Virtually repealed by Factors (Scotland) Act, 1890[3]

17. Short title

This Act may be cited as the Factors Act, 1889.

Schedule repealed by Statute Law Revision Act, 1908[2]

---

[1] Substituted by Bankruptcy Act, 1988 (No. 27), s. 77

[2] 8 Edw. 7 c. 49

[3] 53 & 54 Vict. c. 40

The Partnership Act, 1890
53 & 54 Victoria, chapter 39[1]

List of Sections

---

[1] Applied to Limited Partnership Act, 1907, 7 Edw. 7 c. 24, s. 7, *post, p. 316*

Partnership Act, 1890

An Act to declare and amend the Law of Partnership.
14th August 1890

Be it enacted ...

Nature of partnership

1. Definition of partnership
(1) Partnership is the relation which subsists between persons carrying on a business in common with a view of profit.
(2) But the relation between members of any company or association which is-
   (a) Registered as a company under the Companies Act, 1862, or any other Act of Parliament[2] for the time being in force and relating to the registration of joint stock companies; or
   (b) Formed or incorporated by or in pursuance of any other Act of Parliament or letters patent, or Royal Charter; or
   (c) A company engaged in working mines within and subject to the jurisdiction of the Stannaries:
is not a partnership within the meaning of this Act.

2. Rules for determining existence of partnership
In determining whether a partnership does or does not exist, regard shall be had to the following rules:
(1) Joint tenancy, tenancy in common, joint property, common property, or part ownership does not of itself create a partnership as to anything so held or owned, whether the tenants or owners do or do not share any profits made by the use thereof.
(2) The sharing of gross returns does not of itself create a partnership, whether the persons sharing such returns have or have not a joint or common right or interest in any property from which or from the use of which the returns are derived.
(3) The receipt by a person of a share of the profits of a business is *prima facie* evidence that he is a partner in the business, but the receipt of such a share, or of a payment contingent on or varying with the profits of a business, does not of itself make him a partner in the business; and in particular-
   (a) The receipt by a person of a debt or other liquidated amount by instalments, or otherwise out of the accruing profits of a business does not of itself make him a partner in the business or liable as such:
   (b) A contract for the remuneration of a servant or agent of a person engaged in a business by a share of the profits of the business does not of itself make the servant or agent a partner

---
[2] Companies Act, 1963 to 1990

in the business or liable as such :

(c) A person being the widow or child of a deceased partner, and receiving by way of annuity a portion of the profits made in the business in which the deceased person was a partner, is not by reason only of such receipt a partner in the business or liable as such:

(d) The advance of money by way of loan to a person engaged or about to engage in any business on a contract with that person that the lender shall receive a rate of interest varying with the profits, or shall receive a share of the profits arising from carrying on the business, does not of itself make the lender a partner with the person or persons carrying on the business or liable as such. Provided that the contract is in writing, and signed by or on behalf of all the parties thereto:

(e) A person receiving by way of annuity or otherwise a portion of the profits of a business in consideration of the sale by him of the goodwill of the business is not by reason only of such receipt a partner in the business or liable as such.

3. Postponement of rights of person lending or selling in consideration of share of profits in case of insolvency.

In the event of any person to whom money has been advanced by way of loan upon such a contract as is mentioned in the last foregoing section, or of any buyer of a goodwill in consideration of a share of the profits of the business, being adjudged a bankrupt, entering into an arrangement to pay his creditors less than twenty shillings in the pound, or dying in insolvent circumstances, the lender of the loan shall not be entitled to recover anything in respect of his loan, and the seller of the goodwill shall not be entitled to recover anything in respect of the share of profits contracted for, until the claims of the other creditors of the borrower or buyer for valuable consideration in money or money's worth have been satisfied.

4. Meaning of firm

(1) Persons who have entered into partnership with one another are for the purposes of this Act call collectively a firm, and the name under which their business is carried on is called the firm-name.

(2) In Scotland a firm is a legal person distinct from the partners of whom it is composed, but an individual partner may be charged on a decree or diligence directed against the firm, and on payment of the debts is entitled to relief *pro rata* from the firm and its other members.

Partnership Act, 1890
Relations of partners to persons dealing with them

5. Power of partner to bind the firm
Every partner is an agent of the firm and his other partners for the purpose of the business of the partnership; and the acts of every partner who does any act for carrying on in the usual way business of the kind carried on by the firm of which he is a member bind the firm and his partners, unless the partner so acting has in fact no authority to act for the firm in the particular matter, and the person with whom he is dealing either knows that he has no authority, or does not know or believe him to be a partner.

6. Partners bound by acts on behalf of firm
An act or instrument relating to the business of the firm and done or executed in the firm-name, or in any other manner showing an intention to bind the firm, by any person thereto authorised, whether a partner or not, is binding on the firm and all the partners.
Provided that this section shall not affect any general rule of law relating to the execution of deeds or negotiable instruments.

7. Partners using credit of firm for private purposes
Where one partner pledges the credit of the firm for a purpose apparently not connected with the firm's ordinary course of business, the firm is not bound, unless he is in fact specially authorised by the other partners; but this section does not affect any personal liability incurred by an individual partner.

8. Effect of notice that firm will not be bound by acts of partners
If it has been agreed between the partners that any restriction shall be placed on the power of any one or more of them to bind the firm, no act done in contravention of the agreement is binding on the firm with respect to persons having notice of the agreement.

9. Liability of partners
Every partner in a firm is liable jointly with the other partners, and in Scotland severally also, for all debts and obligations of the firm incurred while he is a partner; and after his death his estate is also severally liable in a due course of administration for such debts and obligations, so far as they remain unsatisfied, but subject in England or Ireland to the prior payment of his separate debts.

10. Liability of the firm for wrongs
Where, by any wrongful act or omission of any partner acting in the ordinary course of the business of the firm, or with the authority of his co-partners, loss or injury is caused to any person not being a

Partnership Act, 1890

partner in the firm, or any penalty is incurred, the firm is liable therefor to the same extent as the partner so acting or omitting to act.

11. Misapplication of Money or property received for or in custody of the firm

In the following cases; namely-

(a) Where one partner acting within the scope of his apparent authority receives the money or property of a third person and misapplies it; and

(b) Where a firm in the course of its business receives money or property of a third person, and the money or property so received is misapplied by one or more of the partners while it is in the custody of the firm; the firm is liable to make good the loss.

12. Liability for wrongs joint and several

Every partner is liable jointly with his co-partners and also severally for everything for which the firm while he is a partner therein becomes liable under either of the two last preceding sections.

13. Improper employment of trust property for partnership purposes _

If a partner, being a trustee, improperly employs trust-property in the business or on the account of the partnership, no other partner is liable for the trust-property to the persons beneficially interested therein:

Provided as follows:-

(1) This section shall not affect any liability incurred by any partner by reason of his having notice of a breach of trust; and

(2) Nothing in this section shall prevent trust money from being followed and recovered from the firm if still in its possession or under its control.

14. Persons liable by "holding out"

(1) Every one who by words spoken or written or by conduct represents himself, or who knowingly suffers himself to be represented, as a partner in a particular firm, is liable as a partner to any one who has on the faith of any such representation given credit to the firm, whether the representation has or has not been made or communicated to the person so giving credit by or with the knowledge of the apparent partner making the representation or suffering it to be made.

(2) Provided that where after a partner's death the partnership business is continued in the old firm name, the continued use of that name or of the deceased partner's name as part thereof shall not of

142

itself make his executors or administrators estate or effects liable for any partnership debts contracted after his death.

15. Admissions and representations of partners

An admission or representation made by any partner concerning the partnership affairs, and in the ordinary course of its business, is evidence against the firm.

16. Notice to acting partners to be notices to the firm

Notice to any partner who habitually acts in the partnership business of any matter relating to partnership affairs operates as notice to the firm, except in the case of a fraud on the firm committed by or with the consent of that partner.

17. Liabilities of incoming and outgoing partners

(1) A person who is admitted as a partner into an existing firm does not thereby become liable to the creditors of the firm for anything done before he became a partner.

(2) A partner who retires from a firm does not thereby cease to be liable for partnership debts or obligations incurred before his retirement.

(3) A retiring partner may be discharged from any existing liabilities, by an agreement to that effect between himself and the members of the firm as newly constituted and the creditors, and this agreement may be either express or inferred as a fact from the course of dealing between the creditors and the firm as newly constituted.

18. Revocation of continuing guarantee by change in the firm

A continuing guaranty or cautionary obligation given either to a firm or to a third person in respect of the transactions of a firm is, in the absence of agreement to the contrary, revoked as to future transactions by any change in the constitution of the firm to which, or of the firm in respect of the transactions of which, the guaranty or obligation was given.

Relations of partners to one another

19. Variation by consent of terms of partnership

The mutual rights and duties of partners, whether ascertained by agreement or defined by this Act, may be varied by the consent of all the partners, and such consent may be either express or inferred from a course of dealing.

20. Partnership property

(1) All property and rights and interests in property originally brought into the partnership stock or acquired, whether by purchase or otherwise, on account of the firm, or for the purposes and in the course of the partnership business, are called in this Act partnership property, and must be held and applied by the partners exclusively for the purposes of the partnership and in accordance with the partnership agreement.

(2) Provided that the legal estate or interest in any land, or in Scotland the title to and interest in any heritable estate, which belongs to the partnership shall devolve according to the nature and tenure thereof, and the general rules of law thereto applicable, but intrust, so far as necessary, for the persons beneficially interested in the land under this section.

(3) Where co-owners of an estate or interest in any land, or in Scotland of any heritable estate, not being itself partnership property, are partners as to profits made by the use of that land or estate, and purchase other land or estate out of the profits to be used in like manner, the land or estate so purchased belongs to them, in the absence of an agreement to the contrary, not as partners but as co-owners for the same respective estates and interests as are held by them in the land or estate first mentioned at the date of the purchase.

21. Property bought with partnership money

Unless the contrary intention appears, property bought with money belonging to the firm is deemed to have been bought on account of the firm.

22. Conversion into personal estate of land held as partnership property

Where land or any heritable interest therein has become partnership property, it shall, unless the contrary intention appears, be treated as between the partners (including the representatives of a deceased partner), and also as between the heirs of a deceased partner and his executors or administrators, as personal or moveable and not real or heritable estate.

23. Procedure against partnership property for a partner's separate judgment debt

(1)[3] .. a writ of execution shall not issue against any partnership property except on a judgment against the firm.

(2) The High court, or a judge thereof, or the Chancery Court of the country palatine of Lancaster, or a county court, may, on the application by summons of any judgment creditor of a partner, make

---

[3] Deletion: by Statute Law Revision Act, 1908, 8 Edw. 7 c. 49

Partnership Act, 1890

an order charging that partner's interest in the partnership property and profits with payment of the amount of the judgment debt and interest thereon, and may by the same or a subsequent order appoint a receiver of that partner's share of profits (whether already declared or accruing), and of any other money which may be coming to him in respect of the partnership, and direct all accounts and inquiries, and give all other orders and directions which might have been directed or given if the charge had been made in favour of the judgment creditor by the partner, or which the circumstances of the case may require.

(3) The other partner or partners shall be at liberty at any time to redeem the interest charged, or in case of a sale being directed, to purchase the same.

(4) This section shall apply in the case of a cost-book company as if the company were a partnership within the meaning of this Act.

(5) This section shall not apply to Scotland.

24. Rules as to interests and duties of partners subject to special agreements

The interest of partners in the partnership property and their rights and duties in relation to the partnership shall be determined, subject to any agreement express or implied between the partners, by the following rules:

(1) All the partners are entitled to share equally in the capital and profits of the business, and must contribute equally towards the losses whether of capital or otherwise sustained by the firm.

(2) The firm much indemnify every partner in respect of payment made and personal liabilities incurred by him-

    (a) In the ordinary and proper conduct of the business of the firm; or

    (b) In or about anything necessarily done for the preservation of the business or property of the firm.

(3) A partner making, for the purpose of the partnership, any actual payment or advance beyond the amount of capital which he has agreed to subscribe, is entitled interest at the rate of five per cent. per annum from the date of the payment or advance.

(4) A partner is not entitled, before the ascertainment of profits, to interest on the capital subscribed by him.

(5) Every partner may take part in the management of the partnership business.

(6) No partner shall be entitled to remuneration for acting in the partnership business.

(7) No person may be introduced as a partner without the consent of all existing partners.

(8) Any difference arising as to ordinary matters connected with

the partnership business may be decided by a majority of the partners, but no change may be made in the nature of the partnership business without the consent of all existing partners.

(9) The partnership books are to be kept at the place of business of the partnership (or the principal place, if there is more than one), and very partner may, when he thinks fit, have access to and inspect and copy any of them.

25. Expulsion of partner

No majority of the partners can expel any partner unless a power do so has been conferred by express agreement between the partners.

26. Retirement from partnership at will

(1) Where no fixed term has been agreed upon for the duration of the partnership, any partner may determine the partnership at any time on giving notice of his intention so to do to all the other partners.

(2) Where the partnership has originally been constituted by deed, a notice in writing, signed by the partner giving it, shall be sufficient for this purpose.

27. Where partnerships for term is continued over, continuance on old terms presumed

(1) Where a partnership entered into for a fixed term is continued after the term has expired, and without any express new agreement, the rights and duties of the partners remain the same as they were at the expiration of the term, so far as is consistent with the incidents of a partnership at will.

(2) A continuance of the business by the partners or such of them as habitually acted therein during the term, without any settlement or liquidation of the partnership affairs, is presumed to be a continuance of the partnership.

28. Duty of partners to render accounts, &c.

Partners are bound to render true accounts and full information of all things affecting the partnership to any partner or his legal representatives.

29. Accountability of partners for private profits

(1) Every partner must account for the firm for any benefit derived by him without the consent of the other partners from any transaction concerning the partnership, or from any use by him of the partnership property name or business connexion.

(2) This section applies also to transactions undertaken after a partnership has been dissolved by the death of a partner, and before

the affairs thereof have been completely wound up, either by any surviving partner or by the representatives of the deceased partner.

30. Duty of partner not to compete with firm
If a partner, without the consent of the other partners carries on any business of the same nature as and competing with that of the firm, he must account for and pay over to the firm all profits made by him in that business.

31. Rights of assignee of share in partnership
(1) An assignment by any partner of his share in the partnership, either absolute or by way of mortgage or redeemable charge, does not, as against the other partners, entitle the assignee, during the continuance of the partnership, to interfere in the management or administration of the partnership business or affairs, or to require any accounts of the partnership transaction, or to inspect the partnership books, but entitles the assignee only to receive the share of profits to which the assigning partner would otherwise be entitled, and the assignee must accept the account of profits agreed to by the partners.

(2) In case of a dissolution of the partnership, whether as respects all the partners or as respects the assigning partner, the assignee is entitled to receive the share of the partnership assets to which the assigning partner is entitled as between himself and the other partners, and, for the purpose of ascertaining that share, to an account as from the date of the dissolution.

Dissolution of partnership, and its consequences

32. Dissolution by expiration or notice
Subject to any agreement between the partners, a partnership is dissolved-
- (a) If entered into for a fixed term, by the expiration of that term:
- (b) If entered into for a single adventure or undertaking, by the termination of that adventure or undertaking:
- (c) If entered into for an undefined time, by any partner giving notice to the other or others of his intention to dissolve the partnership.

  In the last-mentioned case the partnership is dissolved as from the date mentioned in the notice as the date of dissolution, or, if no date is so mentioned, as from the date of the communication of the notice.

33. Dissolution by bankruptcy death, or charge
(1) Subject to any agreement between the partners, very partnership

is dissolved as regards all the partners by the death or bankruptcy[4] of any partner.

(2) A partnership may, at the option of the other partner, be dissolved if any partner suffers his share of the partnership property to be charged under this Act for his separate debt.

34. Dissolution by illegality of partnership

A partnership is in very case dissolved by the happening of any event which makes it unlawful for the business of the firm too be carried on or for the members of the firm to carry it on in partnership.

35. Dissolution by the Court

On application by a partner the Court may decree a dissolution of the partnership in any of the following cases:

(a) When a partner is found lunatic by inquisition, or in Scotland by cognition, or is shown to the satisfaction of the Court to be of permanently unsound mind, in either of which cases the application may be made as well on behalf of that partner by his committee or next friend or person having title to intervene as by any other partner:

(b) When a partner, other than the partner suing, becomes in any other way permanently incapable of performing his part of the partnership contract:

(c) When a partner, other than the partner suing, has been guilty of such conduct as, in the opinion of the Court, regard being had to the nature of the business, is calculated to prejudicially affect the carrying on of the business:

(d) When a partner, other than the partner suing, wilfully or persistently commits a breach of the partnership agreement, or otherwise so conducts himself in matters relating to the partnership business that it is not reasonably practicable for the other partner or partners to carry on the business in partnership with him:

(e) When the business of the partnership can only be carried on at a loss:

(f) Whenever in any case circumstances have arisen which, in the opinion of the Court, render it just and equitable that the partnership be dissolved.

36. Rights of persons dealing with firm against apparent member of firm

(1) Where a person deals with a firm after a change in its

---

[4] The Bankruptcy Act, 1988 (No. 27), at sections 30 to 37 and section 138 makes provision for the procedure in bankruptcy in partnership cases.

constitution he is entitled to treat all apparent members of the old firm as still being members of the firm until he has notice of the change.

(2) An advertisement in the London Gazette as to a firm whose principal place of business is in England or Wales, in the Edinburgh Gazette as to a firm whose principal place of business is in Scotland, and in *Iris Oifigiúil* [5] as to a firm whose principal place of business is in Ireland, shall be notice as to persons who had not dealings with the firm before the date of the dissolution or change so advertised.

(3) The estate of a partner who dies, or who becomes bankrupt, or of a partner who, not having been known to the person dealing with the firm to be a partner, retires form the firm, is not liable for partnership debts contracted after the date of the death, bankruptcy, or retirement respectively.

37. Rights of partners to notify dissolution

On the dissolution of a partnership or retirement of a partner any partner may publicly notify the same, and may require the other partner or partners to concur for that purpose in all necessary or proper acts, if any, which cannot be done without his or their concurrence.

38. Continuing authority of partners for purpose of winding up

After the dissolution of a partnership the authority of each partner to bind the firm, and the other rights and obligations of the partner, continue notwithstanding the dissolution so far as may be necessary to wind up the affairs of the partnership, and to complete transaction begun but unfinished at the time of the dissolution, but not otherwise.

Provided that the firm is in no case bound by the acts of a partner who has become bankrupt; but this proviso does not affect the liability of any person who has after the bankruptcy represented himself or knowingly suffered himself to be represented as a partner of the bankrupt.

39. Rights of partners as to application of partnership property

On the dissolution of a partnership every partner is entitled, as against the other partners in the firm, and all persons claiming through them in respect of their interests as partners, to have the property of the partnership applied in payment of the debts and liabilities of the firm, and to have the surplus assets after such payment applied in payment of what may be due to the partners respectively after deducting what may be due from them as partners to the firm; and for that purpose any partner or his representatives

---

[5] Construction of the Dublin Gazette, Adaptation of Enactments Act, 1922 (No. 2), s. 4

may on the termination of the partnership apply to the court to wind up the business and affairs of the firm.

40. Apportionment of premium where partnership prematurely dissolved

Where one partner has paid a premium to another on entering into a partnership for a fixed term, and the partnership is dissolved before expiration of that term otherwise than by the death of a partner, the Court may order the repayment of the premium, or of such part thereof as it thinks just, having regard to the terms of partnership contract and to the length of time during which the partnership has continued; unless

(a) the dissolution is, in the judgment of the Court, wholly or chiefly due to the misconduct of the partner who paid the premium, or

(b) the partnership has been dissolved by an agreement containing no provision for a return of any part of the premium.

41. Rights where partnership dissolved for fraud or misrepresentation

Where a partnership contract is rescinded on the ground of the fraud or misrepresentation of one of the parties thereto, the party entitled to rescind is, without prejudice to any other right, entitled-

(a) to a lien on, or right of retention of, the surplus of the partnership assets, after satisfying the partnership liabilities, for any sum of money paid by him for the purchase of a share in the partnership and for any capital contributed by him, and is (b) to stand in the place of the creditors of the firm for any payments made by him in respect of the partnership liabilities, and

(c) to be indemnified by the person guilty of the fraud or making the representation against all the debts and liabilities of the firm.

42. Right of outgoing partner in certain cases to share profits made after dissolution

(1) Where any member of a firm has died or otherwise ceased to be a partner, and the surviving or continuing partners carry on the business of the firm with its capital or assets without any final settlement of accounts as between the firm and the outgoing partner or his estate, then, in the absence of any agreement to the contrary, the outgoing partner or his estate is entitled at the option of himself or his representative to such share of the profits made since the dissolution as the Court may find to be attributable to the use of his

share of the partnership assets, or to interest at the rate of five per cent. per annum on the amount of his share of the partnership assets.

(2) Provided that where by the partnership contract an option is given to surviving or continuing partners to purchase the interest of a deceased or outgoing partner, and that option is duly exercised, the estate of the deceased partner, or the outgoing partner or his estate, as the case may be, is not entitled to any further or other share of profits; but if any partner assuming to act in exercise of the option does not in all material respects comply with the terms thereof, he is liable to account under the foregoing provisions of this section.

43. Retiring or deceased partner's share to be a debt

Subject to any agreement between the partners, the amount due from surviving or continuing partners to an outgoing partner or the representatives of a deceased partner in respect of the outgoing or deceased partner's share is a debt accruing at the date of the dissolution or death.

44. Rule for distribution of assets on final settlement of accounts

In settling accounts between the partners after a dissolution of partnership, the following rules shall, subject to any agreement, be observed:

(a) Losses, including losses and deficiencies of capital, shall be paid first out of profits, next out of capital, and lastly, if necessary, by the partners individually in the proportion in which they were entitled to share profits:

(b) The assets of the firm including the sums, if any, contributed by the partner to make up losses or deficiencies of capital, shall be applied in the following manner and order:

   1. In paying the debts and liabilities of the firm to persons who are not partners therein:
   2. In paying to each partner rateably what is due from the firm to him for advances as distinguished from capital:
   3. In paying to each partner rateably what is due from the firm to him in respect of capital:
   4. The ultimate residue, if any, shall be divided among the partners in the proportion in which profits are divisible.

Supplemental

45. Definitions of "court" and "business"

In this Act, unless the contrary intention appears -

The expression "court" includes every court and judge having jurisdiction in the case:

The expression "business" includes very trade, occupation, or profession.

46. Saving for rules of equity and common law
The rules of equity and of common law applicable to partnership shall continue in force except except so far as they are inconsistent with the express provisions of this Act.

47. Provision as to bankruptcy in Scotland
(1) In the application of this Act to Scotland the bankruptcy of a firm or of an individual shall mean sequestration under the Bankruptcy (Scotland) Acts, and also in the case of an individual the issue against him of a decree of *cessio bonorum.*

(2) Nothing in this Act shall alter the rules of the law of Scotland relating to the bankruptcy of a firm or of the individual partners thereof.

48. Repealed by Statute Law Revision Act, 1908[6]

49. Repealed by Statute Law Revision Act, 1908.

50. Short title
This Act may be cited as the Partnership Act, 1890.

Schedule

Repealed by Statute Law Revision Act, 1908.

---

[6] 8 Edw. 7 c. 49

Merchandise Marks Act, 1891
54 & 55 Victoria, chapter 15

An Act to amend the Merchandise Marks Act, 1887
11th May 1891

1. Customs entry to be a trade description.
The customs entry relating to imported goods shall, for the purposes of the Merchandise Marks Act, 1887[1], be deemed to be a trade description applied to the goods.

2. Repealed by Merchandise Marks Act, 1931 (No. 48) s. 35, sch.

3. Short title
This Act may be cited as the Merchandise Marks Act, 1891, and the Merchandise Marks Acts, 1887, and this Act may be cited together as the Merchandise Marks Acts, 1887 and 1891.

---

[1] 50 & 51 Vict. c. 28, *ante*

Statutes Revised on Commercial Law

The Industrial and Provident Societies Act, 1893
56 & 57 Victoria, chapter 39

List of Sections

Industrial and Provident Society Act, 1893

An Act to consolidate and amend the Laws relating to Industrial and Provident Societies.[1]
12th September 1893

Preamble repealed by Statute Law Revision Act, 1908[2]

Preliminary.
1. Short title
This Act may be cited as the Industrial and Provident Societies Act, 1893

2.[3] Extent of Act
This Act .... shall extend to .... Ireland ....

3. Existing societies.[4]
Every incorporated society now existing which has been registered or certified under any Act relating to industrial and provident societies shall be deemed to be a society registered under this Act, and its rules shall, so far as the same are not contrary to any express provision of this Act, continue in force until altered or rescinded.

Registration of Societies

4.[5] Societies which may be registered.[6]
A society which may be registered under this Act (herein called an industrial and provident society) is a society for carrying on any industries, businesses, or trades specified in or authorised by its rules, whether wholesale or retail, and including dealings of any description with land. Provided that -

---

[1] Rstrct. Creamery Act, 1928 (No. 26), ss. 6-8; limit on shareholding removed in pt. Creamery Act, 1928 (No. 26), s. 11; powers of regd. co-op. socy. ext. Agricultural Credit Act, 1929 (No. 30), s. 29; applied to credit unions save in so far as is otherwise provided, Credit Union Act, 1966 (No. 19), s. 3(1); applic. rstrct. Mergers, Take-overs and Monopolys (Control) Act, 1978 (No. 17), s. 14(1).

[2] 8 Edw. 7 c. 49

[3] Amended: Statute Law Revision Act, 1908, 8 Edw. 7 c. 49, s. 80, sch.

[4] Rstrct.: Credit Union Act, 1966 (No. 19), s. 3(2)

[5] Excl. Housing (Ireland) Act, 1919, 9 & 10 Geo. 5 c. 45, s. 14(2)

[6] Ext.: Credit Union Act, 1966 (No. 19), s. 2(1)

(a)[7] No member other than a registered society shall have or claim any interest in the shares of the society exceeding the amount specified hereunder for the class of society (as defined in the Industrial and Provident Societies (Financial Limits) Regulations, 1985) to which it belongs :

£100,000[8] in the case of a class A society, a class B society or a class C society:

£250,000 in the case of a class D society:

£6,000 in the case of a class E society, a class F society or a class G society, and

(b) In regard to the business of banking, the society shall be subject to the provisions herein-after contained.[9]

5.[10] Condition of registration

With respect to the registry of new societies, the following provisions shall have effect:-

(1) No society can be registered under this Act which does not consist of seven persons at least: none of whom in the case of a credit union is less than twenty-one years of age.[11]

(2) For the purpose of registry an application to register the society, signed by seven members and the secretary, and two printed copies of the rules, shall be sent to the registrar.

(3) No society shall be registered under a name identical with that under which any other existing society is registered, or so nearly resembling such name as to be likely, or in any name likely, in the opinion of the registrar, to mislead the members or the public as to its identity, and no society shall change its name except in the manner herein-after provided.

(4) A society registered under the Industrial and Provident Societies Act, 1852, and not registered under the Industrial and Provident Societies Acts, 1862, 1867, or 1876, may obtain from the registrar an acknowledgment of registry under this Act.

(5) The word "limited" shall be the last word in the name of every society registered under this Act.

(6) A society carrying or intending to carry on business in more than one part of the United Kingdom shall be registered in the part in which its registered office, as herein mentioned, is situate; but

---

[7] Text to be construed as printed here: see S. I. 1985/392, reg. 3

[8] As now to be construed: S. I. 246/1990

[9] Note: Credit Union Act, 1966 (No. 19), s. 36(1), regarding non-application of certain provisions

[10] Modified: Industrial and Provident Societies (Amendment) Act, 1913, 3 & 4 Geo. 5 c. 31, s. 11

[11] As amended: Credit Union Act, 1966 (No. 19), s. 37, 39(2), sch. pt. 1

copies of the rules of the society and of all amendments of the same shall, when registered, be sent to the registrar of each of the other parts to be recorded by him, and until such rules are so recorded the society shall not be entitled to any of the privileges of this Act in the part in which such rules have not been recorded, and until such amendments are so recorded the same shall not take effect in such part.

6. Acknowledgment of registry.[14]

The registrar, on being satisfied that a society has complied with the provisions as to registry in force under this Act, shall issue to such society an acknowledgment of registry.

7. Appeals from refusal to register.[14]

(1)[12] If the registrar refuses to register the society, or any rules or amendments of rules, the society may appeal from such refusal as follows:-

(a) ... England....

(b) In .... Ireland, to the Chief Registrar, and if he refuses .... to the High Court in Ireland.

(2) If the refusal of registry is overruled on appeal, an acknowledgment of registry shall thereupon be given to the society by the registrar.

8. Effect of acknowledgment of registry.

The acknowledgment of registry shall be conclusive evidence that the society therein mentioned is duly registered, unless it is proved that the registry of the society has been suspended or cancelled.

Cancelling and Suspension of Registry

9. Cancelling and suspension of registry.

(1) The registrar may cancel the registry of a society by writing under his hand or seal:

(a) If at any time it is proved to his satisfaction that the number of the members of the society has been reduced to less than seven, or that an acknowledgment of registry has been obtained by fraud or mistake, or that the society has ceased to exist;

(b) If he thinks fit, at the request of a society, to be evidenced in such manner as he shall from time to time direct;

(bb) Where the society has been wound up by the High Court under the Industrial and Provident Societies Act, 1893 to

---

[12] Substituted: Industrial and Provident Societies (Amendment) Act, 1895, 58 & 59 Vict. c. 30, ss. 3, 4.

1978[13];

(bc) Where the society has ceased to function or where it has suspended its business for a period of not less than six months[13].

(c) With the approval of the Treasury, on proof to his satisfaction that the society exists for an illegal purpose, or has wilfully and after notice from a registrar violated any of the provisions of this Act.

(2) The registrar, in any case in which he might, with the approval of the Treasury, cancel the registry of a society, may suspend the same, by writing under his hand or seal, for any term not exceeding three months, and may, with the approval of the Treasury, renew such suspension from time to time for the like period.

(3) Not less than two months previous notice in writing, specifying briefly the ground of any proposed cancelling or suspension of registry, shall be given by the registrar to a society before the registry of the same can be cancelled (except at its request) or suspended; and notice of every cancelling or suspension shall be published in the Gazette, and in some local newspaper circulating in or about the locality in which the registered office of the society is situated, as soon as practicable after the same takes place.

(4) A society may appeal from the cancelling of its registry, or from any suspension of the same which is renewed after three months, in manner herein provided for appeals from the registrar's refusal to register.

(5) A society whose registry has been suspended or cancelled shall from the date of publication in the Gazette of notice of such suspension or cancelling (but, if suspended, only whilst such suspension lasts, and subject also to the right of appeal hereby given) absolutely cease to enjoy as such the privileges of a registered society, but without prejudice to any liability actually incurred by such society, which may be enforced against the same as if such suspension or cancelling had not taken place.

Rules

10. Rules and amendments.

(1)[14] The rules of a society registered under this Act shall contain provisions in respect of the several matters mentioned in the Second Schedule to this Act.

(2) An amendment of a rule of a society registered under this Act shall not be valid until the same has been registered under this Act,

---

[13] Ins. Industrial & Provident Societies (Amendment) Act, (No. 23), 1978 s. 34

[14] Non applic. Credit Union Act, 1966 (No. 19), ss. 36(1), 39(2)

for which purpose two copies of the same, signed by three members and the secretary, shall be sent to the registrar.

(3) The Registrar shall, on being satisfied that any amendment of a rule is not contrary to the provisions of this Act, issue to the society an acknowledgment of registry of the same, which shall be conclusive evidence that the same is duly registered.

(4) A copy of the rules of a registered society shall be delivered by the society to every person on demand, on payment of a sum not exceeding one shilling.

(5) The rules of a registered society, or any schedule thereto, may set forth the form of any instrument necessary for carrying the purposes of the society into effect.

(6)[14] The rules of every society registered under this Act shall provide for the profits being appropriated to any purposes stated therein or determined in such manner as the rules direct.

Duties of Registered Societies.

11. Registered office.

Every registered society shall have a registered office to which all communications and notices shall be addressed, and shall send to the registrar notice of the situation of such office, and of every change therein.

12. Publication of name.

Every registered society shall paint or affix, and keep painted or affixed, its registered name on the outside of every office or place in which the business of the society is carried on, in a conspicuous position, in letters easily legible, and have its registered name engraven in legible characters on its seal, and have its registered name mentioned in legible characters in all notices, advertisements, and other official publications of the society, and in all bills of exchange, promissory notes, endorsements, cheques, and orders for money or goods, purporting to be signed by or on behalf of such society, and in all bills of parcels, invoices, receipts, and letters of credit of the society.

13.[15] Audit

The auditors shall have access to all the books, deeds, documents, and accounts of the society, and shall examine the balance sheets showing the receipts and expenditure, funds and effects of the society, and verify the same with the books, deeds, documents, accounts and vouchers relating thereto, and shall either sign the

[15] Deletion: Industrial and Provident Societies (Amendment) Act, 1913, 3 & 4 Geo. 5 c. 31, s. 12(3), sch.

same as found by them to be correct, duly vouched, and in accordance with law, or specially report to the society in what respects they find them incorrect, unvouched, or not in accordance with law.

14. Annual returns.

(1) Every registered society shall once in every year, not later than the thirty-first day of March, send to the registrar an annual return of the receipts and expenditure, funds and effects, of the society as audited.

(2) The annual return -
   (a) shall be signed by the auditor or auditors; and
   (b) shall show separately the expenditure in respect of the several objects of the society; and
   (c)[16]shall be made up from the date of its registration or last annual return to that of its last published balance sheet, unless the last-mentioned date is more than four months before or more than one month after the thirty-first day of December, in which case it shall be made up to the said thirty-first day of December inclusive; and[17]
   (d) shall state whether the audit has been conducted by a Public Auditor appointed as by this Act is provided, and by whom .. [18] ..

15. Supply of copies of annual returns.

Every registered society shall supply gratuitously to every member or person interested in the funds of the society, on his application, a copy of the last annual return of the society for the time being.

16. Copy of last Balance Sheet.

Every registered society shall keep a copy of the last balance sheet for the time being, together with the report of the auditors, always hung up in a conspicuous place at the registered office of the society.

---

[16] Substituted by Industrial and Provident Societies (Amendment) Act, 1913, 3 & 4 Geo. 5 c. 31, ss. 3(1), 12(3), sch.

[17] The Credit Union Act, 1966 (No. 19), at section 7(4) provides :
The financial year of a credit union shall end on the 31st day of December ...

[18] Deletion: Industrial and Provident Societies (Amendment) Act, 1913, 3 & 4 Geo. 5 c. 31, s. 12(3), sch.

Industrial and Provident Society Act, 1893
Inspection of Books.

17. Inspection of books by members.

(1) Save as provided by this Act, no member or person shall have any right to inspect the books of a registered society, notwithstanding anything in the existing rules relating to such inspection.

(2) Any member or person having an interest in the funds of a registered society shall be allowed to inspect his own account and the books containing the names of the members at all reasonable hours at the registered office of the society, or at any place where the same are kept, subject to such regulations as to the time and manner of such inspection as may be made from time to time by the general meetings of the society.

(3) A registered society may, by any rules registered after this Act is passed, authorise the inspection of any of its books therein mentioned, in addition to the said books containing the names of members, under such conditions as are thereby imposed, so that no person, unless he be an officer of the society, or be specially authorised by a resolution thereof, shall have the right to inspect the loan or deposit account of any other member without his written consent.

18. Inspection of books by order of registrar.

(1) The registrar may, if he thinks fit, on the application of ten members of a registered society, each of whom has been a member of the society for not less than twelve months immediately preceding the date of the application, appoint an accountant or actuary to inspect the books of the society, and to report thereon.

(2) Provided as follows,-

   (a) the applicants shall deposit with the registrar such sum as a security for the costs of the proposed inspection as the registrar may require; and

   (b) all expenses of and incidental to any such inspection shall be defrayed by the applicants, or out of the funds of the society, or by the members or officers, or former members or officers, of the society in such proportions as the registrar may direct.

(3) A person appointed under this section shall have power to make copies of any books of the society, and to take extracts therefrom, at all reasonable hours, at the registered office of the society, or at any place where the books are kept.

(4) The registrar shall communicate the results of any such inspection to the applicants and to the society.

19. Conditions of banking by societies.[14]

(1) No registered society which has any withdrawable share capital shall carry on the business of banking.

(2) Every registered society which carries on the business of banking shall on the first Mondays in February and August in each year make out and keep conspicuously hung up in its registered office, and every other office or place of business belonging to it where the business of banking is carried on, a statement in the form in the Third Schedule, or as near thereto as the circumstances admit.

(3) The taking deposits of not more than ten shillings in any one payment, nor more than twenty pounds for any one depositor, payable on not less than two clear days notice, shall not be included in the business of banking within the meaning of this Act; but no society which takes such deposits shall make any payment of withdrawable capital while any claim due on account of any such deposit is unsatisfied.

Returns and Documents

20. Form and deposit of documents.

Every return and other document required for the purposes of this Act shall be made in such form and shall contain such particulars as the chief registrar prescribes, and shall be deposited and registered or recorded, with or without observations thereon, in such manner as the chief registrar directs.

Privileges of Societies

21. Incorporation of society with limited liability.

The registration of a society shall render it a body corporate by the name described in the acknowledgment of registry, by which it may sue and be sued, with perpetual succession and a common seal, and with limited liability; and shall vest in the society all property for the time being vested in any person in trust for the society; and all legal proceedings pending by or against the trustees of any such society may be prosecuted by or against the society in its registered name without abatement.

22. Rules to bind members.

The rules of a registered society shall bind the society and all members thereof and all persons claiming through them respectively to the same extent as if each member had subscribed

165

his name and affixed his seal thereto, and there were contained in such rules a covenant on the part of such member, his heirs, executors, administrators, and assigns, to conform thereto, subject to the provisions of this Act: Provided that a society registered at the time when this Act comes into operation, or the members thereof, may respectively exercise any power given by this Act, and not made to depend on the provisions of its rules, notwithstanding any provision contained in any rule thereof registered before this Act was passed.

23. Remedy for debts from members.

(1) All moneys payable by a member to a registered society shall be a debt due from such member to the society, and shall be recoverable as such either in the county court of the district in which the registered office of the society is situate, or in that of the district in which such member resides, at the option of the society.

(2)[19] A registered society shall have a lien on the shares, deposits, dividends or interest on deposits of any member for any debt due to it by him, and may set off any sum credited to the member thereon in or towards the payment of such debt.

24. Repealed by Income Tax Act, 1918[20], s. 238, sch. 7

25 Power of nomination for sums not exceeding [22] . . .

(1) A member of a registered society not being under the age of sixteen years may, by writing under his hand delivered at or sent to the registered office of the society during the lifetime of such member or made in any book kept thereat, nominate any person or persons to or among whom there shall be transferred at his decease such property in the society as may be his at the time of his decease (whether in shares, loans, or deposits, or otherwise), or so much thereof as is specified in such nomination, if the nomination does not comprise the whole. If on the death of the nominator the amount of his property in the society comprised in the nomination exceeds £6,000[21] the nomination shall be valid to the extent of the sum of £6,000[21], but not further or otherwise:

Provided that a person so nominated shall not be an officer or servant of the society unless such officer or servant is the husband, wife, father, mother, child, brother, sister, nephew, or niece of the nominator.

(2) A nomination so made may be revoked or varied by a subsequent nomination signed and delivered or sent or made as aforesaid or by any similar document in the nature of a revocation or variation under the hand of the nominator so delivered sent or made as aforesaid, but shall not be revocable or variable by the will of the nominator or any codicil thereto.

(3) The society shall keep a book wherein the names of all persons so nominated and all revocations or variations (if any) of such nominations shall be recorded, and the property comprised in any such nomination to an amount not

---

[19] As amended by Credit Union Act, 1966 (No. 19), s. 37, sch. pt. I

[20] 8 & 9 Geo. 5 c. 40

[21] To be construed as such: S. I. 392/1985, reg. 4.

exceeding £6,000 shall be payable or transferable to the nominee although the rules of the society declare the shares not to be transferable.

(4) The marriage of a member of a society shall operate as a revocation of any nomination made by him before such marriage, provided that, in the event of an officer of a society having transferred any property of a member to a nominee, in ignorance of a marriage contracted subsequent to the date of the nomination, the receipt of the nominee shall be a valid discharge to the society, and the society shall be under no liability to any other person claiming such property.

26.[22] Proceedings on the death of a nominator.

(1) On receiving satisfactory proof of the death of a nominator, the committee of the society shall, subject to the limitation on amount herein-before provided, either transfer the property comprised in the nomination in manner directed by the nomination, or pay to every person entitled thereunder the full value of the property given to him, unless the shares comprised in the nomination, if transferred as directed by the nominator, would raise the share capital of any nominee to a sum exceeding £6,000[23] in which case they shall pay him the value of such excess.

(2) Where a nominee who is nominated under the provisions of this Act is under sixteen years of age, the society may pay the sum nominated to either parent, or to a guardian of the nominee, or to any other person of full age who will undertake to hold the same on trust for the nominee or to apply the same for his benefit and whom the society may think a fit and proper person for the purpose, and the receipt of such parent, guardian, or other person shall be a sufficient discharge to the society for all moneys so paid.

27. Provisions for intestacy.

(1) If any member of a registered society entitled to property therein in respect of shares, loans, or deposits, not exceeding in the whole, at his death, £3,000[23], dies intestate, without having made any nomination thereof then subsisting, the committee may, without letters of administration, distribute the same among such persons as appear to them, on such evidence as they deem satisfactory, to be entitled by law to receive the same ..[24] ..

(2) If any such member is illegitimate and leaves no widow, widower, or issue, the committee shall deal with his property in the society as the Treasury shall direct.

---

[22] Substituted by Industrial and Provident Societies (Amendment) Act, 1913, 3 & 4 Geo. 5 c. 31, ss. 5, 12(3), sch.

[23] To be construed as such: S. I. 392/1985, reg. 6

[24] Repealed: Industrial and Provident Societies (Amendment) Act, 1913, 3 & 4 Geo. 5 c. 31, s. 12(3), sch.

28. Repealed by Credit Union Act, 1966 (No. 19), s. 37 sch, pt. I

29. Power to deal with the property of insane or lunatic members.

Where a member or person claiming through a member of a society is insane, and no committee of his estate or trustee of his property has been duly appointed, the society may, when it is proved to the satisfaction of the committee that it is just and expedient so to do, pay the amount of the shares, loans, and deposits ..[25].. belonging to such member or person, to any person whom they shall judge proper to receive the same on his behalf, whose receipt shall be a good discharge to the society for any sum so paid.

30. Payments to persons apparently entitled valid.

All payments or transfers made by the committee of a registered society, under the provisions of this Act with respect to payments or transfers to or on behalf of deceased or insane members, to any person who at the time appears to the committee to be entitled thereunder, shall be valid and effectual against any demand made upon the committee or society by any other person.

31. Transfer of stock standing in name of trustee.

(1) When any person in whose name any stock belonging to a registered society transferable at the Bank of England or Bank of Ireland is standing, either jointly with another or others or solely, as a trustee therefor, is absent from Great Britain or Ireland respectively, or becomes bankrupt, or files any petition or executes any deed for liquidation of his affairs by assignment or arrangement, or for composition with his creditors, or becomes a lunatic, or is dead, or has been removed from his office of trustee, or if it be unknown whether such person is living or dead, the chief registrar, on application in writing from the secretary and three members of the society, and on proof satisfactory to him, may direct the transfer of the stock into the names of any other persons as trustees for the society.

(2) The transfer shall be made by the surviving or continuing trustees, and if there be no such trustee, or if such trustees refuse or be unable to make such transfer, and the chief registrar so directs, then by the Accountant-General or Deputy or Assistant Accountant-General of the Bank of England or Bank of Ireland, as the case may be.

(3) The Banks of England and Ireland are hereby indemnified for

[25] Repealed: Industrial and Provident Societies (Amendment) Act, 1913, 3 & 4 Geo. 5 c. 31, ss. 7, 12(3), sch.

anything done by them or any of their officers in pursuance of this provision against any claim or demand of any person injuriously affected thereby.

32. Membership of minors.

A person under the age of twenty-one but above the age of sixteen may be a member of a registered society, unless provision be made in the rules thereof to the contrary, and may, subject to the rules of the society, enjoy all the rights of a member (except as by this Act provided), and execute all instruments and give all acquittances necessary to be executed or given under the rules, but shall not be a member of the committee, trustee, manager or treasurer of the society.

33. Promissory notes and bills of exchange.

A promissory note or bill of exchange shall be deemed to have been made, accepted, or endorsed on behalf of any society if made, accepted, or endorsed in the name of the society, or by or on behalf or account of the society, by any person acting under the authority of the society.

34. Register of members or shares.

Any register or list of members or shares kept by any society shall be *prima facie* evidence of any of the following particulars entered therein:-

   (a) The names, addresses, and occupations of the members, the number of shares held by them respectively, the numbers of such shares, if they are distinguished by numbers, and the amount paid or agreed to be considered as paid on any such shares;

   (b) The date at which the name of any person, company or society was entered in such register or list as a member.

   (c) The date at which any such person, company, or society ceased to be a member.

35. Contracts how made, varied, or discharged.

Contracts on behalf of a registered society may be made, varied, or discharged as follows:-

   (a) Any contract, which if made between private persons would be by law required to be in writing, and if made according to the English law to be under seal, may be made on behalf of the society in writing under the common seal of the society, and may in the same manner be varied or discharged;

   (b) Any contract, which if made between private persons would be by law required to be in writing and signed by the persons to be charged therewith, may be made on behalf of the society in writing by any person acting under the express or implied authority of the society, and may in the same manner be varied or discharged;

(c) Any contract under seal which, if made between private persons, might be varied or discharged by a writing not under seal, signed by any person interested therein, may be similarly varied or discharged on behalf of the society by a writing not under seal, signed by any person acting under the express or implied authority of the society;

(d) Any contract, which if made between private persons would be by law valid though made by parol only and not reduced into writing, may be made by parol on behalf of the society by any person acting under the express or implied authority of the society, and may in the same manner be varied or discharged;

(e) A signature, purporting to be made by a person holding any office in the society, attached to a writing whereby any contract purports to be made, varied, or discharged by or on behalf of the society, shall *prima facie* be taken to be the signature of a person holding at the time when the signature was made the office so stated.

All contracts which may be or have been made, varied, or discharged according to the provisions contained in this section, shall, so far as concerns the form thereof, be effectual in law and binding on the society and all other parties thereto, their heirs, executors, or administrators as the case may be.

Property and Funds of Registered Society

36. Holding of land.

A registered society may (if its rules do not direct otherwise) hold, purchase, or take on lease in its own name any land, and may sell, exchange, mortgage, lease, or build upon the same, or grant bonds and dispositions on security or other heritable securities over the same (with power to alter and pull down buildings and again rebuild) and no purchaser, assignee, mortgagee, tenant, or bond-holder shall be bound to inquire as to the authority for any such sale, exchange, mortgage, or lease by the society, and the receipt of the society shall be a discharge for all moneys arising from or in connection with such sale, exchange, mortgage, lease, or heritable security.

37. Provision as to copyholds.

Where any registered society is entitled in equity to any hereditaments of copyhold or customary tenure, either absolutely or by way of mortgage or security, the lord of the manor of which the same are held shall from time to time, if the society so require, admit such persons (not to exceed three) as such society appoints to be trustees on its behalf, as tenants in respect of such hereditaments, on payment of the usual fines, fees, and other dues payable on the admission of a single tenant, or may admit the society as tenant in respect of the same on payment of such special fine or compensation, in lieu of fine and fees, as may be agreed upon between such lord and the society.

38. Investments by societies.

(1) A registered society may invest any part of its capital in or upon any security authorised by its rules, and also, if the rules do not direct otherwise -

(a) in or upon any security in which trustees are for the time being authorised by law to invest; and

(b) in or upon any mortgage, bond, debenture, debenture stock, corporation stock, annuity, rentcharge, rent, or other security (not being securities payable to bearer) authorised by or under any Act of Parliament passed or to be passed of any local authority as defined by section thirty-four of the Local Loans Act, 1875; and

(c) in the shares or on the security of any other society registered or deemed to be registered under this Act, or under the Building Societies Acts, or of any company registered under the Companies Acts or incorporated by Act of Parliament or by charter, provided that no such investment be made in the shares of any society or company other than one with limited liability.

(2) A society so investing shall be deemed to be a person within the meaning of the Companies Acts, and of the Building Societies Acts.

(3) Any investments made before the passing of this Act, which would have been valid if this Act had then been in force, are hereby ratified and confirmed.

39. Power to invest in savings banks.

A society (not being one chargeable with income tax in pursuance of this Act) may invest its capital and funds, or any part thereof to any amount, in any savings bank certified under the Trustee Savings Banks Act, 1863, or in a post office savings bank.

40. Advances to members.

The rules of a registered society may provide for advances of money to members on the security of real or personal property, or in the case of a society registered to carry on banking business in any manner customary in the conduct of such business.

41. Societies members of other bodies corporate may vote by proxy.

A registered society which has invested any part of its capital in the shares or on the security of any other body corporate may appoint as proxy any one of its members although such member is not personally a shareholder of such other body corporate. The proxy shall, during the continuance of his appointment, be taken in virtue thereof as holding the number of shares held by the society by whom he is appointed for all purposes except the transfer of any such shares, or the giving receipts for any dividends thereon.

42. Any body corporate may hold shares in a society.

Any other body corporate may, if its regulations permit, hold shares by its corporate name in a registered society.

Discharge of Mortgages by Receipt endorsed.

43. Discharge of mortgages by receipt endorsed.

In .... Ireland -

(1) A receipt in full, signed by two members of the committee, and countersigned by the secretary, of a registered society, for all moneys secured to the society on the security of any property to which such receipt relates, and being in the Form A. in the Third Schedule to this Act, or in any other form specified in the rules of the society or any schedule thereto, if endorsed on or annexed to any mortgage or assurance, shall vacate the same and vest the property therein comprised in the person entitled to the equity of redemption thereof without any formal reconveyance or surrender.

(2) If such mortgage or other assurance has been registered under any Act for the registration or record of deeds or titles, or is of copyholds or lands of customary tenure, and is entered on any court rolls, the registrar under such Act, or recording officer, or steward of the manor, or keeper of the register, shall, on production of such receipt verified by oath or statutory declaration of any person, enter satisfaction on the register or on the court rolls respectively of such mortgage or of the charge made by such assurance, and shall grant a certificate, either upon such mortgage or assurance or separately to the like effect, which certificate shall be received in evidence in all courts and proceedings without further proof; and such registrar, recording officer, steward, or keeper of the register shall be entitled, for making the said entry and granting the said certificate, to a fee of two shillings and sixpence, which in Ireland shall be paid by stamps and applied in accordance with the Public Offices Fees Act, 1879.

44. Relates to Scotland only.

45. Receipt in case of society in liquidation.

Where a registered society is in liquidation, the signature to such a receipt as aforesaid of the liquidator or liquidators for the time being, described as such, shall have the same effect, and shall be entitled to the same exemption from stamp duty, as would under this Act attach to a similar receipt signed as aforesaid if the society were not in liquidation.

46. Execution of deeds.

(1) Any deed or writ to which any registered society is a party shall be held to be duly executed on behalf of such society in Scotland if it is either executed in conformity with the present law thereof or is sealed with the common seal of the society, subscribed on its behalf by two members of the committee and the secretary of the society, whether such subscription is attested by witnesses or not.

(2) On payment of all moneys intended to be secured to a society by any of the aforesaid securities, the debtor or his successor or representatives shall be entitled to a receipt in the appropriate form provided by this Act.

Officers in receipt or charge of Money.

47. Security by officers.

Every officer of a registered society having receipt or charge of money, if the rules of the society require, shall, before taking upon himself the execution of his office, become bound, either with or without a surety as the committee may require, in a bond according to one of the forms set forth in the Third Schedule to this Act, or such other form as the committee of the society approve, or give the security of a guarantee society, in such sum as the committee directs, conditioned for his rendering a just and true account of all moneys received and paid by him on account of the society at such times as its rules appoint, or as the society or the committee thereof require him to do, and for the payment by him of all sums due from him to the society.

48. Accounts of officers.

(1) Every officer of a registered society having receipt or charge of money, or his executors or administrators, shall, at such times as by the rules of the society he should render account, or upon demand made, or notice in writing given or left at his last or usual place of residence, give in his account as may be required by the society, or by the committee thereof, to be examined and allowed or disallowed

by them, and shall, on the like demand or notice, pay over all moneys and deliver all property for the time being in his hands or custody to such person as the society or the committee appoint; and in case of any neglect or refusal to deliver such account, or to pay over such moneys or to deliver such property in manner aforesaid, the society may sue upon the bond or security before mentioned, or may apply to the county court (which may proceed in a summary way), or to a court of summary jurisdiction, and the order of either such court and the order of either such court shall be final and conclusive.

(2) This section shall apply to every servant of a registered society in receipt or charge of money in every case where he is not engaged under a special agreement to account.

Disputes.

49. Decision of disputes.[26]

(1) Every dispute between a member of a registered society, or any person aggrieved who has for not more than six months ceased to be a member of a registered society, or any person claiming through such member or person aggrieved, or claiming under the rules of a registered society, and the society or an officer thereof, shall be decided in manner directed by the rules of the society, if they contain any such direction, and the decision so made shall be binding and conclusive on all parties without appeal, and shall not be removable into any court of law or restrainable by injunction; and application for the enforcement thereof may be made to the county court.

(2) The parties to a dispute in a society may, by consent (unless the rules of such society expressly forbid it), refer such dispute to the chief registrar, or to the assistant registrar in Scotland or Ireland, who shall with the consent of the Treasury, either by himself or by any other registrar, hear and determine such dispute, and shall have power to order the expenses of determining the same to be paid either out

---

[26] Note Credit Union Act, 1966 (No. 19), s. 36(2) :

Section 49 of the Principal Act shall, in its application to a dispute concerning the expulsion of a member by a credit union or a proposed transfer of shares by a member of a credit union, have effect as if subsection (1) and (4) to (6) were deleted and as if, for the words from "and such determination" in subsection (2) to the end of that subsection, the following were substituted :

"And such determination and order shall be binding and conclusive on all parties without appeal, and shall not be removable into any court of law or restrainable by injunction, and application for the enforcement thereof may be made to the judge of the Circuit Court assigned to the circuit in which the registered office of the society is situate"

of the funds of the society or by such parties to the dispute as he shall think fit, and such determination and order shall have the same effect and be enforceable in like manner as a decision made in the manner directed by the rules of the society.

(3) The chief or other registrar to whom any dispute is referred may administer oaths, and may require the attendance of all parties concerned and of witnesses, and the production of all books and documents relating to the matter in question; and any person refusing to attend, or to produce any documents, or to give evidence before such chief or other registrar, shall be guilty of an offence under this Act.

(4) Where the rules of a society direct that disputes shall be referred to justices, the dispute shall be determined by a court of summary jurisdiction:

Provided that in every case of dispute cognisable under the rules of a society by a court of summary jurisdiction, it shall be lawful for the parties thereto to enter into a consent referring such dispute to the county court, which may hear and determine the matter in dispute.

(5) Where the rules contain no direction as to disputes, or where no decision is made on a dispute within forty days after application to the society for a reference under its rules, the member or person aggrieved may apply either to the county court, or to a court of summary jurisdiction, which may hear and determine the matter in dispute.

(6) Notwithstanding anything contained .... in any .... Act, the court and the chief or other registrar shall not be compelled to state a special case on any question of law arising in the case, but the court or chief or other registrar, may, at the request of either party, state a case for the opinion in .... Ireland of the Supreme Court of Judicature .... on any question of law, and may also grant to either party such discovery as to documents and otherwise, or such inspection of documents, ... as might be granted by any court of law or equity; such discovery to be made on behalf of the society by such officer of the same as such court or registrar may determine.

Inspection of Affairs.

50. Power to appoint inspectors.

(1) Upon the application of one-tenth of the whole number of members of a registered society, or of one hundred members in the case of a society exceeding one thousand members, the chief registrar, or, in the case of societies registered and doing business exclusively in .... Ireland, the assistant registrar for .... Ireland, ... but with the consent of the Treasury in every case, may-

(a) appoint an inspector or inspectors to examine into and report

175

on the affairs of such society; or

(b) call a special meeting of the society.

(2) The application under this section shall be supported by such evidence, for the purpose of showing that the applicants have good reason for requiring such inspection to be made or meeting to be called, and that they are not actuated by malicious motives in their application, and such notice thereof shall be given to the society, as the chief registrar shall direct.

(3) The chief registrar or such assistant registrar may, if he think fit, require the applicants to give security for the costs of the proposed inspection or meeting before appointing any inspector or calling such meeting.

(4) All expenses of and incidental [or preliminary[27]] to any such inspection or meeting shall be defrayed by the members applying for the same, or out of the funds of the society, or by the members or officers, or former members or officers, of the society in such proportions as the chief registrar or such assistant registrar shall direct.

(5) An inspector appointed under this section may require the production of all or any of the books, accounts, securities, and documents of the society, and may examine on oath its officers, members, agents, and servants in relation to its business, and may administer an oath accordingly.

(6) The chief registrar or such assistant registrar may direct at what time and place a special meeting under this section is to be held, and what matters are to be discussed and determined at the meeting, and the meeting shall have all the powers of a meeting called according to the rules of the society, and shall in all cases have power to appoint its own chairman, any rule of the society to the contrary notwithstanding.

Change of Name :   Amalgamation :   Conversion

51. Meaning of special resolution.[28]

For the purposes of this Act a special resolution shall mean a resolution which is -

---

[27] Inserted: Industrial and Provident Societies (Amendment) Act, 1913, 3 & 4 Geo. 5 c. 31, s. 9

[28] The Industrial and Provident Society (Amendment) Act, 1971 (No. 31), s. 1 provides: The Industrial and Provident Society Act, 1893, shall have effect, in relation to the amalgamation of two or more registered societies each of which has amongst its objects and is engaged in the manufacture of butter, cream or any other dairy product, as if "if not less than three fourths" were deleted in section 51(a)

(a) passed by a majority of not less than three-fourths[28] of such members of a registered society for the time being entitled under the rules to vote as may have voted in person, or by proxy where the rules allow proxies, at any general meeting of which notice, specifying the intention to propose the resolutions, has been duly given according to the rules; and

(b) confirmed by a majority of such members for the time being entitled under the rules to vote as may have voted in person, or by proxy where the rules allow proxies, at a subsequent general meeting of which notice has been duly given, held not less than fourteen days nor more than one month from the day of the meeting at which such resolution was first passed.

At any meeting mentioned in this section a declaration by the chairman that the resolution has been carried shall be deemed conclusive evidence of the fact.

52. Power to change name.

A registered society may, by special resolution, with the approval in writing of the chief registrar, or, in the case of societies registered and doing business exclusively in .... Ireland, the assistant registrar for .... Ireland ...., change its name; but no such change shall affect any right or obligation of the society, or of any member thereof, and any pending legal proceedings may be continued by or against the society notwithstanding its new name.

53.[29] Amalgamation and transfer of engagements.

(1) Any two or more registered societies may, by special resolution of both or all such societies, become amalgamated together as one society, with or without any dissolution or division of the funds of such societies or either of them, and the property of such societies shall become vested in the amalgamated society without the necessity of any form of conveyance other than that contained in the special resolution amalgamating the societies.

(2) Any registered society may by special resolution transfer its engagements to any other registered society which may undertake to fulfil the engagements of such society.

(3)[30] Notwithstanding subsection (1) and (2) of this section, a credit union shall not amalgamate with or transfer its enjoyments to any other registered society unless that society is a credit union the members of which have the same common bond as have the members of the first mentioned credit union.

[29] Modified: Industrial and Provident Societies (Amendment) Act, 1913, 3 & 4 Geo. 5 c. 31, s. 8

[30] Inserted: Credit Union Act, 1966 (No. 19), s. 37, sch., pt. 1

54. Conversion of society into company.[14]

(1) A registered society may by special resolution determine to convert itself into a company under the Companies Acts, or to amalgamate with or transfer its engagements to any such company.

(2) If a special resolution for converting a registered society into a company contains the particulars by the Companies Acts required to be contained in the Memorandum of Association of a company, and a copy thereof has been registered at the central office, a copy of such resolution under the seal or stamp of the central office shall have the same effect as a Memorandum of Association duly signed and attested under the said Act.

(3) If a registered society is registered as, or amalgamates with, or transfers all its engagements to, a company, the registry of such society under this Act shall thereupon become void, and the same shall be cancelled by the chief registrar or by the assistant registrar for .... Ireland under his direction; but the registration of a society as a company shall not affect any right or claim for the time being subsisting against such society or any penalty for the time being incurred by such society; and, for the purpose of enforcing any such right, claim, or penalty, the society may be sued and proceeded against in the same manner as if it had not become registered as a company; and every such right or claim, or the liability to such penalty, shall have priority, as against the property of such company, over all other rights or claims against or liabilities of such company.

55. Conversion of company into society.[14]

(1) A company registered under the Companies Acts may, by a special resolution, determine to convert itself into a registered society, and, for this purpose, in any case where the nominal value of its shares held by any member other than a registered society exceeds two hundred pounds, may, by such resolution, provide for the conversion of the excess of such share capital over two hundred pounds into a transferable loan stock bearing such rate of interest as may thereby be fixed, and repayable on such conditions only as are in such resolution determined.

(2) A resolution for the conversion of a company into a registered society shall be accompanied by a copy of the rules of the society therein referred to, and shall appoint seven persons, members of the company, who, together with the secretary, shall sign the rules, and who may either be authorised to accept any alterations made by the registrar therein, without further consulting the company, or may be required to lay all such alterations before the company in general meeting for acceptance as the resolution may direct.

(3) With the rules a copy of the special resolution for conversion of the company into a registered society shall be sent to the registrar,

who, upon the registration of the society, shall give to it, in addition to the acknowledgement of registry, a certificate similarly sealed or signed that the rules of the society referred to in the resolution have been registered, but in the registered name of the company as a society the word "company" shall not be used.

(4) A copy of the resolution for the conversion of the company into a registered society under the seal of the company, together with the certificate so issued by the registrar, shall be sent for registration to the office of the Registrar of Joint Stock Companies, and, upon the registration of such resolution and certificate, the conversion shall take effect.

(5) Upon the conversion of a company into a registered society the registry of the company under the Companies Acts shall become void, and shall be cancelled by the Registrar of Joint Stock Companies, but the registration of a company as a registered society shall not affect any right or claim for the time being subsisting against the company, or any penalty for the time being incurred by such company, and, for the purpose of enforcing any such right, claim, or penalty, the company may be sued and proceeded against in the same manner as if it had not become registered as a society. And every such right or claim, and the liability to such penalty, shall have priority as against the property of such society over all other rights or claims against or liabilities of the society.

56.[31] Registration of special resolutions.

A copy of every special resolution for any of the purposes mentioned in this Act, signed by the chairman of the meeting at which the resolution was confirmed, and countersigned by the secretary of the society, shall be sent to the central office and

---

[31] The Mergers, Take-overs and Monopolies (Control) Act, 1978 (No. 17), s. 14(3)(a) provides : A copy of a special resolution under section 53 of the Act of 1893, providing for the amalgamation of, or the transfer of the engagements between, two or more societies registered under that Act (being a proposed merger or takeover to which this Act applies) shall not be registered under section 56 of the Act of 1893 until either -

(i) the Minister has stated in writing that he has decided not to make an order under section 9 in relation to the proposed amalgamation or transfer of engagements, or

(ii) the Minister has stated in writing that he has made a conditional order in relation to the proposed amalgamation or transfer of engagements,or

(iii) the relevant period within the meaning of section 6 has elapsed without the Minister having made an order under section 9 in relation to the proposed amalgamation or transfer of engagements,

whichever first occurs.

registered there, and until that copy is so registered the special resolution shall not take effect.

57. Saving for rights of creditors.
An amalgamation or transfer of engagements in pursuance of this Act shall not prejudice any right of a creditor of any registered society party thereto.

Dissolution of Societies.

58.[32] Provisions as to dissolution of societies.
A registered society may be dissolved-
  (a) By an order to wind up the society, or a resolution for the winding up thereof, made as is directed in regard to companies by the Companies Acts, 1862 to 1890, the provisions whereof shall apply to any such order or resolution, except that the term "registrar" shall for the purposes of such winding up have the meaning given to it by this Act; or
  (b) By the consent of three-fourths of the members, testified by their signatures to an instrument of dissolution.

Industrial and Provident Societies

59. Transfer of winding up from county court.
Any proceedings in the winding up of a registered society which at the passing of this Act are pending in any county court may, on application made by or on behalf of the registrar, with the consent of the Treasury, be transferred to the High Court, and thereupon the Companies (Winding-Up) Act, 1890, shall, so far as applicable, apply thereto accordingly.

60. Liability of members in winding up.
Where a registered society is wound up in pursuance of an order or resolution the liability of a present or past member of the society to contribute for payment of the debts and liabilities of the society, the expenses of winding up, and the adjustment of the rights of contributories amongst themselves, shall be qualified as follows:-
  (a) No individual, society, or company, who or which has ceased to be a member for one year or upwards prior to the commencement of the winding up, shall be liable to contribute;

---
[32] Modified: Industrial and Provident Societies (Amendment) Act, 1913, 3 & 4 Geo. 5 c. 31, s. 8

(b) No individual, society, or company shall be liable to contribute in respect of any debt or liability contracted after he or it ceased to be a member ;

(c) No individual, society, or company, not a member, shall be liable to contribute, unless it appears to the court that the contributions of the existing members are insufficient to satisfy the just demands on the society ;

(d) No contribution shall be required from any individual, society, or company exceeding the amount, if any, unpaid on the shares in respect of which he or it is liable as a past or present member ;

(e) An individual, society, or company shall be taken to have ceased to be a member, in respect of any withdrawable shares withdrawn, from the date of the notice or application for withdrawal.

61. Provisions as to instrument of dissolution.
Where a society is terminated by an instrument of dissolution :-

(a) The instrument of dissolution shall set forth the liabilities and assets of the society in detail, the number of members and the nature of their interests in the society respectively, the claims of creditors (if any) and the provisions to be made for their payment, and the intended appropriation or division of the funds and property of the society, unless the same be stated in the instrument of dissolution to be left to the award of the chief registrar;

(b) Alterations in the instrument of dissolution may be made with the like consents as herein-before provided, and testified in the same manner;

(c) A statutory declaration shall be made by three members and the secretary of the society that the provisions of this Act have been complied with, and shall be sent to the registrar with the instrument of dissolution; and any person knowingly making a false or fraudulent declaration in the matter shall be guilty of a misdemeanour;

(d) The instrument of dissolution and all alterations therein shall be registered in the manner herein provided for the registry of rules, and shall be binding upon all the members of the society;

(e) The registrar shall cause a notice of the dissolution to be advertised at the expense of the society in the Gazette and in some newspapers circulating in or about the locality in which the registered office of the society is situated; and unless, within three months from the date of the Gazette in which such advertisement appears, a member or other person

181

interested in or having any claim on the funds of the society commences proceedings to set aside the dissolution of the society in the county court of the district[33] where the registered office of the society is situate, and such dissolution is set aside accordingly, the society shall be legally dissolved from the date of such advertisement, and the requisite consents to the instrument of dissolution shall be considered to have been duly obtained without proof of the signatures thereto.

(f) Notice shall be sent to the central office of any proceeding to set aside the dissolution of a society, not less than seven days before it is commenced, by the person by whom it is taken, or of any order setting it aside, within seven days after it is made by the society.

Offences, Penalties, and Legal Proceedings.

62.[34] Offences by societies.
It shall be an offence under this Act if-
(a) a registered society, or an officer or member thereof, or any other person, fails to give any notice, send any return or document, do or allow to be done anything which the society, officer, or member, or person is by this Act required to give, send, do, or allow to be done; or
(b) a registered society, or an officer or member thereof, or any other person, wilfully neglects or refuses to do any act, or to furnish any information required for the purposes of this Act by the chief or other registrar, or by any other person authorised under this Act, or does anything forbidden by this Act ; or
(c) a registered society, or an officer or member thereof, or any other person, makes a return, or wilfully furnishes information in any respect false or insufficient ; or
(d) a registered society carries on the business of banking when it has any withdrawable share capital, or in carrying on such business does not make out and keep conspicuously hung up such statement as is herein-before required, or makes any payment of withdrawable capital contrary to the provisions of this Act.

---

[33]Construed as reference to the judge of the circuit: Courts (Supplemental Provisions) Act, 1961 (No. 39), s. 22(4)(a), sch 5.

[34] Substituted; Industrial and Provident Societies (Amendment) Act, 1913, 3 & 4 Geo. 5 c. 31, ss. 10, 12(3), sch.

63. Offences by societies to be also offences by officers, &c.

Every offence by a society under this Act shall be deemed to have been also committed by every officer of the same bound by the rules thereof to fulfil the duty whereof such offence is a breach, or, if there be no such officer, then by every member of the committee of the same, unless such member be proved to have been ignorant of or to have attempted to prevent the commission of such offence; and every act or default under this Act constituting an offence, if continued, shall constitute a new offence in every week during which the same continues.

64. Punishment of fraud or misappropriation.

If any person obtains possession by false representation or imposition of any property of a society, or having the same in his possession withholds or misapplies the same, or wilfully applies any part thereof to purposes other than those expressed or directed in the rules of the society, and authorised by this Act, he shall, on the complaint of the society, or of any member authorised by the society, or the committee thereof, or by the central office, or of the chief registrar or any assistant registrar by his authority, be liable on summary conviction to a fine not exceeding twenty pounds with costs, and to be ordered to deliver up all such property or to repay all moneys applied improperly, and, in default of such delivery or repayment, or of the payment of such fine, to be imprisoned, with or without hard labour, for any time not exceeding three months; but nothing in this section shall prevent any such person from being proceeded against by way of indictment, if not previously convicted of the same offence under this Act.

65. Penalty for falsification.

If any person wilfully makes, orders, or allows to be made any entry or erasure in, or omission from, any balance sheet of a registered society, or any contribution or collecting book, or any return or document required to be sent, produced, or delivered for the purposes of this Act, with intent to falsify the same, or to evade any of the provisions of this Act, he shall be liable to a fine not exceeding fifty pounds.

66. Penalty for not using name of society.

If any officer of a registered society, or any person on its behalf, uses any seal purporting to be a seal of the society, whereon its name is not so engraved as aforesaid, or issues or authorises the issue of any notice, advertisement, or other official publication of the society, or signs or authorises to be signed on behalf of the society any bill of exchange, promissory note, endorsement, cheque, order for money or goods, or issues or authorises to be issued any bills of parcels, invoice, receipt, or letters of credit of the society, wherein its name is not mentioned in manner aforesaid, he shall be liable to a fine not exceeding fifty pounds, and shall further be personally liable to the holder of any such bill or exchange, promissory note, cheque, or order for money or goods for the amount thereof unless the same is duly paid by the society.

67. Delivery of untrue rules.

It shall be an offence under this Act if any person, with intent to mislead or defraud, gives to any other person a copy of any rules, other than the rules for the time being registered under this Act, on the pretence that the same are existing rules of a registered society, or that there are no other rules of such society, or gives to any person a copy of any rules on the pretence that such rules are the rules of a registered society when the society is not registered.

68. Penalties for ordinary offences.

Every society, officer or member of a society, or other person, guilty of an offence under this Act for which no penalty is expressly provided herein, shall be liable to a fine not exceeding five pounds.

69. Recovery of penalties.

(1) Every fine imposed or to be imposed by this Act, or by any regulations under this Act, or by the rules of a registered society, shall be recovered summarily.

(2) Any such fine, if imposed by this Act or by any regulations thereunder, shall be recoverable at the suit of the chief registrar, or of any assistant registrar, or of any person aggrieved, and, if imposed by the rules of a registered society shall be recoverable at the suit of the society.

(3)[35] Any costs or expenses ordered or directed by the chief or other registrar to be paid by any person under this Act shall be recoverable summarily before a court of summary jurisdiction as a civil debt.

(4) Where proceedings are taken against a society for the recovery of any fine under this Act, the summons or other process shall be sufficiently served by leaving a true copy thereof at the registered office of the society, or, if that office is closed, by posting the copy on the outer door of that office.

70. Appeals from summary decisions.

(1) In . . Ireland any party may appeal to quarter sessions from

---

[35] S-s. (3) (4), inserted, Industrial and Provident Societies (Amendment) Act, 1913, 3 & 4 Geo. 5 c. 31, s. 11.

any order or conviction made by a court of summary jurisdiction under this Act.

(2) In Scotland ...

Supplemental

71. Remuneration of county court officers.

The registrar and high bailiffs of the county courts shall be remunerated for the duties to be performed by them under this Act in such manner as the Treasury, with the consent of the Lord Chancellor, from time to time order and direct.

72. Public auditors.

The Treasury may appoint public auditors for the purposes of this Act, and may determine the rates of remuneration to be paid by registered societies for the services of such auditors, ..[36] ......

73. Fees.[37]

(1) The Treasury may determine a scale of fees to be paid for matters to be transacted or for the inspection of documents under this Act.

(2) All fees received by any registrar under or by virtue of this Act shall be paid into the Exchequer.

74. Regulations for carrying out Act.[38]

(1) The Treasury may make regulations respecting registry and procedure under this Act, and the forms to be used for such registry, and the duties and functions of the registrar, and the inspection of documents kept by the registrar under this Act, and generally for carrying this Act into effect.

(2) All such regulations shall be laid before both Houses of Parliament within ten days after the making thereof if Parliament is then sitting, or, if not then sitting, then within ten days from the then next assembling of Parliament.

(3) Until otherwise provided by such regulations, the forms contained in the Fourth Schedule of this Act shall be used.

75. Evidence of documents

Every copy of rules or other instrument or document, copy or extract of an instrument or document, bearing the seal or stamp of the central office, shall be received in evidence without further proof;

---

[36] Repealed, Industrial and Provident Societies (Amendment) Act, 1913, 3 & 4 Geo. 5 c. 31, s. 12(3), sch.

[37] Am. S.I. 291/1983

[38] S.R. & O. 731/1894 as am. S.R. & O. 1551/1914; Forms, S.I. 351/1986

and every document purporting to be signed by the chief or any assistant registrar, or any inspector or Public Auditor under this Act, shall, in the absence of any evidence to the contrary, be received in evidence without proof of the signature.

76. Duties of the Registrars. 38 & 39 Vict. c. 60.

Sub-sections six, seven, eight, and nine of section ten of the Friendly Societies Act, 1875, relating to the duties of the chief registrar and assistant registrars, shall, so far as the same are applicable to industrial and provident societies, be incorporated with this Act.

77. & 78. Relates to Channel Islands only.

79. Definitions

In this Act, if not inconsistent with the context, the following terms shall have the meanings herein-after respectively assigned to them:-

"The Registrar" shall mean, ... for .... Ireland, the assistant registrar of friendly societies; ....

"the central office" shall mean the central office so established; and

"chief registrar" and "assistant registrar" shall mean chief registrar and assistant registrar of friendly societies respectively;

"Land" shall include hereditaments and chattels real; ....

"Property" shall include all real and personal estate (including books and papers);

"Registered society" shall mean a society registered or deemed to be registered under this Act;

"Amendment of rule" shall include a new rule, and a resolution rescinding a rule;

"Rules" shall mean the registered rules for the time being, and shall include any registered amendment of rules;

"The committee" shall mean the committee of management or other directing body of a society;

"Persons claiming through a member" shall include the heirs, executors, or administrators, and assigns of a member, and also his nominees where nomination is allowed;

"Officer"[14] shall extend to any treasures, secretary, member of the committee, manager or servant, other than a servant appointed by the committee, of a society;

"Meeting" shall include (where the ruled of the society so allow) a meeting of delegates appointed by members;

"Office" shall mean the registered office for the time being of a society;

"Gazette" shall mean....the Dublin Gazette[39] for Ireland.

80. Repealed by Statute Law Revision Act, 1908[40]

Schedule I
Repealed by Statute Law Revision Act, 1908

Schedule II[14]

Section 10

Matters to be provided for by the rules of societies
registered under this Act.

1. Object, name, and registered offices of the society.
2. Terms of admission of the members, including any society or
company investing funds in the society under the provisions of this
Act.
3. Mode of holding meetings, scale and right of voting, and of
making, altering, or rescinding rules.
4. The appointment and removal of a committee of management,
by whatever name, of managers or other officers, and their respective
powers and remuneration.
5. Determination of the amount of interest, not exceeding two
hundred pounds sterling, in the shares of the society which any
member other than a registered society may hold.
6. Determination whether the society may contract loans or receive
money on deposit subject to the provisions of this Act from members
or others; and, if so, under what conditions, on what security, and to
what limits of amount.
7. Determination whether the shares or any of them shall be
transferable; and provision for the form of transfer and registration
of the shares, and for the consent of the committee thereto;
determination whether the shares or any of them shall be
withdrawable, and provision for the mode of withdrawal and for
payment of the balance due thereon on withdrawing from the society.
8. Provision for the audit of accounts and for the appointment of
auditors or a public auditor.
9. Determination whether and how members may withdraw from
the society, and provision for the claims of the representatives of

---

[39] To be construed as *Iris Oifigúil*; Adaptation of Enactments Act, 1922 (No. 2),
s. 4
[40] 8 Edw. 7 c. 49

deceased members, or the trustees of the property of bankrupt members, and for the payment of nominees.

10. Mode of application of profits.

11. Provision for the custody and use of the seal of the society.

12. Determination whether, and by what authority, and in what manner, any part of the capital may be invested.

Schedule III

Sections 19, 43, 47

Form of statement to be made out by a society carrying on the business of banking.

1. Capital of the society :-
(a) Nominal amount of each share;
(b) Number of shares issued;
(c) Amount paid up on shares.

2. Liabilities of the society on the first day of January (or July) last previous:-
(a) On judgments;
(b) On specialty;
(c) On notes or bills;
(d) On simple contracts;
(e) On estimated liabilities.

3. Assets of the society on the same date:-
(a) Government, or other securities (stating them);
(b) Bills of exchange and promissory notes;
(c) Cash at the bankers;
(d) Other securities

Forms of Bond

(1) In .... Ireland.

(a) *Know all men* by these presents, that we A.B., of one of the officers of the ...., Limited, hereinafter referred to as "the Society", whose registered office is at.................................in the County of ...., and C.D., of .... (as surety on behalf of the said A.B.), are jointly and severally held and firmly bound to the said society in the sum of .... to be paid to the said society, or their certain attorney, for which payment well and truly to be made we jointly and severally bind ourselves, and each of us by himself, our and each of our heirs, executors, and administrators, firmly by these presents.

Sealed with our seals.
Dated the .... day of ....

Whereas the above-bounden A.B. has been duly appointed to the office of .... of the .... Society, and he, together with the above-bounden C.D. as his surety, have entered into the above-written bond, subject to the condition hereinafter contained: Now therefore, the condition of the above-written bond is such, that if the said A.B. do render a just and true account of all moneys received and paid by him on account of the society, at such times as the rules thereof appoint, and do pay over all the moneys remaining in his hands, and assign and transfer or deliver all property (including books and papers) belonging to the society in his hands or custody to such person or persons as the society or the committee thereof appoint, according to the rules of the society, together with the proper and legal receipts or vouchers for such payments, then the above-written bond shall be void, but otherwise shall remain in full force.

Sealed   and   delivered   in   the   presence   of
....

(b)   *Know   all   men*   by   these   presents   that   I
....,
of .... , in the County of .... ,
am firmly bound to ...., Limited, hereinafter referred to as "the Society", whose registered office is at ...., in the County of ...., in the sum of .... pounds sterling to be paid to the said society or their assigns, for which payment to be truly made to the said society or their certain attorney or assigns I bind myself, my heirs, executors, and administrators, by these presents sealed with my seal.

[*And   know further*   that I (we) as surety (sureties) for the above named principal obligor and such obligor are jointly and severally bound to the society in the sum aforesaid to be paid to the society or their assigns, for which payment to be truly made to the society or their certain attorney or assigns we firmly bind ourselves and each of us our and each of our heirs, executors, and administrators by these presents sealed with our seals.]

Dated..................... day of .... 19... .

Industrial and Provident Society Act, 1893

The condition of the above-contained bond is that if the said
....

faithfully execute the office of .... to the society during such time as he continues to hold the same in virtue either of his present appointment, or of any renewal thereof if such office is of a renewable character [without wasting, embezzling, losing, misspending, misapplying, or unlawfully making away with any of the moneys, goods, chattels, wares, merchandise or effects whatsoever of the said society at any time committed to his charge, custody, or keeping by reason or means of his said office], and render a true and full account of all moneys received or paid by him on its behalf as and when he is required by the committee of management of the society for the time being, and pay over all the moneys remaining in his hands from time to time, and assign, transfer, and deliver up all securities, books, papers, property, and effects whatsoever of or belonging to the society in his charge, custody, or keeping, to such person or persons as the said committee may appoint, according to the rules or regulations of the society for the time being, together with the proper or legal receipts or vouchers for such payments; and in all other respects well and faithfully perform and fulfil the said office of .... to the society according to the rules thereof, then the above-contained bond shall be void and of no effect; but otherwise shall remain in full force.

Sealed and delivered by the above-named

[The words between brackets against which we have set out initials being first struck out*] in the presence of us.
. . . .

Forms of receipt to be endorsed on mortgage or further charge.

(1) In .... Ireland.

A.- The .... , Limited, hereby acknowledges to have received all moneys intended to be secured by the within (or above) written deed. Dated this .... day of
....

Members of the Committee.
Secretary

---

*If no words are struck out in the bond or condition, strike out these words and let the witnesses set their initials in the margin.

Industrial and Provident Society Act, 1893
Schedule IV

Section 74

Acknowledgement of registry of society.

The .... , Limited, is registered under the Industrial and Provident Societies Act 1893, this .... day of
....
(Seal or stamp of central office, or signature of Assistant Registrar for .... Ireland)

Acknowledge of registry of amendment of rules.

The foregoing amendment of the rules of the .... , Limited, is registered under the Industrial and Provident Societies Act, 1893, this .... day of ....

(Seal or stamp of central office, or signature of Assistant Registrar for .... Ireland)

The Trustee Act, 1893
56 & 57 Victoria, chapter 53

List of Sections

Part I

Investments

Part II

Various Powers and Duties of Trustees

Appointment of New Trustees

Purchase and Sale

Trustee Act, 1893

16. Repealed

Various Powers and Liabilities.

Part III
Powers of the Court.

Appointment of New Trustees and Vesting Orders.

Trustee Act, 1893

Part I
Investments

1. Authorised investments.[1]

A trustee may, unless expressly forbidden by the instrument (if any) creating the trust, invest any trust funds in his hands, whether at the time in a state of investment or not, in manner following, that is to say:

(a) in securities of the Government (including Savings Certificates);

(b) in securities guaranteed as to capital and interest by the Minister for Finance;

(c) in the stock of the Bank of Ireland;

(d) in securities of the Electricity Supply Board;

(e) in securities of the Agricultural Credit Corporation, Limited;

(f) in securities of Bord na Móna;

(g) on real securities in the State;

(h) in securities or mortgages of any of the following authorities in the State :

(i) the council of a county,

(ii) the corporation of a county borough,

(iii) the corporation of Dun Laoghaire,

(iv) the Dublin Port and Docks Board,

(v) the Cork Harbour Commissioners,

(vi) the Limerick Harbour Commissioners,

(vii) the Waterford Harbour Commissioners;

(i) in debentures or debenture stock, quoted on a Stock Exchange, of any industrial or commercial company registered in the State, provided that the total of the debentures, debenture stock or debentures and debenture stock of the company does not exceed the paid-up share capital (including payments in respect of share premiums) and that a dividend of not less than five per cent. has been paid on the ordinary shares of the company in each of the five years last past before the date of investment;

(ii)[2] subject to section 137(2) of the Central Bank Act, 1989, in an interest bearing deposit account with the Central Bank of Ireland;

(j) in an interest bearing deposit account with any of the

---

[1] As substituted, Trustee (Authorised Investments) Act, 1958 (No. 8), s. 1

[2] Inserted, Central Bank Act, 1989 (No.16), s.137(1), s-s. (2) states that the provision...shall not be construed as imposing an obligation on the Bank to accept trust funds for deposit with it.

following banks[3,4] :

(i)   Bank of Ireland,[5]
(ii)   Guinness & Mahon,
(iv)   Allied Irish Banks Limited,[6]
(vi)   National City Bank, Ltd.,
(vii) Northern Bank, Ltd.,[7]
(x)   Ulster Bank, Ltd.,
(xi)   the Post Office Savings Bank,
(xii) a Trustee Savings Bank in the State;[8]

(k) in British Government securities inscribed or registered in the State,

and may also from time to time vary any such investment.

2. Purchase at a premium of redeemable stocks.

(1) A trustee may under the powers of this Act invest in any of the securities mentioned or referred to in section one of this Act, notwithstanding that the same may be redeemable and that the price exceeds the redemption value.

(2) Repealed by Trustee (Authorised Investments) Act, 1958 (No. 8), s. 6, sch.

(3) A trustee may retain until redemption any redeemable stock, fund, or security which may have been purchased in accordance with the powers of this Act.

---

[3] The Trustee (Authorised Investments) Act, 1958 (No. 8) at section 2(1) provides: The Minister for Finance may by order vary by addition or deletion -

(a) the investments specified in section 1 of the Trustee Act, 1893, as amended by section 1 of this Act, or

(b) where those investments have been varied by order under this subsection, these investments are so varied.

These investments have been added to by the following Statutory Instruments: 285/1967, 241/1969, 377/1974, 41/1977, 344/1977, 407/1979, 58/1983, 224/1985, 372/1986, 327/1990, 75/1992.

[4] Ref., Educational Exchange (Ireland and the United States of America) Act, 1991 (No. 12), s. 7(e), power of commission re. authorisation of funds.

[5] By Statutory Instrument the Hibernian Bank, Ltd., (21/1972) and the National Bank (of Ireland) Limited (20/1972) are to be known as the Bank of Ireland.

[6] By Statutory Instrument the Munster & Leinster Bank, Ltd., (22/1972), the Provincial Bank of Ireland, Ltd., (23/1972) and the Royal Bank of Ireland, Ltd.(24/1972) are to be known as Allied Irish Banks Limited (now AIB Bank).

[7] Now known as the National Irish Bank Limited.

[8] See: S.I. 55/1992 re. TSB Bank.

3. Discretion of trustees.

Every power conferred by the preceding sections shall be exercised according to the discretion of the trustee, but subject to any consent required by the instrument, if any, creating the trust with respect to the investment of the trust funds.

4. Application of preceding sections.

The preceding sections shall apply as well to trusts created before as to trusts created after the passing of this Act, and the powers thereby conferred shall be in addition to the powers conferred by the instrument, if any, creating the trust.

5. Enlargement of express powers of investment.

(1) A trustee having power to invest in real securities, unless expressly forbidden by the instrument creating the trust, may invest and shall be deemed to have always had power to invest -

    (a) on mortgage of property held for an unexpired term of not less than two hundred years, and not subject to a reservation of rent greater than a shilling a year, or to any right of redemption or to any condition for re-entry, except for non-payment of rent; and

    (b) on any charge, or upon mortgage of any charge, made under the Improvement of Land Act, 1864.

(2) A trustee having power to invest in the mortgages or bonds of any railway company or of any other description of company may, unless the contrary is expressed in the instrument authorising the investment, invest in the debenture stock of a railway company or such other company as aforesaid.

(3) A trustee having power to invest money in the debentures or debenture stock of any railway or other company may, unless the contrary is expressed in the instrument authorising the investment, invest in any nominal debentures or nominal debenture stock issued under the Local Loans Act, 1875.

(4) A trustee having power to invest money in securities in the Isle of Man, or in securities of the government of a colony, may, unless the contrary is expressed in the instrument authorising the investment, invest in any securities of the Government of the Isle of Man, under the Isle of Man Loans Act, 1880.

(5) A trustee having a general power to invest trust moneys in or upon the security of shares, stock, mortgages, bonds, or debentures of companies incorporated by or acting under the authority of an Act of Parliament, may invest in, or upon the security of, mortgage debentures duly issued under and in accordance with the provisions of the Mortgage Debenture Act, 1865.

6. Power to invest, notwithstanding drainage charges.

A trustee having power to invest in the purchase of land or on mortgage of land may invest in the purchase, or on mortgage of any land, notwithstanding the same is charged with a rent under the powers of the Public Money Drainage Acts, 1846 to 1856, or the Landed Property Improvement (Ireland) Act, 1847 or by an absolute order made under the Improvement of Land Act, 1864, unless the terms of the trust expressly provide that the land to be purchased or taken in mortgage shall not be subject to any such prior charge.

7. Trustees not to convert inscribed stock into certificates to bearer.

(1) A trustee, unless authorised by the terms of his trust, shall not apply for or hold any certificate to bearer issued under the authority of any of the following Acts, that is to say:

(a)　The India Stock Certificate Act, 1863;

(b)　The National Debt Act, 1870;

(c)　The Local Loans Act, 1875;

(d)　The Colonial Stock Act, 1877.

(2) Nothing in this section shall impose on the Bank of England or of Ireland, or on any person authorised to issue any such certificates, any obligation to inquire whether a person applying for such a certificate is or is not a trustee, or subject them to any liability in the event of their granting any such certificate to a trustee, nor invalidate any such certificate if granted.

8. Loans and investments by trustees not chargeable as breaches of trust.

(1) A trustee lending money on the security of any property on which he can lawfully lend shall not be chargeable with breach of trust by reason only of the proportion borne by the amount of the loan to the value of the property at the time when the loan was made, provided that it appears to the court that in making the loan the trustee was acting upon a report as to the value of the property made by a person whom he reasonably believed to be an able practical surveyor or valuer instructed and employed independently of any owner of the property, whether such surveyor or valuer carried on business in the locality where the property is situate or elsewhere, and that the amount of the loan does not exceed two equal third parts of the value of the property as stated in the report, and that the loan was made under the advice of the surveyor or valuer expressed in the report.

(2) A trustee lending money on the security of any leasehold property shall not be chargeable with breach of trust only upon the ground that in making such loan he dispensed either wholly or partly with the production or investigation of the lessor's title.

(3) A trustee shall not be chargeable with breach of trust only upon the ground that in effecting the purchase of or in lending money upon the security of any property he has accepted a shorter title than the title which a purchase is, in the absence of a special contract, entitled to require, if in the opinion of the court the title accepted be such as a person acting with prudence and caution would have accepted.

(4) This section applies to transfers of existing securities as well as to new securities, and to investments made as well before as after the commencement of this Act, except where an action or other proceeding was pending with reference thereto on the twenty-fourth day of December one thousand eight hundred and eighty-eight.

9. Liability for loss by reason of improper investments.

(1) Where a trustee improperly advances trust money on a mortgage security which would at the time of the investment be a proper investment in all respects for a smaller sum than is actually advanced thereon the security shall be deemed an authorised investment for the smaller sum, and the trustee shall only be liable to make good the sum advanced in excess thereof with interest.

(2) This section applies to investments made as well before as after the commencement of this Act except where an action or other proceeding was pending with reference thereto on the twenty-fourth day of December on thousand eight hundred and eighty-eight.

Part II

Various Powers and Duties of Trustees

Appointment of New Trustees

10. Power of appointing new trustees.

(1) Where a trustee, either original or substituted, and whether appointed by a court or otherwise, is dead, or remains out of the United Kingdom for more than twelve months, or desires to be discharged from all or any of the trusts or powers reposed in or conferred on him, or refuses or is unfit to act therein, or is incapable of acting therein, then the person or persons nominated for the purpose of appointing new trustees by the instrument, if any, creating the trust, or if there is no such person, or no such person able and willing to act, then the surviving or continuing trustees or trustee for the time being, or the personal representatives of the last surviving or continuing trustee, may, by writing, appoint another person or other persons to be a trustee or trustees in the place of the trustee dead, remaining out of the United Kingdom, desiring to be discharged

refusing, or being unfit or being incapable, as aforesaid.

(2) On the appointment of a new trustee for the whole or any part of trust property -

(a) the number of trustees may be increased; and

(b) a separate set of trustees may be appointed for any part of the trust property held on trusts distinct from those relating to any other part or parts of the trust property, notwithstanding that no new trustees or trustee are or is to be appointed for other parts of the trust property, and any existing trustee may be appointed or remain one of such separate set of trustees; or, if only one trustee was originally appointed, then one separate trustee may be so appointed for the first-mentioned part; and

(c) it shall not be obligatory to appoint more than one new trustee where only one trustee was originally appointed, or to fill up the original number of trustees where more than two trustees were originally appointed; but, except where only one trustee was originally appointed, a trustee shall not be discharged under this section from his trust unless there will be at least two trustees to perform the trust; and

(d) any assurance or thing requisite for vesting the trust property, or any part thereof, jointly in the persons who are the trustees, shall be executed or done.

(3) Every new trustee so appointed, as well before as after all the trust property becomes by law, or by assurance, or otherwise, vested in him, shall have the same powers, authorities, and discretions, and may in all respects act, as if he had been originally appointed a trustee by the instrument, if any, creating the trust.

(4) The provisions of this section relative to a trustee who is dead include the case of a person nominated trustee in a will but dying before the testator, and those relative to a continuing trustee include a refusing or retiring trustee, if willing to act in the execution of the provisions of this section.

(5) This section applies only if and as far as a contrary intention is not expressed in the instrument, if any, creating the trust, and shall have effect subject to the terms of that instrument and to any provisions therein contained.

(6) This section applies to trusts created either before or after the commencement of this Act.

11. Retirement of trustee.

(1) Where there are more than two trustees, if one of them by deed declares that he is desirous of being discharged from the trust, and if his co-trustees and such other person, if any, as is empowered to appoint trustees, by deed consent to the discharge of the trustee, and to the vesting in the co-trustees alone of the trust property, then the

trustee desirous of being discharged shall be deemed to have retired from the trust, and shall, by the deed, be discharged therefrom under this Act, without any new trustee being appointed in his place.

(2) Any assurance or thing requisite for vesting the trust property in the continuing trustees alone shall be executed or done.

(3) This section applies only if and as far as a contrary intention is not expressed in the instrument, if any, creating the trust, and shall have effect subject to the terms of that instrument and to any provisions therein contained.

(4) This section applies to trusts created either before or after the commencement of this Act.

12. Vesting of trust property in new or continuing trustees.

(1) Where a deed by which a new trustee is appointed to perform any trust contains a declaration by the appointor to the effect that any estate or interest in any land subject to the trust, or in any chattel so subject, or the right to recover and receive any debt or other thing in action so subject, shall vest in the persons who by virtue of the deed become an are the trustees for performing the trust, that declaration shall, without any conveyance or assignment, operate to vest in those persons, as joint tenants, and for the purposes of the trust, that estate, interest, or right.

(2) Where a deed by which a retiring trustee is discharged under this Act contains such a declaration as is in this section mentioned by the retiring and continuing trustees, an by the other person, if any, empowered to appoint trustees, that declaration shall, without any conveyance or assignment, operate to vest in the continuing trustees alone, as joint tenants, and for the purposes of the trust, the estate, interest, or right to which the declaration relates.

(3) This section does not extend to any legal estate or interest in copyhold or customary land, or to land conveyed by way of mortgage for securing money subject to the trust, or to any such share, stock, annuity, or property as in only transferable in books kept by a company or other body, or in manner directed by or under Act of Parliament.

(4) For purposes of registration of the deed in any registry, the person or persons making the declaration shall be deemed the conveying party or parties, and the conveyance shall be deemed to be made by him or them under a power conferred by this Act.

(5) This section applies only to deeds executed after the thirty-first of December one thousand eight hundred and eighty-one.

13. Power of trustee for sale to sell by auction, &c.

(1) Where a trust for sale or a power of sale of property is vested in a trustee, he may sell or concur with any other person in selling all or any part of the property, either subject to prior charges or not, and either together or in lots, by public auction or by private contract, subject to any such conditions respecting title or evidence of title or other matter as the trustee thinks fit, with power to vary any contract for sale, and to buy in at any auction, or to rescind any contract for sale and to re-sell, without being answerable for any loss.

(2) This section applies only if and as far as a contrary intention is not expressed in the instrument creating the trust or power, and shall have effect subject to the terms of that instrument and to the provisions therein contained.

(3) This section applies only to a trust or power created by an instrument coming into operation after the thirty-first of December one thousand eight hundred and eighty-one.

14. Power to sell subject to depreciatory conditions.

(1) No sale made by a trustee shall be impeached by any beneficiary upon the ground that any of the conditions subject to which the sale was made may have been unnecessarily depreciatory, unless it also appears that the consideration for the sale was thereby rendered inadequate.

(2) No sale made by a trustee shall, after the execution of the conveyance, be impeached as against the purchaser upon the ground that any of the conditions subject to which the sale was made may have been unnecessarily depreciatory, unless it appears that the purchaser was acting in collusion with the trustee at the time when the contract for sale was made.

(3) No purchaser, upon any sale made by a trustee, shall be at liberty to make any objection against the title upon the ground aforesaid.

(4) This section applies only to sales made after the twenty-fourth day of December one thousand eight hundred an eighty-eight.

15. Power to sell under 37 & 38 Vict. c. 78.

A trustee who is either a vendor or a purchaser may sell or buy without excluding the application of section two of the Vendor and Purchaser Act, 1874.

16. Repealed: Married Women's Status Act, 1957 (No. 5), s. 19, sch.

Various Powers and Liabilities.

17. Power to authorise receipt of money by banker or solicitor.

(1) A trustee may appoint a solicitor to be his agent to receive and give a discharge for any money or valuable consideration or property receivable by the trustee under the trust, by permitting the solicitor to have the custody of, and to produce, a deed containing any such receipt as is referred to in section fifty-six of the Conveyancing and Law of Property Act, 1881; and a trustee shall not be chargeable with breach of trust by reason only of his having made or concurred in making any such appointment; and the producing of any such deed by the solicitor shall have the same validity and effect under the said section as if the person appointing the solicitor had not been a trustee.

(2) A trustee may appoint a banker or solicitor to be his agent to receive and give a discharge for any money payable to the trustee under or by virtue of a policy of assurance, by permitting the banker or solicitor to have the custody of and to produce the policy of assurance with a receipt signed by the trustee, and a trustee shall not be chargeable with a breach of trust by reason only of his having made or concurred in making any such appointment.

(3) Nothing in this section shall exempt a trustee from any liability which he would have incurred if this Act had not been passed, in case he permits any such money, valuable consideration, or property to remain in the hands or under the control of the banker or solicitor for a period longer than is reasonably necessary to enable the banker or solicitor (as the case may be) to pay or transfer the same to the trustee.

(4) This section applies only where the money or valuable consideration or property is received after the twenty-fourth day of December one thousand eight hundred and eighty-eight.

(5) Nothing in this section shall authorise a trustee to do anything which he is in express terms forbidden to do, or to omit anything which he is in express terms directed to do, by the instrument creating the trust.

18. Power to insure building.

(1) A trustee may insure against loss or damage by fire any building or other insurable property to any amount (including the amount of any insurance already on foot) not exceeding three equal fourth parts of the full value of such building or property, and pay the premiums for such insurance out of the income thereof or out of the income of any other property subject to the same trust, without obtaining the consent of any person who may be entitled wholly or partly to such income.

(2) This section does not apply to any building or property which a trustee is bound forthwith to convey absolutely to any beneficiary upon being requested to do so.

(3) This section applies to trusts created either before or after the commencement of this Act, but nothing in this section shall authorise any trustee to do anything which he is in express terms forbidden to do, or to omit to do anything which he is in express terms directed to do, by the instrument creating the trust.

19. Power of trustees of renewable leaseholds to renew and raise money for the purpose.

(1) A trustee of any leaseholds for lives or years which are renewable from time to time, either under any covenant or contract, or by custom or usual practice, may, if he thinks fit, and shall, if thereto required by any person having any beneficial interest, present or future, or contingent, in the leaseholds, use his best endeavours to obtain from time to time a renewed lease of the same hereditaments on the accustomed and reasonable terms, and for that purpose may from time to time make or concur in making a surrender of the lease for the time being subsisting, and do all such other acts as are requisite: Provided that, where by the terms of the settlement or will the person in possession for his life or other limited interest is entitled to enjoy the same without any obligation to renew or to contribute to the expense of renewal, this section shall not apply unless the consent in writing of that person is obtained to the renewal on the part of the trustee.

(2) If money is required to pay for the renewal, the trustee effecting the renewal may pay the same out of any money then in his hands in trust for the persons beneficially interested in the lands to be comprised in the renewed lease, and if he has not in his hands sufficient money for the purpose, he may raise the money required by mortgage of the hereditaments to be comprised in the renewed lease, or of any other hereditaments for the time being subject to the uses or trusts to which those hereditaments are subject, and no person advancing money upon a mortgage purporting to be under this power shall be bound to see that the money is wanted, or that no more is raised than is wanted for the purpose.

(3) This section applies to trusts created either before or after the commencement of this Act, but nothing in this section shall authorise any trustee to do anything which he is in express terms forbidden to do, or to omit to do anything which he is in express terms directed to do, by the instrument creating the trust.

20. Power of trustee to give receipts.

(1) The receipt in writing of any trustee for any money, securities, or other personal property or effects payable, transferable, or deliverable to him under any trust or power shall be a sufficient discharge for the same, and shall effectually exonerate the person paying, transferring, or delivering the same from seeing to the application or being answerable for any loss or misapplication thereof.

(2) This section applies to trusts created either before or after the commencement of this Act.

21. Power for executors and trustees to compound, &c. [9]

(1) An executor or administrator may pay or allow any debt or claim on any evidence that he thinks sufficient.

(2) An executor or administrator, or two or more trustees, acting together, or a sole acting trustee where by the instrument, if any, creating the trust a sole trustee is authorised to execute the trusts and powers thereof, may, if and as he or they may think fit, accept any composition or any security, real or personal, for any debt or for any property, real or personal, claimed, and may allow any time for payment for any debt, and may compromise, compound, abandon, submit to arbitration, or otherwise settle any debt, account, claim, or thing whatever relating to the testator's or intestate's estate or to the trust, and for any of those purposes may enter into, give, execute, and do such agreements, instruments of composition or arrangement, releases, and other things as to him or them seem expedient, without being responsible for any loss occasioned by any act or thing so done by him or them in good faith.

(3) This section applies only if and as far as a contrary intention is not expressed in the instrument, if any, creating the trust, and shall have effect subject to the terms of that instrument, and to the provisions therein contained.

(4) This section applies to executorships, administratorships and trusts constituted or created either before or after the commencement of this Act.

22. Powers of two or more trustees.

(1) Where a power or trust is given to or vested in two or more trustees jointly, then, unless the contrary is expressed in the instrument, if any, creating the power or trust, the same may be exercised or performed by the survivor or survivors of them for the time being.

(2) This section applies only to trusts constituted after or created by

---

[9] Repealed in so far as it applies to personal representatives by Succession Act, 1965 (No. 27), ss. 8, 9, sch. 2, pt. 3.

instruments coming into operation after the thirty-first day of December one thousand eight hundred and eighty-one.

23. Exoneration of trustees in respect of certain powers of attorney.

A trustee acting or paying money in good faith under or in pursuance of any power of attorney shall not be liable for any such act or payment by reason of the fact that at the time of the payment or act the person who gave the power of attorney was dead or had done some act to avoid the power if this fact was not known to the trustee at the time of his so acting or paying.

Provided that nothing in this section shall affect the right of any person entitled to the money against the person to whom the payment is made, and that the person so entitled shall have the same remedy against the person to whom the payment is made as he would have had against the trustee.

24. Implied indemnity of trustees.

A trustee shall, without prejudice to the provisions of the instrument, if any, creating the trust, be chargeable only for money and securities actually received by him notwithstanding his signing any receipt for the sake of conformity, and shall be answerable and accountable only for his own acts, receipts, neglects, or defaults, and not for those of any other trustee, nor for any banker, broker, or other person with whom any trust moneys, or securities may be deposited, nor for the insufficiency or deficiency of any securities, nor for any other loss, unless the same happens through his own wilful default; and may reimburse himself, or pay or discharge out of the trust premises, all expenses incurred in or about the execution of his trusts or powers.

Part III
Powers of the Court.

Appointment of New Trustees and Vesting Orders.

25. Power of the Court to appoint new trustees.[10]

(1) The High Court may, whenever it is expedient to appoint a new trustee or new trustees, and it is found inexpedient, difficult, or, impracticable so to do without the assistance of the Court, make an order for the appointment of a new trustee or new trustees either in substitution for or in addition to any existing trustee or trustees, or although there is no existing trustee. In particular and without prejudice to the generality of the foregoing provision, the Court may make an order for the appointment of a new trustee in substitution

[10] Power of court extended, Trustee Act, 1931 (No. 20), ss. 3, 4.

for a trustee who is convicted of felony or is a bankrupt.

(2) An order under this section, and any consequential vesting order or conveyance, shall not operate further or otherwise as a discharge to any former or continuing trustee than an appointment of new trustees under any power for that purpose contained in any instrument would have operated.

(3) Nothing in this section shall give power to appoint an executor or administrator.

26. Vesting orders as to land.

In any of the following cases, namely:-

    (i) Where the High Court appoints or has appointed a new trustee; and

    (ii) Where a trustee entitled to or possessed of any land, or entitled to a contingent right therein, either solely or jointly with any other person, -

        a. is an infant, or

        b. is out of the jurisdiction of the High Court, or

        c. cannot be found; and

    (iii) Where it is uncertain who was the survivor of two or more trustees jointly entitled to or possessed of any land; and

    (iv) Where, as to the last trustee known to have been entitled to or possessed of any land, it is uncertain whether he is living or dead; and

    (v) Where there is no heir or personal representative to a trustee who was entitled to or possessed of land and has died intestate as to that land, or where it is uncertain who is the heir or personal representative or devisee of a trustee who was entitled or possessed of land and is dead; and

    (vi) Where a trustee jointly or solely entitled to or possessed of any land, or entitled to a contingent right therein, has been required, by or on behalf of a person entitled to require a conveyance of the land or a release of the right, to convey the land or to release the right, and has wilfully refused or neglected to convey the land or release the right for twenty-eight days after the date of the requirement;

the High Court may make an order (in this Act called a vesting order) vesting the land in any such person in any such manner and for any such estate as the Court may direct, or releasing or disposing of the contingent right to such person as the Court may direct.

Provided that-

    (a) Where the order is consequential on the appointment of a new trustee the land shall be vested for such estate as the Court may direct in the persons who on the appointment are the trustees; and

(b) Where the order relates to a trustee entitled jointly with another person, and such trustee is out of the jurisdiction of the High Court or cannot be found, the land or right shall be vested in such other person, either alone or with some other person.

27. Orders as to contingent rights of unborn persons.

Where any land is subject to a contingent right in an unborn person or class of unborn persons who, on coming into existence would, in respect thereof, become entitled to or possessed of the land on any trust, the High court may make an order releasing the land from the contingent right, or may make an order vesting in any person the estate to or of which the unborn person or class of unborn persons would, on coming into existence, be entitled or possessed in the land.

28. Vesting order in place of conveyance by infant mortgagee.

Where any person entitled to or possessed of land, or entitled to a contingent right in land, by way of security for money, is an infant, the High Court may make an order vesting or releasing or disposing of the land or right in like manner as in the case of an infant trustee.

29. Vesting order in place of conveyance by heir, or devisee of heir, &c., or personal representative of mortgagee.

Where a mortgagee of land has died without having entered into the possession or into the receipt of the rents and profits thereof, and the money due in respect of the mortgage has been paid to a person entitled to receive the same, or that last-mentioned person consents to any order for the reconveyance of the land, then the High Court may make an order vesting the land in such person or persons in such manner and for such estate as the Court may direct in any of the following cases, namely,-

(a) Where an heir or personal representative or devisee of the mortgagee is out of the jurisdiction of the High Court or cannot be found; and

(b) Where an heir or personal representative or devisee of the mortgagee on demand made by or on behalf of a person entitled to require a conveyance of the land has stated in writing that he will not convey the same or does not convey the same for the space of twenty-eight days next after a proper deed for conveying the land has been tendered to him by or on behalf of the person so entitled; and

(c) Where it is uncertain which of several devisees of the mortgagee was the survivor; and

(d) Where it is uncertain as to the survivor of several devisees of the mortgagee or as to the heir or personal representative of

209

the mortgagee whether he is living or dead; and

(e) Where there is no heir or personal representative to a mortgagee who has died intestate as to the land, or where the mortgagee has died and it is uncertain who is his heir or personal representative or devisee.

30. Vesting order consequential on judgment for sale or mortgage of land.

Where any court gives a judgment or makes an order directing the sale or mortgage of any land, every person who is entitled to or possessed of the land, or entitled to a contingent right therein ....[11] and is a party to the action or proceeding in which the judgment or order is given or made or is otherwise bound by the judgment or order, shall be deemed to be so entitled or possessed, as the case may be, as a trustee within the meaning of this Act; and the High Court may, if it thinks expedient, make an order vesting the land or any part thereof for such estate as that Court thinks fit in the purchaser or mortgagee or in any other person.

31. Vesting order consequential on judgment for specific performance, &c.

Where a judgment is given for the specific performance of a contract concerning any land, or for the partition, or sale in lieu of partition, or exchange, of any land, or generally where any judgment is given for the conveyance of any land either in cases arising out of the doctrine of election or otherwise, the High Court may declare that any of the parties to the action are trustees of the land or any part thereof within the meaning of this Act, or may declare that the interests of unborn persons who might claim under any party to the action, or under the will or voluntary settlement of any person deceased who was during his lifetime a party to the contract or transactions concerning which the judgment is given, are the interests of persons who, on coming into existence, would be trustees within the meaning of this Act, and thereupon the High Court may make a vesting order relating to the rights of those persons, born and unborn, as if they had been trustees.

32. Effect of vesting order.

A vesting order under any of the foregoing provisions shall in the case of a vesting order consequential on the appointment of a new trustee, have the same effect as if the persons who before the appointment were the trustees (if any) had duly executed all proper

---

[11] Words repealed by Trustee Act, 1893, Amendment Act, 1894, 57 & 58 Vict. c. 10, ss. 1-3, *post, p. 251*

conveyances of the land for such estate as the high Court directs, or if there is no such person, or no such person of full capacity, then as if such person had existed and been of full capacity and had duly executed all proper conveyances of the land for such estate as the Court directs, and shall in every other case have the same effect as if the trustee or other person or description or class of persons to whose rights or supposed rights the said provisions respectively relate had been an ascertained and existing person of full capacity, and had executed a conveyance or release to the effect intended by the order.

33. Power to appoint person to convey.
In all cases where a vesting order can be made under any of the foregoing provisions, the High Court may, if it is more convenient, appoint a person to convey the land or release the contingent right, and a conveyance or release by that person in conformity with the order shall have the same effect as an order under the appropriate provision.

34. Effect of vesting order as to copyhold.
(1) Where an order vesting copyhold land in any person is made under this Act with the consent of the lord or lady of the manor, the land shall vest accordingly without surrender or admittance.

(2) Where an order is made under this Act appointing any person to convey any copyhold land, that person shall execute and do all assurances and things for completing the assurance of the land; and the lord and lady of the manor and every other person shall, subject to the customs of the manor and the usual payments, be bound to make admittance to the land and to do all other acts for completing the assurance thereof, as if the persons in whose place an appointment is made were free from disability and had executed and done those assurances and things.

35. Vesting orders as to stock and choses in action.
(1) In any of the following cases, namely:-
  (i) Where the High Court appoints or has appointed a new trustee; and
  (ii) Where a trustee entitled alone or jointly with another person to stock or to a chose in action-
    a. is an infant, or
    b. is out of the jurisdiction of the High Court, or
    c. cannot be found; or
    d. neglects or refuses to transfer stock or receive the dividends or income thereof, or to sue for or recover a chose in action, according to the direction of the person absolutely entitled thereto for twenty-eight days next

after a request in writing has been made to him by the person so entitled, or

e. neglects or refuses to transfer stock or receive the dividends or income thereof, or to sue for or recover a chose in action for twenty-eight days next after an order of the High Court for that purpose has been served on him; or

(iii) Where it is uncertain whether a trustee entitled alone or jointly with another person to stock or to a chose in action is alive or dead,

the High Court may make an order vesting the right to transfer or call for a transfer of stock, or to receive the dividends or income thereof, or to sue for or recover a chose in action, in any such person as the Court may appoint:

Provided that-

(a) Where the order is consequential on the appointment by the Court of a new trustee, the right shall be vested in the persons who, on the appointment, are the trustees; and

(b) Where the person whose right is dealt with by the order was entitled jointly with another person, the right shall be vested in that last-mentioned person either alone or jointly with any other person whom the Court may appoint.

(2) In all cases where a vesting order can be made under this section, the Court may, if it is more convenient, appoint some proper person to make or join in making the transfer.

(3) The person in whom the right to transfer or call for the transfer of any stock is vested by an order of the Court under this Act, may transfer the stock to himself or any other person, according to the order, and the Banks of England and Ireland and all other companies shall obey every order under this section according to its tenor.

(4) After notice in writing of an order under this section it shall not be lawful for the Bank of England or of Ireland or any other company to transfer any stock to which the order relates or to pay any dividends thereon except in accordance with the order.

(5) The High Court may make declarations and give directions concerning the manner in which the right to any stock or chose in action vested under the provisions of this Act is to be exercised.

(6) The provisions of this Act as to vesting orders shall apply to shares in ships registered under the Acts relating to merchant shipping as if they were stock.

36. Persons entitled to apply for orders.

(1) An order under this Act for the appointment of a new trustee or concerning any land, stock, or chose in action subject to a trust, may be made on the application of any person beneficially interested in

the land, stock, or chose in action, whether under disability or not, or on the application of any person duly appointed trustee thereof.

(2) An order under this Act concerning land, stock, or chose in action subject to a mortgage may be made on the application of any person beneficially interested in the equity of redemption, whether under disability or not, or of any person interested in the money secured by the mortgage.

37. Powers of new trustee appointed by Court.

Every trustee appointed by a court of competent jurisdiction shall, as well before as after the trust property becomes by law, or by assurance, or otherwise, vested in him, have the same powers, authorities, and discretions, and may in all respects act as if he had been originally appointed a trustee by the instrument, if any, creating the trust.

38. Power to charge costs on trust estate.

The High Court may order the costs and expenses of and incident to any application for an order appointing a new trustee, or for a vesting order, or of and incident to any such order, or any conveyance or transfer in pursuance thereof, to be paid or raised out of the land or personal estate in respect whereof the same is made, or out of the income thereof, or to be borne and paid in such manner and by such persons as to the Court may seem just.

39. Trustees of charities.

The powers conferred by this Act as to vesting orders may be exercised for vesting any land, stock, or chose in action in any trustee of a charity or society over which the High Court would have jurisdiction upon action duly instituted, whether the appointment of the trustee was made by instrument under a power or by the High Court under its general or statutory jurisdiction.

40. Orders made upon certain allegations to be conclusive evidence, 53 & 54 Vict. c. 5.

Where a vesting order is made as to any land under this Act or under the Lunacy Act, 1890, or under any Act relating to lunacy in Ireland, founded on an allegation of the personal incapacity of a trustee or mortgagee, or on an allegation that a trustee or the heir or personal representative or devisee of a mortgagee is out of the jurisdiction of the High Court or cannot be found, or that it is uncertain which of several trustees or which of several devisees of a mortgagee was the survivor, or whether the last trustee or the heir or personal representative or last surviving devisee of a mortgagee is living or dead, or on an allegation that any trustee or mortgagee has died intestate without an heir or has died and it is not known who is his heir or personal representative or devisee, the fact that the order has been so made shall be conclusive evidence of the matter so alleged in any court upon any question as to the validity of the order; but this section shall not prevent the High Court from directing a reconveyance or the payment of costs occasioned by any such order if improperly obtained.

41. Application of vesting order to land out of England.

The powers of the High Court in England to make vesting orders under this Act shall extend to all land and personal estate in Her Majesty's dominions, except Scotland

Payment into Court by Trustees.

42. Payment into Court by trustees.[12]

(1) Trustees, or the majority of trustees, having in their hands or under their control money or securities belonging to a trust, may pay the same into the high Court; and the same shall, subject to rules of Court, be dealt with according to the orders of the High Court.

(2) The receipt or certificate of the proper officer shall be a sufficient discharge to trustees for the money or securities so paid into Court.

(3) Where any moneys or securities are vested in any persons as trustees, and the majority are desirous of paying the same into court, but the concurrence of the other or others cannot be obtained, the High Court may order the payment into court to be made by the majority without the concurrence of the other or others; and where any such moneys or securities are deposited with any banker, broker, or other depository, the Court may order payment or delivery of the moneys or securities to the majority of the trustees for the purpose of payment into court, and every transfer payment and delivery made in pursuance of any such order shall be valid and take effect as if the same had been made on the authority or by the act of all the persons entitled to the moneys and securities so transferred, paid, or delivered.

Miscellaneous.

43. Power to give judgment in absence of a trustee.

Where in any action the High Court is satisfied that diligent search has been made for any person who, in the character of trustee, is made a defendant in any action, to serve him with a process of the

---

[12] Applied to Dublin and Blessington Steam Tramway (Abandonment) Act, 1932 (No. 13), s. 15, re. payment of money into court.

Court, and that he cannot be found, the Court may hear and determine the action and give judgment therein against that person in his character of a trustee, as if he had been duly served, or had entered an appearance in the action, and had also appeared by his counsel and solicitor at the hearing, but without prejudice to any interest he may have in the matters in question in the action in any other character.

44. Power to sanction sale of land or minerals separately.[13]

(1) Where a trustee [or other person[14]] is for the time being authorised to dispose of land by way of sale, exchange, partition, or enfranchisement, the High Court may sanction his so disposing of the land with an exception or reservation of any minerals, and with or without rights and powers of or incidental to the working, getting, or carrying away of the minerals, or so disposing of the minerals, with or without the said rights or powers, separately from the residue of the land.

(2) Any such trustee [or other person [14]] with the said sanction previously obtained, may, unless forbidden by the instrument creating the trust or direction, from time to time, without any further application to the Court, so dispose of any such land or minerals.

(3) Nothing in this section shall derogate from any power which a trustee may have under the Settled Land Acts, 1882 to 1890, or otherwise.

45. Power to make beneficiary indemnity for breach of trust.

(1) Where a trustee commits a breach of trust at the instigation or request or with the consent in writing of a beneficiary, the High Court may, if it thinks fit, ...[15] make such order as to the Court seems just, for impounding all or any part of the interest of the beneficiary in the trust estate by way of indemnity to the trustee or person claiming through him.

(2) This section shall apply to breaches of trust committed as well before as after the passing of this Act, but shall not apply so as to prejudice any question in an action or other proceeding which was pending on the twenty-fourth day of December one thousand eight hundred and eighty-eight, and is pending at the commencement of this Act.

---

[13] Restricted, Conveyancing Act, 1911, 1-2 Geo. 5 c. 37, s. 4(4)

[14] Inserted by Trustee Act, 1893, Amendment Act, 1894, 57 & 58 Vict. c. 10, s. 3, *post, p. 251*

[15] Repealed by Married Women's Status Act, 1957 (No. 5), s. 19, sch.

46. Jurisdiction of palatine and county courts.

The provisions of this Act with respect to the High Court shall, in their application to cases within the jurisdiction of a palatine court or county court, include that court, and the procedure under this Act in palatine courts and county courts shall be in accordance with the Acts and rules regulating the procedure of those courts.

Part IV.

Miscellaneous and Supplemental.

47. Application to trustees under Settled Land Acts of provisions as to appointment of trustees.

(1) All the powers and provisions contained in this Act with reference to the appointment of new trustees, and the discharge and retirement of trustees, are to apply to and include trustees for the purposes of the Settled Land Acts, 1882 to 1890, whether appointed by the Court or by the Settlement, or under provisions contained in the settlement.

(2) This section applies and is to have effect with respect to an appointment or a discharge and retirement of trustees taking place before as well as after the commencement of this Act.

(3) This section is not to render invalid or prejudice any appointment or any discharge and retirement of trustees effected before the passing of this Act, otherwise than under the provisions of the Conveyancing and Law of Property Act, 1881.

48. Trust estates not affected by trustee becoming a convict.

Property vested in any person on any trust or by way or mortgage shall not, in case of that person becoming a convict within the meaning of the Forfeiture Act, 1870, vest in any such administrator as may be appointed under that Act, but shall remain in the trustee or mortgagee, or survive to his co-trustee or descend to his representative as if he had not become a convict; provided that this enactment shall not affect the title to the property so far as relates to any beneficial interest therein of any such trustee or mortgagee.

49. Indemnity.

This Act, and every order purporting to be made under this Act, shall be a complete indemnity to the Banks of England and Ireland, and to all persons for any acts done pursuant thereto; and it shall not be necessary for the Bank or for any person to inquire concerning the propriety of the order, or whether the Court by which it was made had jurisdiction to make the same.

50. Definitions.

In this Act, unless the context otherwise requires, --

The expression "bankrupt" includes, in Ireland, insolvent:

The expression "contingent right," as applied to land, includes a contingent or executory interest, a possibility coupled with an interest, whether the object of the gift or limitation of the interest, or possibility is or is not ascertained, also a right of entry, whether immediate or future, and whether vested or contingent:

The expressions "convey" and "conveyance" applied to any person include the execution by that person of every necessary or suitable assurance for conveying, assigning, appointing, surrendering, or otherwise transferring or disposing of land whereof he is seised or possessed, or wherein he is entitled to a contingent right, either for his whole estate or for any less estate, together with the performance of all formalities required by law to the validity of the conveyance, including the acts to be performed by married women and tenants in tail in accordance with the provisions of the Acts for abolition of fines and recoveries in England and Ireland respectively, and also including surrenders and other acts which a tenant of customary or copyhold lands can himself perform preparatory to or in aid of a complete assurance of the customary or copyhold land:

The expression "devisee" includes the heir of a devisee and the devisee of an heir, and any person who may claim right by devolution of title of a similar description:

The expression "instrument" includes Act of Parliament:

The expression "land" includes manors and lordships, and reputed manors and lordships, and incorporeal as well as corporeal hereditaments, and any interest therein, and also an undivided share of land:

The expressions "mortgage" and "mortgagee" include and relate to every estate and interest regarded in equity as merely a security for money, and every person deriving title under the original mortgagee:

The expressions "pay" and "payment" as applied in relation to stocks and securities, and in connection with the expression "into court" include the deposit or transfer of the same in or into court:

The expression "possessed" applies to receipt of income of, and to any vested estate less than a life estate, legal or equitable, in possession or in expectancy, in, any land:

The expression "property" includes real and personal property, and any estate and interest in any property, real or personal, and any debt, and any thing in action, and any other right or interest, whether in possession or not:

The expression "rights" includes estates and interest:

The expression "securities" includes stocks, funds, and shares; and so far as relates to payments into court has the same meaning as in the Court of Chancery (Funds) Act, 1872:

The expression "stock" includes fully paid up shares; and, so far as relates to vesting orders made by the Court under this Act, includes any fund, annuity, or security transferable in books kept by any company or society, or by instrument of transfer either alone or accompanied by other formalities, and any share or interest therein:

The expression "transfer," in relation to stock, includes the performance and execution of every deed, power of attorney, act, and thing on the part of the transferor to effect and complete the title in the transferee:

The expression "trust" does not include the duties incident to an estate conveyed by way of mortgage; but with this exception the expressions "trust" and "trustee" include implied and constructive trusts, and cases where the trustee has a beneficial interest in the trust property, and the duties incident to the office of personal representative of a deceased person.

51. Repealed by Statute Law Revision Act, 1908[16]

52. Extent of Act.
This Act does not extend to Scotland.

53. Short title.
This Act may be cited as the Trustee Act, 1893.

54. Repealed by Statute Law Revision Act, 1908[16]

Schedule
Repealed by Statute Law Revision Act, 1908[16]

---

[16] 8 Edw. 7. c. 49

The Sale of Goods Act, 1893
56 & 57 Victoria, chapter 71

<u>List of Sections</u>

Part 1
Formation of the contract

Contract of Sale

Formalities of the Contract

The Price

Conditions and Warranties

Sale of Goods Act, 1893
Part II
Effects of the contract

Transfer of Property between Seller and Buyer

Transfer of Title

Part III
Performance of the contract

Sale of Goods Act, 1893

An Act for codifying the law relating to the Sale of Goods [1,2]
20th February 1893

Part I

Formation of the contract

Contract of Sale

1. Sale and agreement to sell

(1) A contract of sale of goods is a contract whereby the seller transfers or agrees to transfer the property in goods to the buyer for a money consideration, called the price. There may be a contract of sale between one part owner and another.

(2) A contract of sale may be absolute or conditional.

(3) Where under a contract of sale the property in the goods is transferred from the seller to the buyer the contract is called a sale; but where the transfer of the property in the goods is to take place at a future time or subject to some condition thereafter to be fulfilled the contract is called an agreement to sell.

(4) An agreement to sell becomes a sale when the time elapses or the conditions are fulfilled subject to which the property in the goods is to be transferred.

2. Capacity to buy and sell

Capacity to buy and sell is regulated by the general law concerning capacity to contract, and to transfer and acquire property: Provided that where necessaries are sold and delivered to an infant,or minor, or a person who by reason of mental incapacity or drunkenness is incompetent to contract, he must pay a reasonable price therefore.

Necessaries in this section mean goods suitable to the condition in life of such an infant or minor or other person, and to his actual requirements at the time of the sale and delivery.

---

[1] The International Carriage of Goods by Road Act, 1990 (No. 13), s. 3(3) provides that this Act, shall not apply in relation to contracts for the carriage of goods if the carriage is carriage in relation to which C. M. R. (the Convention on the Contract for the International Carriage of Goods by Road, done at Geneva on the 19th day of May, 1956, and the Protocol thereto done at Geneva on the 5th day of July, 1978) applies.

[2] This Act applies to Trading Stamps Act, 1980 (No. 23), s. 8.

Sale of Goods Act, 1893
Formalities of the Contract

3. Contract of sale, how made
Subject to the provision of this Act and of any statute in that behalf, a contract of sale may by made in writing (either with or without seal), or by word of mouth, or partly in writing and partly by word of mouth, or may be implied from the conduct of the parties.

Provided that nothing in this section shall affect the law relating to corporations.

4. Contract of sale for ten pounds and upwards
(1) A contract for the sale of any goods of the value of ten pounds or upwards shall not be enforceable by action unless the buyer shall accept part of the goods so sold, and actually receive the same, or give something in earnest to bind the contract, or in part payment, or unless some note or memorandum in writing of the contract be made and signed by the party to be charged or his agent in that behalf.

(2) The provisions of this section apply to every such contract, not withstanding that the goods may be intended to be delivered at some future time, or may not at the time of such contract be actually made, procured, or provided, fit or ready for delivery, or some act may be requisite for the making or completing thereof, or rendering the same fit for delivery.

(3) There is an acceptance of goods within the meaning of this section when the buyer does any act in relation to the goods which recognises a pre-existing contract of sale whether there be an acceptance in performance of the contract or not.

(4) The provisions of this section do not apply to Scotland.

5. Existing or future goods
(1) The goods which form the subject of a contract of sale maybe either existing goods, owned or possessed by the seller, or goods to be manufactured or acquired by the seller after the making of the contract of sale, in this Act called "future goods".

(2) There may be a contract for the sale of goods, the acquisition of which by the seller depends upon a contingency which may or may not happen.

(3) Where by a contract of sale the seller purports to effect a present sale of future goods, the contract operates as an agreement to sell the goods.

6. Goods which have perished
Where there is a contract for the sale of specific goods and the goods without the knowledge of the seller have perished at the time when the contract is made, the contract is void.

224

7. Goods perishing before sale but after agreement to sell

Where there is agreement to sell specific goods, and subsequently the goods, without any fault on the part of the seller or buyer, perish before the risk passes to the buyer, the agreement is thereby avoided.

The Price

8. Ascertainment of price

(1) The price in a contract of sale may be fixed by the contract, or may be left to be fixed in manner thereby agreed, or may be determined by the course of dealing between the parties.

(2) Where the price is not determined in accordance with the foregoing provisions the buyer must pay a reasonable price. What is a reasonable price is a question of fact dependent on the circumstances of each particular case.

9. Agreement to sell at valuation

(1) Where there is an agreement to sell goods on the terms that the price is to be fixed by the valuation of a third party, and such third party cannot or does not make such valuation, the agreement is avoided; provided that if the goods or any part thereof have been delivered to and appropriated by the buyer he must pay a reasonable price therefore.

(2) Where such third party is prevented from making the valuation by the fault of the seller or buyer, the party not in fault may maintain an action for damages against the party in fault.

Conditions and Warranties

10. Stipulations as to time

(1) Unless a different intention appears from the terms of the contract, stipulations as to time of payment are not deemed to be of the essence of a contract of sale. Whether any other stipulation as to time is of the essence of the contract or not depends on the term of the contract.

(2) In a contract of sale "month" means *prima facie* calender month.

11. When condition to be treated as a warranty[3]

(1) Where a contract of sale is subject to any condition to be fulfilled by the seller, the buyer may waive the condition, or may elect to treat the breach of such condition as a breach of warranty, and not as a ground for treating the contract as repudiated.

(2) Whether a stipulation in a contract of sale is a condition, the

[3] Substituted, Sale of Goods and Supply of Services Act, 1980 (No. 16), s. 10

breach of which may rise to a right to treat the contract as repudiated, or a warranty, the breach of which may give rise to a claim for damages but not to a right to reject the goods and treat the contract as repudiated, depends in each case on the construction of the contract. A stipulation may be a condition, though called a warranty in the contract.

(3) Where a contract of sale is not severable, and the buyer has accepted the goods, or part thereof, the breach of any condition to be fulfilled by the seller can only be treated as a breach of warranty, and not as a ground for rejecting the goods and treating the contract as repudiated, unless there be a term of the contract, express or implied, to that effect.

(4) Nothing in this section shall affect the case of any condition or warranty, fulfilment of which is excused by law by reason of impossibility or otherwise.

12. Implied undertakings as to title, etc.[3]

(1) In every contract of sale, other than one to which subsection (2) applies, there is-

    (a) an implied condition on the part of the seller that, in the case of a sale, he has a right to sell the goods and, in the case of an agreement to sell, he will have a right to sell the goods at the time when the property is to pass, and

    (b) an implied warranty that the goods are free, and will remain free until the time when the property is to pass, from any charge or encumbrance not disclosed to the buyer before the contract is made and that the buyer will enjoy quiet possession of the goods except so far as it may be disturbed by the owner or other person entitled to the benefit of any charge or encumbrance so disclosed.

(2) In a contract of sale, in the case of which there appears from the contract or is to be inferred from the circumstances of the contract an intention that the seller should transfer only such title as he or a third person may have, there is-

    (a) an implied warranty that all charges or encumbrances known to the seller have been disclosed to the buyer before the contract is made, and

    (b) an implied warranty that neither-

        (i) the seller, nor

        (ii) in a case where the parties to the contract intend that the seller should transfer only such title as a third person may have, that person, nor

        (iii) anyone claiming through or under the seller or that third person otherwise than under a charge or encumbrance disclosed to the buyer before the contract is made,

Sale of Goods Act, 1893
will disturb the buyer's quiet possession of the goods.

13. Sale by description[3]
(1) Where there is a contract for the sale of goods by description, there is an implied condition that the goods shall correspond with the description; and if the sale be by sample as well as by description, it is not sufficient that the bulk of the goods corresponds with the sample if the goods do not also correspond with the description.

(2) A sale of goods shall not be prevented from being a sale by description by reason only that, being exposed for sale, they are selected by the buyer.

(3) a reference to goods on a label or other descriptive matter accompanying goods exposed for sale may constitute or form part of a description.

14. Implied undertakings as to quality or fitness[3]
(1) Subject to the provisions of this act and of any statute in that behalf, there is no implied condition or warranty as to the quality or fitness for any particular purpose of goods supplied under a contract of sale.

(2) Where the seller sells goods in the course of a business there is an implied condition that the goods supplied under the contract are of merchantable quality, except that there is no such condition-
   (a) as regards defects specifically drawn to the buyers attention before the contract is made, or
   (b) if the buyer examines the goods before the contract is made, as regards defects which that examination ought to have revealed.

(3) Goods are of merchantable quality if they are as fit for the purpose or purposes for which goods of that kind are commonly bought and as durable as it is reasonable to expect having regard to any description applied to them, the price (if relevant) and all the other relevant circumstances, and any reference in this Act to unmerchantable goods shall be construed accordingly.

(4) Where the seller sells goods in the course of a business and the buyer, expressly or by implication, makes known to the seller any particular purpose for which the goods are being bought, there is an implied condition that the goods supplied under the contract are reasonably fit for that purpose, whether or not that is a purpose for which such goods are commonly supplied, except where the circumstances show that the buyer does not rely, or that it is unreasonable for him to rely, on the seller's skill or judgment.

(5) An implied condition or warranty as to quality or fitness for a particular purpose may be annexed to a contract of sale by usage.

(6) The foregoing provisions of this section apply to a sale by a

227

person who in the course of a business is acting as agent for another as they apply to a sale by a principal in the course of a business, except where that other is not selling in the course of a business and either the buyer knows that fact or reasonable steps are taken to bring it to the notice of the buyer before the contract is made.

15. Sale by Sample[3]
(1) A contract of sale is a contract for sale by sample where there is a term in the contract, express or implied, to that effect.

(2) In the case of a contract for sale by sample-
   (a) there is an implied condition that the bulk shall correspond with the sample in quality:
   (b) There is an implied condition that the buyer shall have a reasonable opportunity of comparing the bulk with the sample:
   (c) There is an implied condition the the goods shall be free from any defect, rendering them unmerchantable, which would not be apparent on reasonable examination of the sample.

Note
The Sale of Goods and Supply of Services Act, 1980 (No.16), provides:

12. Implied warranty for spare parts and servicing
(1) In a contract for the sale of goods there is an implied warranty that spare parts and an adequate after sale service will be made available by the seller in such circumstances as are stated in an offer, description or advertisement by the seller on behalf of the manufacture or on his own behalf and for such period as is so stated or, if no period is so stated, for a reasonable period.

(2) The Minister may, after such consultation with such interested parties as he thinks proper, by order define, in relation to any class of goods described in the order, what shall be a reasonable period for the purpose of subsection (1)

(3) Notwithstanding section 55 (1) of the Act of 1893 (inserted by section 22 of this Act) any terms of a contract exempting from all or any of the provisions of this section shall be void.

13. Implied condition on sale of motor vehicles.
(1) In this section "motor vehicle" means a vehicle intended or adapted for propulsion by mechanical means, including-
   (a) a bicycle or tricycle with an attachment for propelling it by mechanical power, and
   (b) a vehicle the means of propulsion of which is electrical or partly electrical or partly mechanical.

(2) Without prejudice to any other condition or warranty, in every contract for

228

the sale of a motor vehicle (except a contract in which the buyer is a person whose business it is to deal in motor vehicles) there is an implied condition that at the time of delivery of the vehicle under the contract it is free from any defect which would render it a danger to the public, including persons travelling in the vehicle.

(3) Subsection (2) of this section shall not apply where-

    (a) it is agreed between the seller and the buyer that the vehicle is not intended for use in the condition in which it is to be delivered to the buyer under the contract, and

    (b) a document consisting of a statement to that effect is signed by or on behalf of the seller and the buyer and given to the buyer prior to or at the time of such delivery, and it is shown that the agreement referred to in paragraph (a) is fair and reasonable.

(4) Save in a case in which the implied condition as to freedom from defects referred to in subsection (2) is either not incorporated in the contract or has been effectively excluded from the contract pursuant to that subsection, in the case of every sale of a motor vehicle by a person whose business it is to deal in motor vehicles a certificate in writing in such form as the Minister may by regulations prescribe shall be given to the buyer by or on behalf of the seller to the effect that the vehicle is, at the time of delivery, free from any defect which would render it a danger to the public, including persons travelling in the vehicle.

(5) Where and action is brought for breach of the implied condition referred to in subsection (2) by reason of a specific defect in a motor vehicle and a certificate complying with the requirements of this section is not proved to have been given, it shall be presumed unless the contrary is proved that the proven defect existed at the time of delivery.

(6) Regulations under subsection (4) may apply to motor vehicles generally or to motor vehicles of a particular class or description (defined in such manner and by reference to such things as the Minister thinks proper) and different forms of certificate may be prescribed for different classes or descriptions of vehicles.

(7) A person using a motor vehicle with the consent of the buyer of the vehicle who suffers loss as the result of a breach of the condition implied by subsection (2) in the contract of sale may maintain an action for damages against the seller in respect of the breach as if he were the buyer.

Sale of Goods Act, 1893
Part II

Transfer of Property as between Seller and Buyer

16. Goods must be ascertained

Where there is a contract for the sale of unascertained goods no property in the goods is transferred to the buyer unless and until the goods are ascertained.

17. Property passes when intended to pass

(1) Where there is a contract for the sale of specific or ascertained goods the property in them is transferred to the buyer at such time as the parties to the contract intend it to be transferred.

(2) For the purpose of ascertaining the intention of the parties regard shall be had to the terms of the contract, the conduct of the parties, and the circumstances of the case.

18. Rules for ascertaining intention

Unless a different intention appears the following are rules for ascertaining the intention of the parties as to the time at which the property in the goods is to pass to the buyer.

Rule 1 - Where there is an unconditional contract for the sale of specific goods, in a deliverable state, the property in the goods passes to the buyer when the contract is made, and it is immaterial whether the time of payment or the time of delivery, or both, be postponed.

Rule 2 - Where there is a contract for the sale of specific goods and the seller is bound to do something to the goods, for the purpose of putting them into a deliverable state, the property does not pass until such thing be done, and the buyer has notice thereof.

Rule 3 - Where there is a contract for the sale of specific goods in a deliverable state, but the seller is bound to weigh, measure, test, or do some other act or thing with reference to the goods for the purpose of ascertaining the price, the property does not pass until such act or thing be done, and the buyer has notice thereof.

Rule 4 - When goods are delivered to the buyer on approval or "on sale or return" or other similar terms the property therein passes to the buyer:-

  (a) When he signifies his approval or acceptance to the seller or does any other act adopting the transaction:

  (b) If he does not signify his approval or acceptance to the seller but retains the goods without giving notice of rejection, then, if a time has been fixed for the return of the goods, on the expiration of such time, and if no time has been fixed, on the expiration of a reasonable time. What is a reasonable time is a question of fact.

Rule 5 -

(1) Where there is a contract for the sale of unascertained or future goods by description, and goods of that description and in a deliverable state are unconditionally appropriated to the contract, either by the seller with the assent of the buyer, or by the buyer with the assent of the seller, the property in the goods thereupon passes to the buyer. Such assent may be express or implied, and may be given either before or after the appropriation is made:

(2) Where, in pursuance of the contract, the seller delivers the goods to the buyer or to a carrier or other bailee or custodien (whether named by the buyer or not) for the purpose of transmission to the buyer, and does not reserve the right of disposal, he is deemed to have unconditionally appropriated the goods to the contract.

19. Reservation of right of disposal

(1) Where there is a contract for the sale of specific goods or where goods are subsequently appropriated to the contract, the seller may, by the terms of the contract or appropriation, reserve the right of disposal of the goods until certain conditions are fulfilled. In such case, notwithstanding the delivery of the goods to the buyer, or to a carrier or other bailee or custodier for the purpose of transmission to the buyer, the property in the goods does not pass to the buyer until the conditions imposed by the seller are fulfilled.

(2) Where goods are shipped, and by the bill of lading the goods are deliverable to the order of the seller or his agent, the seller is *prima facie* deemed to reserve the right of disposal.

(3) Where the seller of goods draws on the buyer for the price, and transmits the bill of exchange and bill of lading to the buyer together to secure acceptance or payment of the bill of exchange, the buyer is bound to return the bill of lading if he does not honour the bill of exchange, and if he wrongfully retains the bill of lading the property in the goods does not pass to him.

20. Risk *prima facie* passes with property

Unless otherwise agreed, the goods remain at the seller's risk until the property therein is transferred to the buyer, but when the property therein is transferred to the buyer, the goods are at the buyer's risk whether delivery has been made or not.

Provided that where delivery has been delayed through the fault of either buyer or seller the goods are at the risk of the party in fault as regards any loss which might not have occurred but for such fault.

Provided also that nothing in this section shall affect the duties or liabilities of either seller or buyer as a bailee or custodier of the goods of the other party.

21. Sale by person not the owner

(1) Subject to the provisions of this Act where goods are sold by a person who is not the owner thereof, and who does not sell them under the authority or with the consent of the owner, the buyer acquires no better title to the goods than the seller had, unless the owner of the goods is by his conduct precluded from denying the seller's authority to sell.

(2) Provided also that nothing in this Act shall affect-

(a) The provisions of the Factors Acts, or any enactment enabling the apparent owner of goods to dispose of them as if he were the true owner thereof;

(b) The validity of any contract of sale under any special common law or statutory power of sale or under the order of a court of competent jurisdiction.

22. Market overt

(1) Where goods are sold in market overt, according to the usage of the market, the buyer acquires a good title to the goods, provided he buys them in good faith and without notice of any defect or want of title on the part of the seller.

(2) Nothing in this section shall affect the law relating to the sale of horses.

(3) The provisions of this section do not apply to Scotland.

23. Sale under voidable title

When the seller of goods has a voidable title thereto, but his title has not been avoided at the time of the sale, the buyer acquires a good title to the goods, provided he buys them in good faith and without notice of the seller's defect of title.

24. Revesting of property in stolen goods on conviction of offender

(1) Where goods have been stolen and the offender is prosecuted to conviction, the property in the goods so stolen revests in the person who was the owner of the goods, or his personal representative, notwithstanding any intermediate dealing with them, whether by sale in market overt or otherwise.

(2) Notwithstanding any enactment to the contrary, where goods have been obtained by fraud or other wrongful means not amounting to larceny, the property in such goods shall not revest in the person who was the owner of the goods, or his personal representative, by reason only of the convection of the offender.

(3) The provisions of this section do not apply to Scotland.

25. Seller or buyer in possession after sale

(1) Where a person having sold goods continues or is in possession of the goods, or of the documents of title to the goods, the delivery or transfer by that person, or by a mercantile agent acting for him, of the goods or documents of title under any sale, pledge, or other disposition thereof, to any person receiving the same in good faith and without notice of the previous sale, shall have the same effect as if the person making the delivery or transfer were expressly authorised by the owner of the goods to make the same.

(2) Where a person having bought or agreed to buy goods obtains, with the consent of the seller, possession of the goods or the documents of title to the goods, the delivery or transfer by that person, or by a mercantile agent acting for him, of the goods or documents of title, under any sale, pledge, or other disposition thereof, to any person receiving the same in good faith and without notice of any lien or other right of the original seller in respect of the goods, shall have the same effect as if the person making the delivery or transfer were a mercantile agent in possession of the goods or documents of title with the consent of the owner.

(3) In this section the term "mercantile agent" has the same meaning as in the Factors Acts.

26. Effect of writs of execution

(1) A writ of *fieri facias* or other writ of execution against goods shall bind the property in the goods of the execution debtor as from the time when the writ is delivered to the sheriff to be executed; and, for the better manifestation of such time, it shall be the duty of the sheriff, without fee, upon the receipt of any such writ to endorse upon the back thereof the hour, day, month, and year when he received the same.

Provided that no such writ shall prejudice the title to such goods acquired by any person in good faith and for valuable consideration, unless such person had at the time when he acquired his title notice that such writ or any other writ by virtue of which the goods of the execution debtor might be seized, or attached had been delivered to and remained unexecuted in the hands of the sheriff.

(2) In this section the term "sheriff" includes any officer charged with the enforcement of a writ of execution.

(3) The provisions of this section do not apply to Scotland.

Sale of Goods Act, 1893
Part III

Performance of the contract

27. Duties of seller and buyer
It is the duty of the seller to deliver the goods, and of the buyer to accept and pay for them, in accordance with the terms of the contract of sale.

28. Payment and delivery are concurrent conditions
Unless otherwise agreed, delivery of the goods and payment of the price are concurrent conditions, that is to say, the seller must be ready and willing to give possession of the goods to the buyer in exchange for the price, and the buyer must be ready and willing to pay the price in exchange for possession of the goods.

29. Rules as to delivery
(1) Whether it is for the buyer to take possession of the goods or for the seller to send them to the buyer is a question depending in each case on the contract, express or implied, between the parties. Apart from any such contract, express or implied, the place of delivery is the seller's place of business, if he have one, and if not, his residence: Provided that, if the contract be for the sale of specific goods, which to the knowledge of the parties when the contract is made are in some other place, then that place is the place of delivery.

(2) Where under the contract of sale the seller is bound to send the goods to the buyer, but no time for sending them is fixed, the seller is bound to send them within a reasonable time.

(3) Where the goods at the time of sale are in the possession of a third person, there is no delivery by seller to buyer unless and until such third person acknowledges to the buyer that he holds the goods on his behalf; provided that nothing in this section shall affect the operation of the issue or transfer of any document of title to goods.

(4) Demand or tender of delivery may be treated as ineffectual unless made at a reasonable hour. What is a reasonable hour is a question of fact.

(5) Unless otherwise agreed, the expenses of and incidental to putting the good into a deliverable state must be borne by the seller.

30. Delivery of wrong quantity
(1) Where the seller delivers to the buyer a quantity of goods less than he contracted to sell, the buyer may reject them, but if the buyer accepts the goods so delivered he must pay for them at the contract rate.

(2) Where the seller delivers to the buyer a quantity of goods larger

than he contracted to sell, the buyer may accept the goods included in the contract and reject the rest, or he may reject the whole. If the buyer accepts the whole of the goods so delivered he must pay for them at the contract rate.

(3) Where the seller delivers to the buyer the goods he contracted to sell mixed with goods of a different description not included in the contract, the buyer may accept the goods which are in accordance with the contract and reject the rest, or he may reject the whole.

(4) The provisions of this section are subject to any usage of trade, special agreement, or course of dealing between the parties.

31. Instalment deliveries

(1) Unless otherwise agreed, the buyer of goods is not bound to accept delivery thereof by instalments.

(2) Where there is a contract for the sale of goods to be delivered by stated instalments, which are to be separately paid for, and the seller makes defective deliveries in respect of one or more instalments, or the buyer neglects or refuses to take delivery of or pay for one or more instalments, it is a question in each case depending in the terms of the contract and the circumstances of the case, whether the breach of contract is a repudiation of the whole contract or whether it is a severable breach giving rise to a claim for compensation but not to a right to treat the whole contract as repudiated.

32. Delivery to carrier

(1) Where, in pursuance of a contract of sale, the seller is authorised or required to send the goods to the buyer, delivery of the goods to a carrier, whether named by the buyer or not, for the purpose of transmission to the buyer is *prima facie* deemed to be a delivery of the goods to the buyer.

(2) Unless otherwise authorised by the buyer, the seller must make such contract with the carrier on behalf of the buyer as may be reasonable having regard to the nature of the goods and the other circumstances of the case. If the seller omit so to do, and the goods are lost or damaged in course of transit, the buyer may decline to treat the delivery to the carrier as a delivery to himself, or may hold the seller responsible in damages.

(3) Unless otherwise agreed, where goods are sent by the seller to the buyer by a route involving sea transit, under circumstances in which it is usual to insure, the seller must give such notice to the buyer as may enable him to insure them during their sea transit, and, if the seller fails to do so, the goods shall be deemed to be at his risk during such sea transit.

33. Risk where goods are delivered at distant place

Where the seller of goods agrees to deliver them at his own risk at a place other than that where they are when sold, the buyer must, nevertheless, unless otherwise agreed, take any risk of deterioration in the goods necessarily incident to the course of transit.

34. Buyer's right of examining the goods[4]

(1) Where goods are delivered to the buyer, which he has not previously examined, he is not deemed to have accepted them unless and until he has had a reasonable opportunity of examining them for the purpose of ascertaining whether they are in conformity with the contract

(2) Unless otherwise agreed, when the seller tenders delivery of goods to the buyer, he is bound, on request, to afford the buyer a reasonable opportunity of examining the goods for the purpose of ascertaining whether they are in conformity with the contract.

35. Acceptance[4]

The buyer is deemed to have accepted the goods when he intimates to the seller that he has accepted them, or, subject to section 34 of this Act, when the goods have been delivered to him and he does any act in relation to them which is inconsistent with the ownership of the seller or when, without good and sufficient reason, he retains the goods without intimating to the seller that he has rejected them.

36. Buyer not bound to return rejected goods

Unless otherwise agreed, where goods are delivered to the buyer, and he refuses to accept them having the right so to do, he is not bound to return them to the seller, but it is sufficient if he intimates to the seller that he refuses to accept them.

37. Liability of buyer for neglecting or refusing delivery of goods

When the seller is ready and willing to deliver the goods, and requests the buyer to take delivery, and the buyer does not within a reasonable time after such request take delivery of the goods, he is liable to the seller for any loss occasioned by his neglect or refusal to take delivery, and also for a reasonable charge for the care and custody of the goods: Provided that nothing in this section shall affect the rights of the seller where the neglect or refusal of the buyer to take delivery amounts to a repudiation of the contract.

---

[4] Substituted: Sale of Goods and Supply of Services Act, 1980 (No. 16), s. 20

Rights of unpaid seller against the goods

38. Unpaid seller defined

(1) The seller of goods is deemed to be an "unpaid seller" within the meaning of this Act-
  (a) When the whole of the price has not been paid or tendered;
  (b) When a bill of exchange or other negotiable instrument has been received as conditional payment, and the condition on which it was received has not been fulfilled by reason of the dishonour of the instrument or otherwise.

(2) In this Part of this Act the term "seller" includes any person who is in the position of a seller, as, for instance, an agent of the seller to whom the bill of lading has been indorsed, or a consignor or agent who has himself paid, or is directly responsible for, the price.

39. Unpaid seller's rights

(1) Subject to the provisions of this Act, and of any statute in the behalf, notwithstanding that the property in the goods may have passed to the buyer, the unpaid seller of goods, as such, has by implication of law-
  (a) A lien on the goods or right to retain them for the price while he is in possession of them;
  (b) In case of the insolvency of the buyer, a right of stopping the goods in tansitu after he has parted with the possession of them;
  (c) A right of re-sale as limited by this Act.

(2) Where the property in goods has not passed to the buyer, the unpaid seller has, in addition to his other remedies, a right of withholding delivery similar to and co-extensive with his rights of lien and stoppage in transitu where the property has passed to the buyer.

40. Attachment by seller in Scotland

In Scotland a seller of goods may attach the same while in his own hands or possession by arrestment or poinding; and such arrestment or poinding shall have the same operation and effect in a competition or otherwise as an arrestment or poinding by a third party.

Unpaid Seller's Lien

41. Seller's Lien

(1) Subject to the provisions of this Act, the unpaid seller of goods

who is in possession of them is entitled to retain possession of them until payment or tender of the price in the following cases, namely:-

(a) Where the goods have been sold without any stipulation as to credit;

(b) Where the goods have been sold on credit, but the term of credit has expired;

(c) Where the buyer becomes insolvent.

(2) The seller may exercise his right of lien notwithstanding that he is in possession of the goods as agent or bailee or custodier for the buyer.

42. Part delivery

Where an unpaid seller has made part delivery of the goods, he may exercise his right of lien or retention on the remainder, unless such part delivery has been made under such circumstances as to show an agreement to waive the lien or right of retention.

43. Termination of lien

(1) The unpaid seller of goods loses his lien or right of retention thereon-

(a) When he delivers the goods to a carrier or other bailee or custodier for the purpose of transmission to the buyer without reserving the right of disposal of the goods;

(b) When the buyer of his agent lawfully obtains possession of the goods;

(c) By waiver thereof.

(2) The unpaid seller of goods, having a lien or right of retention thereon, does not lose his lien or right of retention by reason only that he has obtained judgment or decree for the price of the goods.

Stoppage in transitu

44. Right of stoppage in transitu

Subject to the provisions of this Act, when the buyer of goods becomes insolvent, the unpaid seller who has parted with the possession of the goods has the right of stopping them in transitu, that is to say, he may resume possession of the goods as long as they are in course of transit, and may retain them until payment or tender of the price.

45. Duration of transit

(1) Goods are deemed to be in course of transit from the time when they are delivered to a carrier by land or water, or other bailee or custodier for the purpose of transmission to the buyer, until the buyer, or his agent in that behalf, takes delivery of them from such

carrier or other bailee or custodier.

(2) If the buyer or his agent in that behalf obtains delivery of the goods before their arrival at the appointed destination, the transit is at an end.

(3) If, after the arrival of the goods at the appointed destination, the carrier or other bailee or custodier acknowledges to the buyer, or his agent, that he holds the goods on his behalf and continues in possession of them as bailee or custodier for the buyer, or his agent, the transit is at an end, and it is immaterial that a further destination for the goods may have been indicated by the buyer.

(4) If the goods are rejected by the buyer, and the carrier or other bailee or custodier continues in possession of them, the transit is not deemed to be at an end, even if the seller has refused to receive them back.

(5) When goods are delivered to a ship chartered by the buyer it is a question depending on the circumstances of the particular case, whether they are in the possession of the master as a carrier, or as agent to the buyer.

(6) Where the carrier or other bailee or custodier wrongfully refuses to deliver the goods to the buyer, or his agent in that behalf, the transit is deemed to be at an end.

(7) Where part delivery of the goods has been made to the buyer, or his agent in that behalf, the remainder of the goods may be stopped in transitu, unless such part delivery has been made under such circumstances as to show an agreement to give up possession of the whole of the goods.

46. How stoppage in transitu is effected

(1) The unpaid seller may exercise his right of stoppage in transitu either by taking actual possession of the goods, or by giving notice of his claim to the carrier or other bailee or custodier in whose possession the goods are. Such notice may be given either to the person in actual possession of the goods or to his principal. In the latter case the notice, to be effectual, must be given at such time and under such circumstances that the principal, by the exercise of reasonable diligence, may communicate it to his servant or agent in time to prevent a delivery to the buyer.

(2) When notice of stoppage in transitu is given by the seller to the carrier, or other bailee or custodier in possession of the goods, he must re-deliver the goods to, or according to the directions of, the seller. The expenses of such re-delivery must be borne by the seller.

47. Effect of sub-sale or pledge by buyer

Subject to the provisions of this Act, the unpaid seller's right of lien or retention or stoppage in transitu is not affected by any sale, or other disposition of the goods which the buyer may have made, unless the seller has assented thereto.

Provided that where a document of title to goods has been lawfully transferred to any person as buyer or owner of the goods, and that person transfers the document to a person who takes the document in good faith and for valuable consideration, then, if such last-mentioned transfer was by way of sale the unpaid seller's right of lien or retention or stoppage in transitu is defeated, and if such last-mentioned transfer was made by way of pledge or other disposition for value, the unpaid seller's right of lien or retention or stoppage in transitu can only be exercised subject to the rights of the transferee.

48. Sale not generally rescinded by lien or stoppage in transitu

(1) Subject to the provisions of this section, a contract of sale is not rescinded by the mere exercise by an unpaid seller of his right of lien or retention or stoppage in transitu.

(2) Where an unpaid seller who has exercised his right of lien or retention or stoppage in transitu re-sells the goods, the buyer acquires a good title thereto as against the original buyer.

(3) Where the goods are of a perishable nature, or where the unpaid seller gives notice to the buyer of his intention to re-sell, and the buyer does not within a reasonable time pay or tender the price, the unpaid seller may re-sell the goods and recover from the original buyer damages for any loss occasioned by his breach of contract.

(4) Where the seller expressly reserves the right of re-sale in case the buyer should make default, and on the buyer making default, re-sells the goods, the original contract of sale is thereby rescinded, but without prejudice to any claim the seller may have for damages.

Part V
Actions for breach of the contract

Remedies of the Seller

49. Action for price

(1) Where, under a contract of sale, the property in the goods has passed to the buyer, and the buyer wrongfully neglects or refuses to pay for the goods according to the terms of the contract, the seller may maintain an action against him for the price of the goods.

(2) Where, under a contract of sale, the price is payable on a day

certain irrespective of delivery, and the buyer wrongfully neglects or refuses to pay such price, the seller may maintain an action for the price, although the property in the goods has not passed, and the goods have not been appropriated to the contract.

(3) Nothing in this section shall prejudice the right of the seller in Scotland to recover interest on the price from the date of tender of the goods, or from the date on which the price was payable, as the case may be.

50. Damages for non-acceptance

(1) Where the buyer wrongfully neglects or refuses to accept and pay for the goods, the seller may maintain an action against him for damages for non-acceptance.

(2) The measure of damages is the estimated loss directly and naturally resulting, in the ordinary course of events, from the buyer's breach of contract.

(3) Where there is an available market for the goods in question the measure of damages is *prima facie* to be ascertained by the difference between the contract price and the market or current price at the time or times when the goods ought to have been accepted, or, if no time was fixed for acceptance, then at the time of the refusal to accept.

Remedies of the Buyer

51. Damages for non-delivery

(1) Where the seller wrongfully neglects or refuses to deliver the goods to the buyer, the buyer may maintain an action against the seller for damages for non-delivery.

(2) The measure of damages is the estimated loss directly and naturally resulting, in the ordinary course of events, from the seller's breach of contract.

(3) Where there is an available market for the goods in question the measure of damages is *prima facie* to be ascertained by the difference between the contract price and the market or current price of the goods at the time or times when they ought to have been delivered, or, if no time was fixed, them at the time of the refusal to deliver.

52. Specific performance

In any action for breach of contract to deliver specific or ascertained goods the court may, if it thinks fit, on the application of the plaintiff, by its judgment or decree direct that the contract shall be performed specifically, without giving the defendant the option of retaining the goods on payment of damages. The judgment or decree may be unconditional, or upon such terms and conditions as to damages, payment of the price, and otherwise, as to the court may seem just, and the application by the plaintiff may be made at any time before judgment or decree.

The provisions of this section shall be deemed to be supplementary to, and not in derogation of, the right of specific implement in Scotland.

53. Remedy for breach of warranty[5]

(1) Subject to subsection (2), where there is a breach of warranty by the seller, or where the buyer elects, or is compelled, to treat any breach of a condition on the part of the seller as a breach of warranty, the buyer is not by reason only of such breach of warranty entitled to reject the goods, but he may-

(a) set up against the seller the breach of warranty in diminution or extinction of the price, or

(b) maintain an action against the seller for damages for thebreach of warranty.

(2) Where-

(a) the buyer deals as consumer[6] and there is a breach of a condition by the seller which, but for this subsection, the buyer would be compelled to treat as a breach of warranty, and

(b) the buyer, promptly upon discovering the breach, makes a request to the seller that he either remedy the breach or replace any goods which are not in conformity with the condition,

then, if the seller refuses to comply with the request or fails to do so within a reasonable time, the buyer is entitled:

(i) to reject the goods and repudiate the contract, or

(ii) to have the defect constituting the breach remedied elsewhere and to maintain an action against the seller for the cost thereby incurred by him.

(3) The onus of proving that the buyer acted with promptness under subsection (2) shall lie on him.

(4) The measure of damages for breach of warranty is the estimated loss directly and naturally resulting, in the ordinary course of events, from the breach of warranty.

(5) In the case of breach of warranty of quality such loss is *prima facia* the difference between the value of the goods at the time of delivery to the buyer and the value they would have had if they had answered to the warranty.

(6) The fact that the buyer has set up the breach of warranty in

---

[5] Substituted: Sale of Goods and Supply of Services Act, 1980 (No. 16), s. 21

[6] See: Sale of Goods and Supply of Services Act, 1980 (No. 16), s. 3 below.

diminution or extinction of the price or that the seller has replaced goods or remedied a breach does not of itself prevent the buyer from maintaining an action for the same breach of warranty if he has suffered further damage.

_____

Note

The Sale of Goods and Supply of Services Act, 1980 (No.16), provides:

3. Dealing as consumer.

(1) In the Act of 1893 and this Act, a party to a contract is said to deal as consumer in relation to another party if-

(a) he neither makes the contact in the course of a business nor holds himself out as doing so, and

(b) the other party does make the contract in the course of a business, and

(c) the goods or services supplied under or in pursuance of the contract are of a type ordinarily supplied for private use or consumption.

(2) On -

(a) a sale by competitive tender, or

(b) a sale by auction -

(i) of goods of a type, or

(ii) by or on behalf of a person of a class defined by the Minister by order,

the buyer is not in any circumstances to be regarded as dealing as consumer.

(3) Subject to this, it is for those claiming that a party does not deal as consumer to show that he does not.

_____

54. Interest and special damages

Nothing in this Act shall affect the right of the buyer or the seller to recover interest or special damages in any case where by law interest or special damages may be recoverable, or to recover money paid where the consideration for payment of it has failed.

55.[7] Exclusion of implied terms and conditions[8]

(1) Subject to the subsequent provisions of this section, where any right, duty or liability would arise under a contract of sale of goods by implication of law, it may be negatived or varied by express agreement, or by the course of dealing between the parties, or by usage if the usage is such as to bind both parties to the contract.

(2) An express condition or warranty does not negative a condition or warranty implied by this Act unless inconsistent therewith.

_____

[7] See: Sale of Goods and Supply of Services Act, 1980 (No. 16), s. 11 below.

[8] Substituted: Sale of Goods and Supply of Services Act, 1980 (No. 16), s. 22.

(3) In the case of a contract of sale of goods, any term of that or any other contract exempting from all or any of the provisions of section 12 of this Act shall be void.

(4) In the case of a contract of sale of goods, any term of that or any other contract exempting from all or any of the provisions of section 13, 14 or 15 of this Act shall be void where the buyer deals as consumer and shall, in any other case, not be enforceable unless it is shown that it is fair and reasonable.

(5) Subsection (4) shall not prevent the court from holding, in accordance with any rule of law, that a term which purports to exclude or restrict any of the provisions of section 13, 14 or 15 of this Act is not a term of the contract.

(6) Any reference in this section to a term exempting from all or any of the provisions of any section of this Act is a reference to a term which purports to exclude or restrict, or has the effect of excluding or restricting, the operation of all or any of the provisions of that section, or the exercise of a right conferred by any provision of that section, or any liability of the seller for breach of a condition or warranty implied by any provision of that section.

(7) Any reference in this section to a term of a contract includes a reference to a term which although not contained in a contract is incorporated in the contract by another term of the contract.

(8) This section is subject to section 61(6) of this Act.

Note

The Sale of Goods and Supply of Services Act, 1980 (No. 16), provides

11. Statements purporting to restrict rights of buyer.

(1) Subsection (2) and (3) apply to any statement likely to be taken as indicating that a right or the exercise of an right conferred by, or a liability arising by virtue of, section 12,13,14 or 15 of the Act of 1893 is restricted or excluded otherwise than under section 55 of that Act.

(2) It shall be an offence for a person in the course of a business to do any of the following things in relation to a statement to which subsection (1) refers:

    (a) to display on any part of any premises a notice that includes any such statement, or

    (b) to publish or cause to be published an advertisement which contains any such statement, or

    (c) to supply goods bearing, or goods in a container bearing, any such statement, or

    (d) otherwise to furnish or to cause to be furnished a document including any such statement.

(3) For the purpose of this section statement to the effect that goods will not be exchanged, or that money will not be refunded, or that only credit notes will

be given for goods returned, shall be treated as a statement to which subsection (1) refers unless it is so clearly qualified that it cannot be construed as applicable in circumstances in which the buyer may be seeking to exercise a right conferred by any provision of a section mentioned in subsection (1).

(4) It shall be a offence for a person in the course of a business to furnish to a buyer goods bearing, or goods in a container bearing, or any document including, any statement, irrespective of its legal effect, which sets out limits or describes rights conferred on a buyer or liabilities to the buyer in relation to goods acquired by him or any statement likely to be taken as such a statement, unless that statement is accompanied by a clear and conspicuous declaration that the contractual rights which the buyer enjoys by virtue of sections 12, 13, 14 and 15 of the Act of 1893 are in no way prejudiced by the relevant statement.

Schedule Fair and Reasonable Terms

1. In determining for the purposes ...section 55 ... if a term is fair and reasonable the test is that it shall be a fair and reasonable one to be included having regard to the circumstances which were, or ought reasonably to have been, known to or in contemplation of the parties when the contract was made.

2. Regard is to be had in particular to any of the following which appear to be relevant:

(a) the strength of the bargaining positions of the parties relative to each other, taking into account (among other things) alternative means by which the customer's requirements could have been met:

(b) whether the customer received an inducement to agree to the term, or in accepting it had an opportunity of entering into a similar contract with other persons, but without having to accept a similar term:

(c) whether the customer knew or ought reasonably to have known of the existence and extent of the term (having regard, among other tings, to any custom of the trade and any previous course of dealing between the parties):

(d) where the term excludes or restricts any relevant liability if some condition is not complied with, whether it was reasonable at the time of the contract to expect that compliance with that condition would be practicable;

(e) whether any goods involved were manufactured, processed or adapted to the special order of the customer.

55A. Conflict of laws[9]

Where the proper law of a contract of sale of goods would, apart from a term that it should be the law of some other country or a term

---
[9] Inserted by Sale of Goods and Supply of Services Act, 1980 (No. 16), s. 23

to the like effect, be the law of Ireland or where any such contract contains a term which purports to substitute, or has the effect of substituting, provisions of the law of some other country for all or any of the provisions of sections 12 to 15 and 55 of this Act, those sections shall, notwithstanding that term but subject to section 61 (6) of this Act, apply to the contract.

56. Reasonable time a question fact

Where, by this Act, any reference is made to a reasonable time the question what is a reasonable time is a question of fact.

57. Rights, &c. enforceable by action

Where any right, duty, or liability is declared by this Act, it may, unless otherwise by this Act provided, be enforced by action.

58. Auction sales

In the case of a sale by auction-

(1) Where goods are put up for sale by auction in lots, each lot is *prima facie* deemed to be the subject of a separate contract of sale:

(2) A sale by auction is complete when the auctioneer announces its completion by the fall of the hammer, or in other customary manner. Until such announcement is made any bidder may retract his bid:

(3) Where a sale by auction is not notified to be subject to a right to bid on behalf of the seller, is shall not be lawful for the seller to bid himself or to employ any person to bid at such sale, or for the auctioneer knowingly to take any bid from the seller or any such person: Any sale contravening this rule may be treated as fraudulent by the buyer:

(4) A sale by auction may be notified to be subject to a reserved or upset price, and a right to bid may also be reserved expressly by or on behalf of the seller. Where a right to bid is expressly reserved, but not otherwise, the seller, or any one person on his behalf, may bid at the auction.

59. Payment into court in Scotland when breach of warranty alleged

In Scotland where a buyer has elected to accept goods which he might have rejected, and to treat a breach of contract as only giving rise to a claim for damages, he may, in an action by the seller for the price, be required, in the discretion of the court before which the action depends, to consign or pay into court the price of the goods, or part thereof, or to give other reasonable security for the due payment thereof.

60. Repealed by Statute Law Revision Act, 1908[10]

61. Savings

(1) The rules in bankruptcy relating to contracts of sale shall continue to apply thereto, notwithstanding anything in this Act contained.

(2) The rules of the common law, including the law merchant, save in so far as they are inconsistent with the express provisions of this Act, and in particular the rules relating to the law of principal and agent and the effect of fraud, misrepresentation, duress or coercion, mistake, or other invalidating cause, shall continue to apply to contracts for the sale of goods.

(3) Nothing in this Act or in any repeal effected thereby shall affect the enactments relating to bills of sale, or any enactment relating to the sale of goods which is not expressly repealed by this Act.

(4) The provision of this Act relating to contracts of sale do not apply to any transaction in the form of a contract of sale which is intended to operate by way of mortgage, pledge, charge, or other security.

(5) Nothing in this Act shall prejudice or affect the landlord's right of hypothec or sequestration for rent in Scotland.

(6)[11]

    (a) Nothing in section 55 or 55A of this Act shall prevent the parties to a contract for the international sale of goods from negativing or varying any right, duty or liability which would otherwise arise by implication of law under sections 12 to 15 of this Act.

    (b) In this subsection 'contract for the international sale of goods' means a contract of sale of goods made by parties whose places of business (or, if they have none, habitual residences) are in the territories of different States and in the case of which one of the following conditions is satisfied:

        (i) the contract involves the sale of goods which are at the time of the conclusion of the contract in the course of carriage or will be carried from the territory of one State to the territory of another; or

        (ii) the acts constituting the offer and acceptance have been effected in the territories of different States; or

        (iii) delivery of the goods is to be made in the territory of a State other than that within whose territory the acts constituting the offer and the acceptance have been effected.

---

[10] 8 Edw. 7, c. 49

[11] Inserted by Sale of Goods and Supply of Services Act, 1980 (No. 16), s. 24

Sale of Goods Act, 1893

62. Interpretation of terms

(1) In this Act, unless the context or subject matter otherwise requires,-

"Action" includes counterclaim and set off, and in Scotland condescendence and claim and compensation:

"Bailee" in Scotland includes custodier:

"Buyer" means a person who buys or agrees to buy goods:

"Contract of sale" includes an agreement to sell as well as a sale:

"Defendant" includes in Scotland defender, respondent, and claimant in a multiplepoinding:

"Delivery" means voluntary transfer of possession from one person to another:

"Document of title to goods" has the same meaning as it has in the Factors Acts:

"Factors Acts" means the Factors Act, 1889, the Factors (Scotland) Act, 1890, and any enactment amending or substituted for the same:

"Fault" means wrongful act or default:

"Future goods" means goods to be manufactured or acquired by the seller after the making of the contract of sale:

"Goods" include all chattels personal other than things in action and money, and in Scotland all corporeal moveables except money. The term includes emblements, industrial growing crops, and things attached to or forming part of the land which are agreed to be severed before sale or under the contract of sale:

"Lien" in Scotland includes right of retention:

"Plaintiff" includes pursuer, complainer, claimant in a multiplepoinding and defendant or defender counterclaiming:

"Property" means the general property in goods, and not merely a special property:

"Quality of goods" includes their state or condition:

"Sale" includes a bargain and sale as well as a sale and delivery:

"Seller" means a person who sells or agrees to sell goods:

"Specific goods" mean goods identified and agreed upon at the time a contract of sale is made:

"Warranty" as regards England and Ireland means an agreement with reference to goods which are the subject of a contract of sale, but collateral to the main purpose of such contract, the breach of which gives rise to a claim for damages, but not to a right to reject the goods and treat the contract as repudiated.

As regards Scotland a breach of warranty shall be deemed to be a failure to perform a material part of the contract.

(2) A thing is deemed to be done "in good faith" within the meaning of this Act when it is in fact done honestly, whether it be done negligently or not.

(3) A person is deemed to be insolvent within the meaning of this

Act who either has ceased to pay his debts in the ordinary course of business, or cannot pay his debts as they become due, whether he has committed an act of bankruptcy or not, and whether he has become a notour bankrupt or not.

(4) Goods are in a "deliverable state" within the meaning of this Act when they are in such a state that the buyer would under the contract be bound to take delivery of them.

63. Repealed by Statute Law Revision Act, 1908[12]

64. Short title
This Act may be cited as the Sale of Goods Act, 1893.

Schedule

Repealed by the Statute Law Revision Act, 1908.

---

[12] 8 Edw. 7 c. 49

Statutes Revised on Commercial Law

The Trustee Act, 1893, Amendment Act, 1894
57 & 58 Victoria, chapter 10

An Act to amend the Trustee Act, 1893
   18th June 1894

Be it enacted ...

1. Amends section 30, Trustee Act, 1893, 56 & 57 Vict. c. 53

2. Extension to Ireland of 56 & 57 Vict. c. 53, s. 41
The powers conferred on the High Court in England by section forty-one of the Trustee Act, 1893, to make vesting orders as to all land and personal estate in Her Majesty's dominions except Scotland, are hereby also given to and may be exercised by the High Court in Ireland.

3. Amends section 44, Trustee Act, 1893, 56 & 57 Vict. c. 53

4. Liability of trustee in case of change of character of investment
A trustee shall not be liable for breach of trust by reason only of his continuing to hold an investment which has ceased to be an investment authorised by the instrument of trust or by the general law.

5. Short title
This Act may be cited as the Trustee Act, 1893, Amendment Act, 1894.

The Industrial and Provident Societies (Amendment) Act, 1895
58 & 59 Victoria, chapter 30

An Act to amend the Industrial and Provident Societies Act, 1893.
6th July 1895

Be it enacted ...

1. Short Title 56 & 57 Vict. c 39 57 & 58 Vict. c. 8[1]
This Act may be cited as the the Industrial and Provident Societies (Amendment) Act, 1895. This Act and the Industrial and Provident Societies Act, 1893 and 1894[1], may be cited together as the Industrial and Provident Societies Acts, 1893 to 1895.

2. Proceedings in Scotland

3. Amends section 7 of 56 & 57 Vict. c. 39

4. Printing of future copies of Principal Act
All copies of the Industrial and Provident Societies Act, 1893 printed after the passing of this Act by any of the several printers to the Queen's most Excellent Majesty duly authorised to print the statutes of the United Kingdom, shall be printed with the substitution required by this Act.

---

[1] The Act of 1894 relates to the Island of Jersey only.

The Life Insurance Companies (Payment into Court) Act, 1896
59 & 60 Victoria, chapter 8

An Act to enable Life Insurance Companies to pay money into Court in certain cases
21st May 1896

1. Short title
This Act may be cited as the Life Insurance Companies (Payment into Court) Act, 1896.

2. Interpretation
In this Act -

The expression "life assurance company" means any corporation, company, or society carrying on the business of life assurance, not being a society registered under the Acts relating to friendly societies;

The expression "life policy" includes any policy not foreign to the business of life assurance.

3. Power to pay money into court
Subject to rules of court any life assurance company may pay into the High Court, or where the head office of the company is situated within the jurisdiction of the Chancery Court of the County Palatine of Lancaster either into that court or into the High Court, any moneys payable by them under a life policy in respect of which, in the opinion of the board of directors, no sufficient discharge can otherwise be obtained.

4. Receipt of officer sufficient discharge
The receipt or certificate of the proper officer shall be a sufficient discharge to the company for the moneys so paid into the court, and such money shall, subject to rules of court, be dealt with according to the orders of the High Court or the Palatine Court, as the case may be.

5. Extent of Act
This Act does not extend to Scotland.

The Friendly Societies Act, 1896
59 & 60 Victoria, chapter 25

<u>List of Sections</u>

The Registry Office

Societies with Branches

Friendly Societies Act, 1896
Property, Funds, and Investments

Officers in Receipt or Charge of Money

Payments on Death generally

Payments on Death of Children

Friendly Societies Act, 1896

An Act to consolidate the law relating to friendly and other societies.[1]

7th August 1896

The Registry Office

1.The registry office[2]

(1) There shall ...[3] be a chief registrar of friendly societies[4] (in this Act called "the chief registrar"), and one or more assistant registrars of friendly societies for England (in this Act called "assistant registrars for England"), and the chief registrar and assistant registrars for England shall ...[3] constitute the central office of the registry of friendly societies.

(2) There shall ...[3] be an assistant registrar of friendly societies for Scotland (in this Act called "assistant registrar for Scotland"), and an assistant registrar of friendly societies for Ireland[3] (in this Act called "assistant registrar for Ireland").

(3) Every chief registrar and assistant registrar shall be appointed by and shall hold his office during the pleasure of the Treasury.

(5)[5] The central office[4] may, with the approval of the Treasury, have attached to it such assistants skilled in the business of an actuary and an accountant as may be required for discharging the duties imposed on the office by this Act.

2. Functions of the central office

(1) The central office shall ...[3] exercise the functions and powers formerly vested-
  (a) as respects trade unions, in the registrar of friendly societies in England; and
  (b) as respects building societies, in the registrar of building societies in England; and
  (c) as respects unincorporated benefit building societies, loan

---

[1] Restricted by Credit Union Act 1966 (No. 19), s. 3(2); by Friendly Societies (Amendment) Act, 1977 (No. 17), s. 3(3) and ss. 8(1), 16, 41 by Workmen's Compensation Act, 1934 (No. 9), s. 62(8)[r. prospectively with savings by Social Welfare (O.I.) Act, 1966 (No. 16), applic. now continued in Social Welfare (Consolidation) Act, 1981 (No. 1).]

[2] Constr. Friendly Societies (Amendment) Act, 1977 (No. 17), s. 5(5)

[3] Deletion by Statute Law Revision Act, 1908, 8 Edw. 7 c. 49

[4] Adaptation made to Registrar of Friendly Societies in Saorstát Éireann; S. R. & O., No. 43 / 1926, par. 5 & 6.

[5] S-s. (4), repealed by Registry of Friendly Societies Act, 1936 (No. 51), s. 4(2)

262

societies, and societies instituted for purposes of science literature or the fine arts, in the barristers appointed to certify the rules of savings banks or friendly societies,

and shall be entitled to receive all fees payable to those registrars and barristers; and all enactments relating to those registrars and barristers shall, so far as respects trade unions and such societies as aforesaid, be construed as applying to the central office.

(2) The central office shall, with the approval of the Treasury-

    (a) prepare and cause to be circulated, for the use of societies, model forms of accounts, balance sheets, and valuations; and

    (b) collect from the returns under this Act and from other sources, and publish and circulate, either generally or in any particular district, or otherwise make known, such information on the subject of the statistics of life and sickness, and the application thereof to the business of friendly societies, and such particulars of their returns and valuations, and such other information useful to the members of or to persons interested in societies registered or capable of being registered under this Act, as the chief registrar may think fit; and

    (c) cause to be constructed and published tables for the payment of sums of money on death, in sickness, or old age, or on any other contingency forming the subject of an assurance authorised under this Act which may appear to be calculable: Provided that the adoption of the tables by a society shall be optional.

3. Functions of assistant registrars generally

(1) The assistant registrars shall except as in this Act provided, be subordinate to the chief registrar.

(2) They shall, within the parts of the United Kingdom for which they are respectively appointed, exercise all functions and powers by this Act given to the registrar, and may also by the written authority of the chief registrar, exercise such of the functions and powers by this Act given to the chief registrar as he may delegate to them.

4. Functions of assistant registrars for Scotland and Ireland

(1) Subject to any regulations to be made under this Act, the assistant registrars for Scotland and Ireland respectively shall[3] exercise the functions and powers formerly vested -

    (a) as respects trade unions, in the registrars of friendly societies in Scotland and Ireland; and

    (b) as respects building societies, in the registrars of building societies in Scotland and Ireland; and

    (c) as respects benefit building societies and societies instituted for purposes of science literature or the fine arts, in Scotland, in the Lord Advocate or his deputes appointed to certify the rules of any such societies, and, in Ireland, in any barristers appointed for the like purpose;

and shall be entitled to receive all fees payable to those registrars, the Lord Advocate or his deputes and those barristers respectively; and all provisions in any Acts of Parliament relating to those persons respectively shall be construed as applying to those assistant registrars.

(2) Subject as aforesaid, the assistant registrars for Scotland and Ireland shall -

 (a) send to the central office copies of all such documents registered or recorded by them as the chief registrar may direct: and

 (b) record such documents and matters as may be sent to them for record from the central office, and such other documents and matters as are in this Act required to be recorded: and

 (c) circulate and publish, or transmit to or from societies registered in Scotland or Ireland respectively, from or to the central office, such information and documents relating to the purposes of this Act as the chief registrar may, with the approval of the Treasury direct: and

 (d) report their proceedings to the chief registrar as he may direct.

(3) An assistant registrar for Scotland or Ireland shall not refuse to record any rules or amendments of rules which have been registered by the central office.

5. Salaries and expenses[2]

The Treasury shall, out of money to be provided by Parliament, pay to the chief and assistant registrars such salaries or other remunerations, and such sums of money for defraying the expenses of office rent, salaries of assistants, clerks, and servants, remuneration for actuaries, accountants, and inspectors, computation of tables, publication of documents, diffusion of information, expenses of prosecutions, travelling expenses and other allowances of the chief or any assistant registrar, and other expenses which may be incurred for carrying out the purposes of this Act, as the Treasury may allow.

6. Report of the chief registrar

The chief registrar shall every year make a report of his proceedings and of those of the assistant registrars, and of the principal matters transacted by him and them and of the valuations returned to or caused to be made by the registrar during the year preceding, and that report shall be laid before Parliament.

The report required by this section shall include particulars relating to credit unions and, in particular, a list of all statutory instruments in operation at the end of the year in question together with explanatory notes regarding such instruments and a copy of such particulars shall be sent free of charge on request to any credit union in the State.[6]

7. Deposit of documents

All documents by this Act required to be sent to the registrar shall be deposited with the rules of the societies to which the documents respectively relate, and shall be registered or recorded by the registrar, with such observations thereon, if any, as the chief registrar may direct.

Registry of Societies.

8. [1] Societies which may be registered[7]

The following societies may be registered under this Act;

(1) Societies (in this Act called friendly societies) for the purpose of providing by voluntary subscriptions of the members thereof, with or without the aid of donations, for -

(a) the relief or maintenance of the members, their husbands, wives, children, fathers, mothers, brothers, or sisters, nephews or nieces, or wards being orphans, during sickness or other infirmity, whether bodily or mental, in old age (which shall mean any age after fifty) or in widowhood, or for the relief or maintenance of the orphan children of members during minority; or

(b) insuring money to be paid on the birth of a member's child or on the death of a member, or for the funeral expenses of the husband, wife, or child of a member, or of the widow of a deceased member, or, as respects persons of the Jewish persuasion, for the payment of a sum of money during the period of confined mourning; or

(c) the relief or maintenance of the members when on travel in search of employment, or when in distressed circumstances, or in case of shipwreck, or loss or damage of or to boats or nets; or

(d) the endowment of members or nominees of members at any

---

[6] Paragraph inserted: Credit Union Act, 1966 (No. 19), s. 37, 39, sch. pt. 2

[7] The Friendly Societies (Amendment) Act, 1977 (No. 17), at section 8 provides : The Minister may by regulation amend sections 8, 41, 56 to 58, 62 and 65 of the Principal Act, or any one or more of those sections, so as to increase by such amount or amounts as he thinks fit any one or more of the amounts specified in those sections.

age; or

(e) the insurance against fire, to any amount not exceeding fifteen pounds, of the tools or implements of the trade or calling of the members

(f) guaranteeing the performance of their duties by officers and servants of the society or any branch thereof.[8]

Provided that a friendly society which contracts with any person for the assurance of an annuity exceeding fifty two[9] pounds per annum, or of a gross sum exceeding £15,000[10] pounds, shall not be registered under this Act:

(2) Societies (in this Act called cattle insurance societies) for the purpose of insurance to any amount against loss of neat cattle, sheep, lambs, swine, horses, and other animals by death from disease or otherwise:

(3) Societies (in this Act called benevolent societies) for any benevolent or charitable purpose:

(4) Societies (in this Act called working-men's clubs) for purposes of social intercourse, mutual helpfulness, mental and moral improvement, and rational recreation:

(5) Societies (in this Act called specially authorised societies) for any purpose which the Treasury may authorise as a purpose to which the provisions of this Act, or such of them as are specified in the authority, ought to be extended.

Provided that where any provisions of this Act are so specified, those provisions only shall be so extended.

8A. Restriction on registration[11]

Notwithstanding section 8 of this Act:

(1) No society shall be registered under this Act for any of the purposes referred to in section 8(1)(a) or section 8(1)(e) of this Act unless the registrar of friendly societies is satisfied that the society is a society to which Article 2.2(b), Article 2.2(c) or Article 3 of Council Directive 73/239/EEC refers.

(2) No society shall be registered under this Act for any of the purposes referred to in section 8(1)(b) or section 8(1)(d) of this Act unless the registrar of friendly societies is satisfied that the society is a society to which Article 2.2, Article 2.3 or Article 3 of Council Directive 79/267/EEC refers, or is a society in respect of which the Minister for Industry and Commerce has indicated that he will issue an authorisation under the European Communities (Life Assurance)

---

[8] Inserted by Friendly Societies Act, 1908, 8 Edw. 7 c. 32, s. 1

[9] Substituted by Friendly Societies (Amendment) Act, 1953 (No. 28), s. 2

[10] Now substituted by S.I. 59/1992, reg. 4, sch.

[11] Inserted by Insurance Act, 1989 (No. 3), s. 28

Regulations, 1984.

(3) No society registered under this Act shall be authorised to carry on any insurance business falling under the description of insurance of Class III, IV or VII of Schedule 1 to the European Communities (Life Assurance) Regulations, 1984, unless it has obtained an authorisation under those regulations for that purpose.

9. Conditions of registration

(1) A society shall not be registered under this Act unless it consists of seven persons at least.

(2) For the purpose of registry there shall be sent to the registrar an application to register the society, signed by seven members and the secretary, and copies of the rules, together with a list of the names of the secretary and of every trustee or other officer intended to be authorised to sue and be sued on behalf of the society.

(3) The rules of the society so sent shall, according to the class in which the society is to be registered, contain provisions in respect of the several matters mentioned in the First Schedule to this Act.

(4) If the list is signed by the secretary and every trustee and other officer named therein, it shall on the registry of the society be evidence that the persons so named have been duly appointed.

10. Name of Society

A society shall not be registered under a name identical with that under which any other existing society is registered or so nearly resembling that name as to be likely, or in any name likely, in the opinion of the registrar, to deceive the members or the public as to its nature or its identity.

11. Acknowledgment of registry

The registrar, on being satisfied that a society has complied with the provisions of this Act as to registry, shall issue to that society an acknowledgment of registry specifying the designation of the society, according to the classification set forth in this Act, and this acknowledgment shall be conclusive evidence that the society therein mentioned is duly registered, unless it is proved that the registry of the society has been suspended or cancelled.

12. Appeals from refusal to register

(1) From a refusal to register a society an appeal shall lie as follows:-

    (a) if the assistant registrar for Scotland or for Ireland refuses to register, the society may appeal to the chief registrar, and if he refuses, to the Court of Session in Scotland, or to the High Court in Ireland:

(b) if the central office refuse, the society may appeal to the High Court in England.

(2) If the refusal to register is overruled on appeal, the registrar shall give an acknowledgment of registry to the society.

13. Registry of amendment of rules

(1) An amendment of a rule made by a registered society shall not be valid until the amendment has been registered under this Act, for which purpose copies of the amendment, signed by three members and the secretary, shall be sent to the registrar.

(2) The registrar shall, on being satisfied that any amendment of a rule is not contrary to the provisions of this Act, issue to the society an acknowledgment of registry of the amendment, and that acknowledgment shall be conclusive evidence that the amendment is duly registered.

(3) The provisions of this Act as to appeals from a refusal to register a society shall apply to a refusal to register an amendment of a rule.

14. Registry of societies carrying on business in more than one part of the United Kingdom

(1) A society carrying or intending to carry on business in more than one part of the United Kingdom shall be registered in the part in which its registered office is situate; but the rules and registered amendments of rules of any such society shall be recorded by the registrars of the other parts, and for that purpose copies of the rules and amendments shall be sent to those registrars.

(2) Until the rules are so recorded the society shall not be entitled to any of the privileges of this Act in the part of the United Kingdom in which the rules have not been recorded, and until the amendments of rules are recorded they shall not take effect in that part.

15. Registry of dividing societies

A society (other than a benevolent society or working-men's club) shall not be disentitled to registry by reason of any rule for or practice of dividing any part of the funds thereof if the rules of the society contain distinct provision for meeting all claims upon the society existing at the time of division before any such division takes place.

16. [1] Registry of societies assuring annuities

A society assuring a certain annuity shall not be entitled to registry, unless the tables of contributions for the assurance, certified by the actuary to the National Debt Commissioners, or by some actuary approved by the Treasury, who has excerised the profession of actuary for at least five years, are sent to the registrar with the application for registry.

Societies with Branches

17. Registry of Societies with branches

(1) Where a society has branches, the application for registry shall be accompanied with -

(a) a list of all the branches, and notice of the place where the registered office of each branch is situate, and

(b) if any branch is to have trustees or officers authorised to sue and be sued on its behalf, other than the trustees or officers authorised to sue and be sued on behalf of the society, a list of the names of all such trustees or officers, distinguishing the branches for which they are authorised to sue and be sued; and

(c) if the rules of all the branches (in this Act called branch rules) are or are intended to be identical, a statement to that effect, and copies of those rules; and

(d) if the branch rules are not or are not intended to be identical, a statement to that effect, and copies of all branch rules.

(2) A society having a fund under the control of a central body to which every branch is bound to contribute may be registered as a single society, and where any such society has branches in more than one part of the United Kingdom the provision of this Act as to the registry of societies doing business in more than one such part shall apply to that society.

18. Establishment of new branches

(1) There shall be sent under the hand of the secretary of a registered society to the registrar -

(a) notice of the establishment of every new branch of the society; and

(b) notice of the place where the registered office of the branch is situate; and

(c) if the branch is to have trustees or officers authorised to sue and be sued on its behalf other than the trustees or officers authorised to sue and be sued on behalf of the society, a list of the name of such trustees or officers; and

(d) a statement whether or not the rules of the branch are identical with those of the other branches of the society, and if not so, a copy of the rules of the branch.

(2) Where the rules of the new branch are not identical with those of the other branches of the society, the society shall not be entitled

269

to any of the privileges of this Act in respect of that branch until that branch has been registered in the part of the United Kingdom in which the registered office of the branch is to be situate.

19. Application of previous provisions to branches
The provisions of this Act as to -
   (a) the acknowledgement of registry of societies and amendments of rules; and
   (b) appeals from refusals to register societies and amendments of rules and the result thereof; and
   (c) the registry of amendments of rules; and
   (d) evidence of registry and of the appointment of trustees and officers
shall apply to branches and amendments of branch rules.

20. Requisites for registry of branches as societies
(1) A body which has been registered as a branch of a society shall not be registered as a society except on production to the registrar of a certificate under the hand of the chief secretary or other principal officer of the society of which it was a branch, that the body has wholly seceded or has been expelled from the society.

(2) An appeal shall lie from the refusal of the chief secretary or other principal officer of the society, or his omission after three months from the receipt of a request in writing made on behalf of the body to grant a certificate, to the High Court in England or Ireland or the the Court of Session in Scotland.

21. Name of seceding or expelled branch
A body which, having been a branch of a society, has wholly seceded or been expelled from that society shall not thereafter use the name of that society or any name implying that it is a branch thereof, or the number by which it was designated as such branch.

22. Contributions from one society to another
(1) A registered society or branch may contribute to the funds and take part by delegates or otherwise in the government of any other registered society or registered branch of a society, as provided in the rules of that first-named society or branch, without becoming a branch under this Act of that other society or branch.

(2) This section shall in respect of contributing to the funds and taking part in the government of a medical society, that is to say, a society for the purpose of relief in sickness by providing medical attendance and medicine, extend to any registered trade union or branch of a registered trade union.

(3) A registered society or trade union or branch shall not

withdraw from contributing to the funds of any such medical society except on three months notice to the society and on payment of all contributions accrued or accruing due to the date of the expiration of the notice.

Consequences of Registry

23. Subscription not recoverable at law
Save as provided by section thirty-one of this Act, the subscription of a person being or having been a member of a registered society or branch shall not be recoverable at law.

24. Registered office
(1) Every registered society and branch shall have a registered office to which all communications and notices may be addressed, and shall send to the registrar notice of the situation of that office, and of every change therein.

(2) In the case of a branch the notice shall be sent to the registrar through an officer appointed in that behalf by the society of which the branch forms part.

25. Appointment of trustees
(1) Every registered society and branch shall have one or more trustees.

(2) The trustees shall be appointed at a meeting of the society or branch, and by a resolution of a majority of the members present and entitled to vote thereat.

(3) The society or branch shall send to the registrar a copy of every resolution appointing a trustee, signed by the trustee so appointed, and by the secretary of the society or branch.

(4) The same person shall not be secretary or treasurer of a registered society or branch, and a trustee of that society or branch.

(5) In the case of a branch the copy of the resolution shall be sent to the registrar through an officer appointed in that behalf by the society of which the branch forms part.

26. Audit
(1) Every registered society and branch shall once at least in every year submit its accounts for audit either to one of the public auditors appointed as in this Act mentioned, or to two or more persons appointed as the rules of the society or branch provide.

(2) The auditors shall have access to all the books and accounts of the society or branch, and shall examine the annual return mentioned in this Act, and verify the annual return with the accounts and vouchers relating thereto, and shall either sign the annual return as

found by them to be correct, duly vouched, and in accordance with law, or specially report to the society or branch in what respects they find it incorrect, unvouched, or not in accordance with law.

27. Annual returns

(1) Every registered society and branch shall once in every year, not later than the thirty-first day of May, send to the registrar a return (in this Act called the annual return) of the receipts and expenditure, funds, and effects of the society or branch as audited.

(2) The annual return must -

(a) show separately the expenditure in respect of the several objects of the society or branch; and

(b) be made out to the thirty-first day of December then last inclusively; and

(c) state whether the audit has been conducted by a public auditor appointed as by this Act provided, and by whom, and, if by persons other than a public auditor, state the name, address, and calling or profession of every such person, and the manner in which, and the authority under which, he is appointed.

(3) the society or branch shall, together with the annual return, send a copy of any special report of the auditors.

(4) In the case of a branch the annual return shall be sent to the registrar through an officer appointed in that behalf by the Society of which the branch forms part.

28. Quinquennial valuation

(1) Every registered society and branch shall, except as in this section provided, once at least in every five years either -

(a) cause it assets and liabilities to be valued by a valuer to be appointed by the society or branch and send to the registrar a report on the condition of the society or branch; or

(b) send to the registrar a return of the benefits assured and contributions receivable from all the members of the society or branch, and of all its funds and effects, debts and credits, accompanied by such evidence in support thereof as the chief registrar prescribes.

(2) If the society or branch sends to the registrar such report as aforesaid, the report must -

(a) be signed by the valuer; and

(b) state the address and calling or profession of the valuer; and

(c) contain an abstract to be made by the valuer of the results of his valuation, together with a statement containing such information with respect to the benefits assured and the contributions receivable by the society or branch, and of its funds and effects, debts and credits, as the registrar may require.

(3) If the society or branch sends to the registrar such return as aforesaid he shall cause the assets and liabilities of the society or branch to be valued and reported on by some actuary, and shall send to the society or branch a copy of the report and an abstract of the results of the valuation.

(4) Provided that this section shall not apply to -

(a) a benevolent society, working-men's club, cattle insurance society or branch thereof, or

(b) a specially authorised society or branch unless it is so directed in the authority for registering that society or branch.

(5) Provided also that the chief registrar may with the approval of the Treasury dispense with the provisions of this section in respect of societies or branches to whose purposes or to the nature of whose operations he may deem those provisions inapplicable.

29. Copy of last balance sheet

Every registered society and branch shall keep a copy of the last annual balance sheet, and of the last quinquennial valuation, together with any special report of the auditors, always hung up in a conspicuous place at the registered office of the society or branch.

30. Public auditors and valuers

(1) For the purpose of audits and valuations to be made under this Act the Treasury may appoint public auditors and valuers and may determine the rates of remuneration to be paid by societies and branches for the services of those auditors and valuers; but the employment of those auditors and valuers shall not be compulsory.

(2) The Treasury may out of money to be provided by Parliament pay to the public auditors and valuers such remuneration (if any) as the Treasury may allow.

31. Registered cattle insurance and other societies

(1) The rules of a registered cattle insurance society or branch, and of such specially authorised societies or branches thereof as the Treasury may allow to take the benefit of this section, shall bind the society or branch and the members thereof, and all persons claiming through them respectively, to the same extent as if each member had subscribed his name and affixed his seal thereto, and there were in the rules contained a covenant on the part of himself, his heirs, executors, and administrators, to conform to the rules subject to the provisions of this Act.

(2) All sums of money payable by a member to such society or branch as aforesaid shall be deemed to be a debt due from the

member to the society or branch, and shall be recoverable as such in the county court of the district in which the member resides.

Privileges of Registered Societies

32. Exception of societies from corresponding Societies Acts, &c.

(1) A registered society or branch or a meeting of a registered society or branch shall not be affected by any of the provisions of the Unlawful Societies Act, 1799, or of the Seditions Meetings Act, 1817, if in the society or branch or at the meeting no business is transacted other than that which directly and immediately relates to the objects of the society or branch as declared in the rules thereof; but the society or branch, and all officers thereof shall, on request in writing by two justices of the peace, give to such justices full information of the nature, objects, proceedings, and practices of the society or branch.

(2) If the society or branch when so required fails to give such information as aforesaid, the provisions of those Acts shall, so far as applicable, be in force in respect of the society or branch.

33. Exemptions from stamp duty

Stamp duty shall not be chargeable upon any of the following documents:-

- (a) Draft or order or receipt given by or to a registered society or branch in respect of money payable by virtue of its rules or of this Act:
- (b) Letter or power of attorney granted by any person as trustee for the transfer of any money of a registered society or branch invested in his name in the public funds:
- (c) Bond given to or on account of a registered society or branch or by the treasurer or other officer thereof:
- (d) Policy of insurance or appointment or revocation of appointment of agent or other document required or authorised by this Act or by the rules of a registered society or branch.

34. Transfer of stock standing in name of trustee

(1) In any of the following cases, namely :-

- (i) where a person being or having been a trustee of a registered society or branch, and whether appointed before or after the registry thereof, in whose name any stock belonging to that society or branch transferable at the Bank of England or Bank of Ireland is standing, either jointly with another or others, or solely -
  - (a) is absent from the British Islands; or

(b) becomes bankrupt or files any petition or executes any deed for liquidation of his affairs by assignment or arrangement, or for composition with his creditors; or

(c) becomes lunatic or is dead; or

(d) has been removed from his office of trustee; or

(ii) if it is unknown whether such person is living or dead, the chief registrar may, on application in writing from the secretary and three members of the society or branch, and on proof satisfactory to him, direct the transfer of the stock into the names of any other persons as trustees for the society or branch.

(2) The transfer shall be made by the surviving or continuing trustees, or if there is no such trustee, or if the trustees refuse or are unable to make the transfer, and the chief registrar so directs, then by the Accountant General or Deputy or Assistant Accountant General of the Bank of England or Bank of Ireland, as the case may be.

(3) The Bank of England and the Bank of Ireland are hereby indemnified for anything done by them or any of their officers in pursuance of this section against any claim or demand of any person injuriously affected thereby.

35. Priority on death, bankruptcy, &c. of officer

(1) In the following cases, namely -

(a) upon the death or bankruptcy of any officer of a registered society or branch having in his possession by virtue of his office any money or property belonging to the society or branch; or

(b) if any execution, attachment, or other process is issued, or action or diligence raised against any such officer or against his property,

His heirs, executors, or administrators, or trustee in bankruptcy, or the sheriff or other person executing the process or the party using the action or diligence respectively shall, upon demand in writing of the trustees of the society or branch, or of any two of them, or of any person authorised by the society or branch, or by the committee thereof to make the demand, pay the money, and deliver over the property to the trustees of the society or branch in preference to any other debt or claim against the estate of the officer.

(2) In this section the expression "bankruptcy" shall include liquidation of a debtor's affairs by arrangement in England, *cessio bonorum* of a debtor in Scotland, and a petition for arrangement with creditors in Ireland; and the expression "trustee in bankruptcy" shall include a judicial factor in Scotland, and an assignee in Ireland.

36. Membership of minors

(1) The rules of a registered society or branch may provide for the admission of a person under twenty-one years[13] of age ..[14] .. as a member.

(2) Any such member may, if he is over sixteen years of age by himself, and if he is under that age by his parent or guardian, execute all instruments and give all acquittances necessary to be executed or given under the rules, but shall not be a member of the committee, or a trustee, manager, or treasurer of the society or branch.

37. Subscriptions to hospitals

A registered society or branch may subscribe out of its funds to any hospital, infirmary, charitable or provident institution, any annual or other sum which may be necessary to secure to members of the society or branch and their families the benefits of the hospital, infirmary, or other institution, according to its rules.

Rights of Members

38. Right to supply of copies of the rules

Every registered society and branch shall deliver to every person on demand, on payment of a sum not exceeding one shilling, a copy of the rules of the society or branch.

39. Right to supply of copies of annual return

Every registered society and branch shall supply gratuitously to every member or person interested in its funds, on his application, either
    (a) a copy of the last annual return of the society or branch; or
    (b) a balance sheet or other document duly audited containing the same particulars as to the receipts and expenditure, funds, and effects, of the society or branch as are contained in the annual return.

40. Inspection of books by members

A member or person having an interest in the funds of a registered society or branch may inspect the books at all reasonable hours at the registered office of the society or branch, or at any place where the books are kept, except that the member or person shall not, unless he is an officer of the society or branch, or is specially authorised by a resolution of the society or branch to do so, have the right to inspect the loan account of any other member without the written consent of that member.

[13] To be construed as of full age: see Age of Majority Act, 1985 (No. 2), s. 2(3)

[14] Deletion by Friendly Societies Act, 1908, 8 Edw. 7 c. 32, s. 2

41.[1] Limitation of benefits[7]

(1) A member, or person claiming through a member, of a registered friendly society or branch, shall not be entitled to receive more than £15,000[15] pounds by way of gross sum, together with any bonuses or additions declared upon assurances not exceeding that amount, or (except as provided by this Act) fifty two[16] pounds a year by way of annuity, from any one or more such societies or branches.

(2) Any such society or branch may require a member, or person claiming through a member, to make and sign a statutory declaration that the total amount to which that member or person is entitled from one or more such societies or branches does not exceed the sums aforesaid.

42. Accumulation of surplus of contributions

The rules of a registered society or branch may provide for accumulating at interest, for the use of any member, any surplus of his contributions to the funds of the society or branch which may remain after providing for any assurance in respect of which they are paid and for the withdrawal of the accumulations.

43. Militiamen and volunteers

(1) A person shall not, by reason of his enrolment or service in the militia or as a naval coast volunteer, Royal Naval volunteer, naval artillery volunteer, or in any corps of yeomanry or volunteers whatsoever, lose or forfeit any interest in a friendly society or branch whether registered or unregistered which he possesses at the time of his being so enrolled or serving, or be fined for absence from or non-attendance at any meeting of the society or branch, if his absence or non-attendance is occasioned by the discharge of his military or naval duty as certified by his commanding officer, any rules of the society or branch to the contrary notwithstanding.

(2) A dispute between any such society or branch and person by reason of that enrolment or service shall be decided by a court of summary jurisdiction.

(3) If the rules of a society or branch certified before the twenty-third day of July one thousand eight hundred and fifty-five, and in force at the time of the enrolment or service, provide that a member shall be deprived of any benefit by reason of that enrolment or service, the society or branch may require of the member a contribution exceeding the rate of contribution otherwise payable by him to an amount not exceeding one tenth of that rate during the time the member is serving out of the United Kingdom, or may

---

[15] Now substituted by S.I. 59/1992, reg. 4, sch.

[16] Substituted by Friendly Societies Act, 1908, 8 Edw. 7 c. 32, s. 3

suspend all claim of the member to any benefits assured by the society or branch, and all claim of the society or branch to any contributions payable by the member, during the time only he is serving out of the United Kingdom, but so that if he returns to the United Kingdom he shall forthwith be replaced on the same footing as before he went abroad on service.

Property, Funds, and Investments

44. Investment of funds

(1) The trustees of a registered society or branch may, with the consent of the committee or of a majority of the members present and entitled to vote in general meeting, invest the funds of the society or branch, or any part thereof, to any amount in any of the following ways:

(a) in the Post Office Savings Bank, or in any savings bank certified under the Trustee Savings Bank Act, 1863; or

(b) in the public funds; or

(c) with the National Debt Commissioners as in this Act provided; or

(d) in the purchase of land, or in the erection or alteration of offices or other buildings thereon; or

(e) upon any other security expressly directed by the rules of the society or branch, not being personal security, except as in this act authorised with respect to loans; or

(f) In any investment in which trustees are for the time being by law authorised to invest trust funds.[17]

(2) The rules of a society with branches and of any branch thereof may provide for the investment of funds of the society or of that branch by the trustees of any branch, or by the trustees of the society, and the consent required for any such investment shall be the consent of the committee, or of such majority as aforesaid of the society or branch by whom the funds are invested.

45. Loans to assured members

(1) A registered society and, subject to the rules of the society, a registered branch may advance to a member of at least one full year's standing any sum not exceeding one half of the amount of an assurance on his life, on the written security of himself and two satisfactory sureties for repayment.

(2) The amount so advanced, with all interest thereon, may be deducted from the sum assured, without prejudice in the meantime to the operation of the security.

---

[17] Inserted by Friendly Societies Act, 1908, 8 Edw. 7 c. 32, s. 4

46. Loans out of separate loan fund

A registered society may, out of any separate loan fund to be formed by contributions or deposits of its members, make loans to members on their personal security, with or without sureties, as may be provided by the rules, subject to the following restrictions: [18]

    (a) a loan shall not at any time be made out of money contributed for the other purposes of the society:

    (b) a member shall not be capable of holding any interest in the loan fund exceeding two hundred pounds:*

    (c) a society shall not make any loan to a member on personal security beyond the amount fixed by the rules, or make any loan which, together with any money owing by a member to the society, exceeds fifty pounds:*

    (d) a society shall not hold at any one time on deposit from its members any money beyond the amount fixed by the rules, and the amount so fixed shall not exceed two thirds of the total sums owing to the society by the members who have borrowed from the loan fund.

47. Holding of land

(1) A registered society or branch may (if the rules thereof so provide) hold, purchase, or take on lease in the names of the trustees of the society or branch any land, and may sell, exchange, mortgage, lease, or build upon that land (with power to alter and pull down buildings and again rebuild), and a purchaser, assignee, mortgagee, or tenant shall not be bound to inquire as to the authority for any sale, exchange, mortgage, or lease by the trustees, and the receipt of the trustees shall be a discharge for all sums of money arising from or in connexion with the sale, exchange, mortgage, or lease.

(2) A branch of a registered society need not for the purposes of this section be separately registered.

(3) Nothing in this section shall authorise a benevolent society to hold land exceeding one acre in extent.

48. Copyholds

Where a registered society or branch is entitled in equity to any hereditaments of copyhold or customary tenure, either absolutely or by way of mortgage or security, the lord of the manor of which the hereditaments are held shall, if the society or branch so requires, admit not more than three trustees of the society or branch as tenants in respect of such hereditaments, on payment of the usual fines, fees, and other dues payable on the admission of a single tenant.

---

[18]Pw. to alter rstrct., Friendly Societies (Amendment) Act, 1977 (No. 17), s. 2

 * Shall have effect as: £5,000 (b), £2,500 (c), in relation to certified societies within the meaning of s. 8(1)(b) & (5), S.I. 59/1992, reg. 3

49. Vesting of property

(1) All property belonging to a registered society, whether acquired before or after the society is registered, shall vest in the trustees for the time being of the society, for the use and benefit of the society and the members thereof, and of all persons claiming through the members according to the rules of the society.

(2) The property of a registered branch of a society shall vest wholly or partly in the trustees for the time being of that branch or of any other branch of which that branch forms part (or, if the rules of the society so provide, in the trustees for the time being of the society), for the use and benefit either of the members of any such branch and persons claiming through those members, or of the members of the society generally, and persons claiming through them, according to the rules of the society.

(3) The trustees shall not be liable to make good any deficiency in the funds of the society or branch, but shall be liable only for sums of money actually received by them respectively on account of the society or branch.

50. Devolution on death

Upon the death, resignation, or removal of a trustee of a registered society or branch, the property vested in that trustee shall, without conveyance or assignment, and whether the property is real or personal, vest, as personal estate subject to the same trusts, in the succeeding trustees of that society or branch either solely or together with any surviving or continuing trustees, and, until the appointment of succeeding trustees, shall so vest in the surviving or continuing trustees only, or in the executors or administrators of the last surviving or continuing trustee, except that stocks and securities in the public funds of Great Britain and Ireland shall be transferred into the names of the succeeding trustees, either solely or jointly with any surviving or continuing trustees.

51. Description in legal proceedings

In all legal proceedings whatsoever concerning any property vested in the trustees of a registered society or branch, the property may be stated to be the property of the trustees in their proper names as trustees for the society or branch without further description.

52. Investments with the National Debt Commissioners

(1) A registered society or branch may pay to the account of the National Debt Commissioners at the Bank of England or the Bank of Ireland, as the case may require, any sum of money not less than fifty pounds upon a declaration of the trustees of the society or branch, or any two of them, that the money belongs exclusively to

the society or branch.

(2) The cashier of the Bank shall receive all such sums of money and place them to the account of the Commissioners in the book of the bank names "The Fund for Friendly Societies."

(3) A sum of money paid in upon a false declaration shall be forfeited to the Commissioners, and applied by them in the manner directed by section twelve of the Savings Banks Act, 1891.

(4) The provisions of sections twenty-one, twenty-two, twenty-four, twenty-five, twenty-six, twenty-seven, and twenty-eight of the Trustee Savings Banks Act, 1863, as to the regulation of receipts, certificates, and orders, shall apply to money paid under this section.

(5) A society or branch so investing money with the Commissioners shall be entitled to a receipt entitling to interest at the following rates:-

To a friendly society or branch legally established before the twenty-eighth of July one thousand eight hundred and twenty-eight, which had invested funds with the Commissioners before the twenty-third of July on thousand eight hundred and fifty-five, a rate of interest in respect of any assurance made before the fifteenth of August one thousand eight hundred and fifty of -	Threepence per centum per diem.
To a friendly society or branch legally established between the twenty-eight of July one thousand eight hundred and twenty-eight and the fifteenth of August one thousand eight hundred and fifty, which had invested funds with the Commissioners before the twenty-third of July one thousand eight hundred and fifty-five, a rate of interest in respect of any assurance made before the fifteenth of August one thousand eight hundred and fifty of -	Twopence halfpenny per centum per diem.
To a friendly society or branch legally established before the twenty-eighth of June one thousand eight hundred and eighty-eight, which had invested funds with the Commissioners before the first day of January one thousand eight hundred and ninety-six, a rate of interest in respect of any assurance made on or before the said twenty-eighth day of June of -	Twopence per centum per diem.

To a society or branch in respect of any investment with the Commissioners, other than as herein-before in this section mentioned, a rate of interest of -	Two pounds fifteen shillings per centum per annum.

(6) A society or branch withdrawing money so invested with the Commissioners shall not be entitled to make any further deposit without their consent.

(7) A society or branch so investing money with the Commissioners shall furnish such returns as may be required by the Commissioners, in respect of the funds deposited with them, and the assurances to which those funds relate.

(8) A society or branch having funds invested with the Commissioners at a rate higher than two pounds fifteen shillings per centum per annum shall retain at that rate so much only of its funds as arises from assurances made before the date applicable to that rate, after deducting all benefit payments and management expenses incurred on account of those assurances; and whenever the society or branch fails to satisfy the Commissioners of its title to retain at that rate any part of its funds, the Commissioners shall require the withdrawal thereof, or the transfer thereof to the rate of twopence per centum per diem, or two pounds fifteen shillings per centum per annum, as the case may require, and in default of withdrawal within thirty days, shall transfer the same in their books accordingly, and shall notify the transfer to the society or branch.

(9) Whenever it appears to the Commissioners that all the members of a society or branch assured before the fifteenth day of August one thousand eight hundred and fifty have died or ceased to be members the Commissioners shall forthwith transfer in their books to the rate of two pence per centum per diem, or two pounds fifteen shillings per centum per annum, as the case may require, all funds of the society or branch remaining invested at any higher rate, and shall notify the transfer to the society or branch.

53. Discharge of mortgages by receipt endorsed

(1) A receipt under the hands of the trustees of a registered society or branch, countersigned by the secretary, for all sums of money secured to the society or branch by any mortgage or other assurance, being in the form prescribed by this Act, if endorsed upon or annexed to the mortgage or other assurance, shall vacate the mortgage or assurance and vest the property therein comprised in the person entitled to the equity of redemption of that property, without reconveyance or resurrender.

(2) If the mortgage or other assurance has been registered under any Act for the registration or record of deeds or titles, or is of

copyholds or of lands of customary tenure and entered on any court rolls, the registrar under any such Act, or recording officer, or steward of the manor, or keeper of the register, shall on production of the receipt, verified by oath of any person, enter satisfaction of the mortgage or charge made by the assurance on the register or court rolls, and shall grant a certificate, either upon the mortgage or assurance, or separately to the like effect.

(3) The certificate shall be received in evidence in all courts and proceedings without further proof.

(4) The person making the entry shall be entitled for making the said entry and granting the said certificate to a fee of two shillings and sixpence, which in Ireland shall be paid by stamps and applied in accordance with the Public Offices Fees Act, 1879.

(5) This section shall not extend to Scotland or the Island of Jersey.

Officers in Receipt or Charge of Money

54. Security by officers

Every officer of a registered society or branch having receipt or charge of money shall, if the rules of the society or branch so require, before taking upon himself the execution of his office, become bound with one sufficient surety at the least in a bond or give the security of a guarantee society, in such sum as the society or branch directs, conditioned for his rendering a just and true account of all sums of money received and paid by him on account of the society or branch at such times as its rules appoint, or as the society or branch or the trustees or committee thereof require him to do, and for the payment by him of all sums due from him to the society or branch.

55. Accounts of officers

(1) Every officer of a registered society or branch having receipt or charge of money shall, at such times as by the rules of the society or branch he should render account, or upon demand made, or notice in writing given or left at his last or usual place of residence, give in his account as may be required by the society or branch, or by the trustees or committee thereof, to be examined and allowed or disallowed by them, and shall, on the like demand or notice, pay over all sums of money and deliver all property in his hands or custody to such person as the society or branch, or the committee or the trustees, appoint.

(2) In case of any neglect or refusal to deliver the account, or to pay over the sums of money or to deliver the property in manner aforesaid, the trustees or authorised officers of the society or branch may sue upon the bond or security before mentioned, or may apply

to the county court or to a court of summary jurisdiction, and the order of either such court shall be final and conclusive.

Payments on Death generally

56. Power of member to dispose of sums payable on his death by nomination[7]

(1) A member of a registered society (other than a benevolent society or working-men's club) or branch thereof, not being under the age of sixteen years, may, by writing under his hand delivered at or sent to the registered office of the society or branch, or made in a book kept at that office, nominate a person to whom any sum of money payable by the society or branch on the death of that member, not exceeding £10,000[19], shall be paid at his decease.

(2) The sum of money payable by the society or branch on the death of a member, shall include sums of money contributed to or deposited in the separate loan account and the sums of money accumulated for the use of the member under the provisions of this Act with interest thereon.

(3) The person so nominated must not be an officer or servant of the society or branch, unless that officer or servant is the husband, wife, father, mother, child, brother, sister, nephew, or niece of the nominator.

(4) A nomination so made may be revoked and varied by any similar document under the hand of the nominator, deliver, sent, or made as aforesaid.

(5) The marriage of a member of a society or branch shall operate as a revocation of any nomination theretofore made by that member under this section.

(6)[20] A nomination or a variation or revocation of a nomination by writing under the hand of a member of a registered branch and delivered at or sent to the registered office of that branch, or made in a book kept at that office, shall be effectual notwithstanding that the money to which the nomination relates or some part thereof is not payable by that branch, but is payable by the society or some other branch.

57. Proceedings on death of a nominator[7]

(1) On receiving satisfactory proof of the death of a nominator, the society or branch shall pay to the nominee the amount due to the deceased member, not exceeding the said sum of £10,000[22]

---

[19] Now substituted by S.I. 74/1988

[20] Inserted by Friendly Societies Act, 1908, 8 Edw. 7 c. 32, s. 5

(2) The receipt of a nominee over sixteen years of age for any amount so paid shall be valid.[21]

58. Intestacy[7]

(1) If any member of a registered society or branch, entitled from the funds thereof to a sum not exceeding £10,000[22] dies intestate and without having made any nomination thereof then subsisting, the society or branch may, without letters of administration, distribute the sum among such persons as appear to a majority of the trustees, upon such evidence as they may deem satisfactory, to be entitled by law to receive that sum, subject. ...[23]

(2) If any such member is illegitimate, the trustees may pay the sum of money which that member might have nominated to or among the persons who, in the opinion of a majority of them, would have been entitled thereto if that member had been legitimate, or if there are no such persons, the society or branch shall deal with the money as the Treasury may direct.

59. Deleted; Credit Union Act, 1966 (No. 19), s. 37, 39(2) sch. pt. 2

60. Validity of payments

(1) A payment made by a registered society or branch, under the foregoing provisions of this Act with respect to payments on death generally to the person who at the time appears to a majority of the trustees to be entitled thereunder, shall be valid and effectual against any demand made upon the trustees or the society or branch by any other person, but the next of kin or lawful representative of the deceased member shall have remedy for recovery of the money, so paid as aforesaid, against the person who has received that money.

(2) Where the society or branch has paid money to a nominee in ignorance of a marriage subsequent to the nomination, the receipt of the nominee shall be a valid discharge to the society or branch.

61. Certificates of death

(1) A registered society or branch shall not pay any sum of money upon the death of a member or other person whose death is or ought to be entered in any register of deaths, except upon the production of a certificate of that death under the hand of the registrar of deaths or other person having care of the register of deaths in which that death is or ought to be entered.

(2) This section shall not apply to deaths at sea, nor to a death by

---

[21] S-s. (3)&(4), r. Friendly Societies (Amendment) Act, 1953 (No. 28), s. 4(b).

[22] Now substituted by S. I. 74/1988

[23] Deletion: Friendly Societies (Amendment) Act, 1953 (No. 28), s. 5.

colliery explosion or other accident where the body cannot be found, nor to any death certified by a coroner or procurator fiscal to be the subject of a pending inquest or inquiry.

Payments on Death of Children

62. Limitation of amount payable[7]

A society or branch, whether registered or unregistered, shall not insure or pay on the death of a child under five years of age any sum of money which, added to any amount payable on the death of that child by any other society or branch, exceeds £1,000[24], or on the death of a child under ten years of age any sum of money which, added to any amount payable on the death of that child by any other society or branch, exceeds £1,000[24].

63. Person to whom payment may be made

A society or branch, whether registered or unregistered, shall not pay any sum on the death of a child under ten years of age except to the parent of the child, or to the personal representative of the parent, and upon the production by the parent or his personal representative of a certificate of death issued by the registrar of deaths, or other person having the care of the register of deaths, containing the particulars mentioned in this Act.

64. Particulars of certificates

(1) Where application is made for a certificate of the death of a child for the purpose of obtaining a sum of money from a society or branch, the name of the society or branch, and the sum sought to be obtained therefrom shall be stated to the registrar of deaths.

(2) The registrar of deaths shall write on or at the foot of the certificate the words "to be produced to the   society or branch (naming the same) said to be liable for payment of the sum of   £. (stating the same)."

(3) All certificates of the same death shall be numbered in consecutive order.

65. Cases in which certificates may be given[7]

(1) A registrar of deaths shall not give any one or more certificates of death for the payment in the whole of any sum of money exceeding £1,000[24] on the death of a child under five years, or for the payment in the whole of a sum exceeding £1,000[24] on the death of a child under ten years.

(2) A registrar of deaths shall not grant any such certificate unless

---

[24] As now amended, S. I. 74/1988

the cause of death has been previously entered in the register of deaths on the certificate of a coroner or of a registered medical practitioner who attended the deceased child during its last illness, or except upon the production of a certificate of the probable cause of death under the hand of a registered medical practitioner, or of other satisfactory evidence thereof.

66. Inquiries by societies

A society or branch, whether registered or unregistered, to which is produced a certificate of the death of a child which does not purport to be the first shall, before paying any money thereon, inquire whether any and what sums of money have been paid on the same death by any other society or branch.

67. Saving as to insurable interests

Nothing in this Act respecting payments on the death of children shall apply to insurances on the lives of children of any age, where the person insuring has an interest in the life of the person insured.

Disputes

68. Decision of disputes

(1) Every dispute between -
  (a) a member or person claiming through a member or under the rules of a registered society or branch, and the society or branch or an officer thereof; or
  (b) any person aggrieved who has ..[25] . ceased to be a member of a registered society or branch, or any person claiming through such person aggrieved, and the society or branch, or an officer thereof; or
  (c) any registered branch of any society or branch and the society or branch of which it is a branch; or
  (d) an officer of any such registered branch and the society or branch of which that registered branch is a branch; or
  (e) any two or more registered branches of any society or branch, or any officers thereof respectively,
shall be decided in manner directed by the rules of the society or branch, and the decision so given shall be binding and conclusive on all parties without appeal, and shall not be removable into any court of law or restrainable by injunction; and application for the enforcement thereof may be made to the county court.

(2) The parties to a dispute in a registered society or branch may, by consent (unless the rules of the society or branch expressly forbid it), refer the dispute to the chief registrar, or in Scotland or Ireland to

---

[25] Words deleted: Friendly Societies Act, 1908, 8 Edw. 7 c. 32, s. 6

the assistant registrar.

(3) The chief or other registrar to whom a dispute is referred shall, with the consent of the Treasury, either by himself or by any other registrar, hear and determine the dispute, and shall have power to order the expenses of determining the dispute to be paid either out of the funds of the society or branch, or by such parties to the dispute as he may think fit, and his determination and order shall have the same effect and be enforceable in like manner as a decision made in the manner directed by the rules of the society or branch.

(4) The chief or other registrar to whom a dispute is referred may administer oaths, and may require the attendance of all parties concerned, and of witnesses, and the production of all books and documents relating to the matter in question.

(5) Where the rules of a registered society or branch direct that disputes shall be referred to justices, the dispute shall be determined by a court of summary jurisdiction, or, if the parties thereto consent, by the county court.

(6) Where the rules contain no direction as to disputes, or where no decision is made on a dispute within forty days after application to the society or branch for a reference under its rules, the member or person aggrieved may apply either to the county court, or to a court of summary jurisdiction, and the court to which application is so made may hear and determine the matter in dispute; but in the case of a society with branches the said forty days shall not begin to run until application has been made in succession to all the bodies entitled to determine the dispute under the rules of the society or branch, so however that no rules shall require a greater delay than three months between each successive determination.

(7) Notwithstanding anything contained in the Arbitration Act, 1889, or in any other Act, the court and the chief or other registrar or any arbitrator or umpire to whom a dispute is referred under the rules of a registered society or branch shall not be compelled to state a special case on any question of law arising in the case but the court, or chief or other registrar, may, at the request of either party, state a case for the opinion in England or Ireland of the Supreme Court, and in Scotland of either division of the Inner House of the Court of Session, on any question of law, and may also grant to either party such discovery as to documents and otherwise, or such inspection of documents, and in Scotland may grant warrant for the recovery of documents and examination of havers, as might be granted by any court of law or equity, and the discovery shall be made on behalf of the society or branch by such officer thereof as the court or registrar may determine.

(8)[26] In this section the expression 'dispute' includes any dispute

---

[26] Inserted by Friendly Societies Act, 1908, 8 Edw. 7 c. 32, s. 6

arising on the question whether a member or person aggrieved is entitled to be or to continue to be a member or to be reinstated as a member, but, save as aforesaid, in the case of a person who has ceased to be a member, does not include any dispute other than a dispute on a question between him and the society or branch or an officer thereof which arose whilst he was a member, or arises out of his previous relation as a member to that society or branch.

Change of Name, Amalgamation, and Conversion of Societies

69. Power to change name

(1) A registered society may, by special resolution, with the approval in writing of the chief registrar, or in the case of societies registered and doing business exclusively in Scotland or Ireland the assistant registrar for Scotland or Ireland respectively, change its name, and shall not change its name in any other manner.

(2) Any such change of name shall not affect any right or obligation of the society, or of any member thereof, and any pending legal proceedings may be continued by or against the trustees of the society, or any other officer who may sue or be sued on behalf of the society, notwithstanding its new name.

70. Amalgamation and transfer of engagements

(1) Any two or more registered societies may, by special resolution of both or all such societies, become amalgamated together as one society, with or without any dissolution or division of the funds of those societies or either of them.

(2) A registered society may, by special resolution, transfer its engagements to any other registered society which may undertake to fulfil the engagements of that society.

(3) A special resolution by a registered friendly society for an amalgamation or transfer of engagements under this Act shall not be valid without -

(a) the assent thereto of five-sixths in value of the members, given either at the meetings at which the resolution is, according to the provisions of this Act, passed and confirmed, or at one of them, or, if the members were not present thereat, in writing; and

(b) the written consent of every person receiving or entitled to any relief, annuity, or other benefit from the funds of the society, unless the claim of that person is first duly satisfied, or adequate provision is made for satisfying that claim.

(4) Provided that on application of the trustees or committee of a registered friendly society desiring to amalgamate or transfer its engagements, and upon notice of that application being published in the Gazette, the chief registrar, after hearing the trustees or committee

and any other persons whom he considers entitled to be heard upon the application, may, with the consent of the Treasury, order that any of the assents, consents, and conditions required by this Act, or by any regulations made under this Act, be dispensed with, and may confirm the amalgamation or transfer.

(5) A registered society consisting wholly of members under twenty-one years of age, and a registered society or branch or branches of a society having members above twenty-one years of age, may, by resolutions registered in the manner required for the registration of an amendment of rules, become amalgamated together as one society or branch, or provide for distributing among several branches the members of a society consisting wholly of members under twenty-one years of age, and the other provisions of this section shall not apply to that amalgamation.

(6) The value of members shall be ascertained by giving one vote to every member, and an additional vote for every five years that he has been a member, but to no one member more than five votes in the whole.

(7) If any member of a friendly society which has amalgamated or transferred its engagements, or if any person claiming any relief, annuity, or other benefit, from the funds thereof, is dissatisfied with the provision made for satisfying his claim, that member or person may apply to the county court of the district within which the chief or any other place of business of the society is situate for relief or other order, and that court shall have the same powers in the matter as in regard to the settlement of disputes under this Act.

71. Conversion of society into company

(1) A registered society may, by special resolution, determine to convert itself into a company under the Companies Acts, 1862 to 1890[27], or to amalgamate with or transfer its engagements to any such company.

(2) If a special resolution for converting a society into a company contains the particulars required by the Companies Acts, 1862 to 1890, to be contained in the memorandum of association of a company, and a copy thereof has been registered at the central office, a copy of that resolution under the seal or stamp of the central office shall have the same effect as a memorandum of association duly signed and attested under the said Acts.

(3) If a society is registered as, or amalgamates with, or transfers all its engagements to, a company, the registry of the society under this Act shall thereupon become void, and shall be cancelled by the chief registrar or by the assistant registrar for Scotland or Ireland under his

---

[27] To be construed as reference to Companies Acts, 1963 to 1990: see Interpretation Act, 1889, 52 & 53 Vict. c. 63, s. 38(1)

direction; but the registration of a society as a company shall not affect any right or claim subsisting against that society, or any penalty incurred by that society; and for the purpose of enforcing any such right, claim, or penalty, the society may be sued and proceeded against in the same manner as if it had not become registered as a company; and every such right or claim, or the liability to any such penalty, shall have priority, as against the property of the company, over all other rights or claims against or liabilities of the company.

72. Saving for right of creditors

An amalgamation or transfer of engagements in pursuance of this Act shall not prejudice any right of a creditor of either or any society party thereto.

73. Conversion of society into branch

(1) A registered society may, by a resolution passed by a majority of the members or delegates present and entitled to vote at any general meeting, of which notice specifying the intention to propose any such resolution has been duly given according to the rules, determine to become a branch of any other registered society, and also, if thought fit, of any registered branch thereof.

(2) If the rules of the society do not comply with all the provisions of this Act and of the Treasury regulations in respect of the registry of branches, the meeting at which any such resolution is passed may amend the rules so as to bring the rules into compliance with this Act and with the Treasury regulations.

(3) A copy of the rules of the society marked to show the amendments, if any, made at the meeting, and two copies of the resolution and of such amendment of rules, if any, as aforesaid, each signed by the chairman of the meeting and by the secretary of the society so determining to become a branch of another society, and countersigned by the secretary of that other society, shall be sent to the registrar.

(4) If the registrar finds that the rules, with or without such amendment as aforesaid, comply with the provisions of this Act and of the Treasury regulations, he shall cancel the registry of the first-mentioned society and register it as a branch of that other society, and also, if so specified in the resolution before mentioned, of any branch of that other society, without further request or notice, and shall register such amendment of rules without further application or evidence, and until such registry as aforesaid the resolution shall not take effect.

(5) An advertisement of any cancelling of registry under this section shall not be requisite.

(6) The rules of a society which becomes a branch under this section shall, so far as they are not contrary to any express provision of this Act or of the Treasury regulations, and subject to any such amendment thereof as aforesaid, continue in force as the rules of the branch until amended.

(7) This section shall apply only to societies registered before the first day of January one thousand eight hundred and seventy-six.

74. Meaning of special resolution

For the purposed of this Act a special resolution shall mean a resolution which is -

(a) passed by a majority of not less than three fourths of such members of a registered society, entitled under the rules to vote as may be present in person or by proxy (where the rules allow proxies) at any general meeting of which notice specifying the intention to propose that resolution has been duly given according to the rules; and

(b) confirmed by a majority of such members entitled under the rules to vote as may be present in person or by proxy (where the rules allow proxies), at a subsequent general meeting of which notice has been duly given, held not less than fourteen days nor more than one month from the day of the meeting at which such resolution was first passed.

At any meeting mentioned in this section a declaration by the chairman that the resolution has been carried shall be conclusive evidence of the fact.

75.[28] Registration of special resolutions

A copy of every special resolution for any of the purposes mentioned in this Act, signed by the chairman of the meeting and countersigned by the secretary, shall be sent to the central office and registered there, and until that copy is so registered the special resolution shall not take effect.

Inspection : Cancelling and Suspension of Registry: Dissolution

76. Inspectors and special meetings

(1) Upon the application -

(a) of one fifth of the whole number of members of a registered society; or

(b) in the case of a registered society of one thousand members and not exceeding ten thousand, of one hundred members; or

---

[28] See Mergers, Take-overs and Monopolies (Control) Act, 1978 (No. 17), s. 14, 4(a)

(c) in the case of a registered society of more than ten thousand members, of five hundred members,

the chief registrar, or in cases of societies registered and doing business exclusively in Scotland or in Ireland the assistant registrars for Scotland and Ireland respectively, but with the consent of the Treasury in every case, may -

    (a) appoint an inspector or inspectors to examine into and report on the affairs of the society; or

    (b) call a special meeting of the society.

(2) The application under this section shall be supported by such evidence, for the purpose of showing that the applicants have good reason for requiring an inspection to be made or meeting to be called, and that they are not actuated by malicious motives in their application, and such notice thereof shall be given to the society, as the chief registrar directs.

(3) The chief or assistant registrar may, if he thinks fit, require the applicants to give security for the costs of the proposed inspection or meeting, before appointing any inspector or calling the meeting.

(4) All expenses of and incidental [or preliminary[29]] to any such inspection or meeting shall be defrayed by the members applying therefor or out of the funds of the society, or by the members or officers, or former members or officers, of the society in such proportions as the chief or assistant registrar directs.

(5) An inspector appointed under this section may require the production of all or any of the books and documents of the society, and may examine on oath its officers, members, agents, and servants in relation to its business, and may administer such oath accordingly.

(6) The chief or assistant registrar may direct at what time and place a special meeting under this section is to be held and what matters are to be discussed and determined at that meeting, and the meetings shall have all the powers of a meeting called according to the rules of the society, and shall in all cases have power to appoint its own chairman, any rule of the society to the contrary notwithstanding.

(7) This section shall not apply to a society with branches, except with the consent of the central body of that society.

77. Cancelling and suspension of registry

(1) The chief registrar, or, in the case of a society registered and doing business in Scotland or Ireland exclusively, the assistant registrar for Scotland or Ireland, may -

    (a) if he thinks fit, at the request of a society, to be evidenced in such manner as he may direct: or

---

[29] Inserted by Friendly Societies Act, 1908, 8 Edw. 7 c. 32, s. 7

(b) with the approval of the Minister[30], on proof to his satisfaction that an acknowledgment of registry has been obtained by fraud or mistake, or that a society exists for an illegal purpose, or has wilfully and after notice from a registrar whom it may concern violated any of the provisions of this Act, or regulations under the Friendly Societies Act, 1896 to 1977[30], or has ceased to exist,

by writing under his hand cancel the registry of a society.

(2) The chief or assistant registrar, in any case in which he might, with the approval of the Treasury, cancel the registry of a society, may, by writing under his hand, suspend the registry for any term not exceeding three months, and may, with the approval of the Treasury, renew the suspension for the like period.

(3) Unless the chief or assistant registrar has given to a registered society not less than two months previous notice in writing, specifying briefly the ground of any proposed cancelling or suspension, the registry of the society shall not be cancelled (except at its request) or suspended.

(4) where the registry of a society has been cancelled or suspended, notice thereof shall forthwith be advertised.

(5) Where the registry of a society has been suspended or cancelled, the society shall from the time of the suspension or cancelling (but if suspended, only while the suspension lasts, and subject also to the right of appeal given by this section) absolutely cease to enjoy as such the privileges of a registered society, but without prejudice to any liability actually incurred by the society, and any such liability may be enforced against the society as if the suspension or cancelling had not taken place.

(6) A society may appeal from the cancelling of its registry, or from any suspension thereof which is renewed after six months, as follows: -

(a) from the assistant registrar for Scotland or Ireland to the chief registrar, and from him to the Court of Session in Scotland or the High Court in Ireland respectively; and

(b) from the chief registrar, in cases not relating exclusively either to Scotland or to Ireland, to the High Court in England.

78. Dissolution of societies

(1) Subject to the provision of this Act as to the dissolution of societies with branches, a registered society or branch may terminate or be dissolved in any of the following ways:-

(a) upon the happening of any event declared by the rules to be the termination of the society or branch; or

(b) as respects societies or branches other than friendly societies

---

[30] Amended: Friendly Societies (Amendment) Act, 1977 (No. 17), s. 6

or branches, by the consent of three-fourths of the members, testified by their signatures to the instrument of dissolution; or

(c) as respects friendly societies or branches, by the consent of five-sixths in value of the members (including honorary members, if any), testified by their signatures to the instrument of dissolution, and also by the written consent of every person receiving or entitled to receive any relief, annuity, or other benefit from the funds of the society or branch, unless the claim of that person is first duly satisfied, or adequate provision made for satisfying that claim, and, in the case of a branch, with the consent of the central body of the society, or in accordance with the general rules of the society; or

(d) by the award of the chief registrar or assistant registrars in the cases specified in this Act.

(2) The provisions of this Act as to the method of calculating the value of members and the remedy of members and persons dissatisfied with the provisions made for satisfying their claims in the case of the amalgamation or transfer of engagements of a registered friendly society shall apply to the dissolution of a registered friendly society or branch.

79. Instrument of dissolution

When a registered society or branch is terminated by an instrument of dissolution:-

(1) The instrument shall set forth -

(a) the liabilities and assets of the society or branch in detail; and

(b) the number of members and the nature of their interest in the society or branch; and

(c) the claims of creditors (if any), and the provision to be made for their payment; and

(d) the intended appropriation or division of the funds and property of the society or branch, unless the appropriation or division is stated in the instrument of dissolution to be left to the award of the chief registrar.

(2) Alterations in the instrument of dissolution may be made with the like consents as are in this Act required for the dissolution of a society or branch, testified in the same manner.

(3) A statutory declaration shall be made by one of the trustees, or by three members and the secretary of the society or branch, that the provisions of this Act have been complied with, and shall be sent to the registrar with the instrument of dissolution.

(4) The instrument shall not in the case of a registered friendly society or branch direct or contain any provision for a division or

appropriation of the funds of the society or branch, or any part thereof, otherwise than for the purpose of carrying into effect the objects of the society or branch as declared in the rules thereof, unless the claim of every member or person claiming any relief, annuity, or other benefit from the funds thereof is first duly satisfied, or adequate provisions are made for satisfying those claims.

(5) The instrument of dissolution and all alterations therein shall be registered in manner in this Act provided for the registry of amendments of rules, and shall be binding upon all the member of the society or branch.

(6) The registrar shall cause a notice of the dissolution to be advertised at the expense of the society or branch, and, unless within three months from the date of the Gazette in which the advertisement appears, a member or other person interested in or having any claim on the funds of the society or branch commences proceedings to set aside the dissolution of the society or branch, and the dissolution is set aside accordingly, the society or branch shall be legally dissolved from the date of that advertisement, and the requisite consents to the instrument of dissolution shall be considered to have been duly obtained without proof of the signatures thereto.

80. Dissolution by award

(1) Upon the application made in writing under their hands -
    (a) of one-fifth of the whole number of members of a registered society or branch; or
    (b) in the case of a registered society or branch of one thousand members and not exceeding ten thousand, of one hundred members; or
    (c) in the case of a registered society or branch of more than ten thousand members, of five hundred members,

the chief registrar may by himself, or by any assistant registrar, or by any actuary or public auditor whom the chief registrar may appoint in writing under his hand, investigate the affairs on the society or branch, but shall give not less than one[31] months previous notice in writing to the society or branch whose affairs are to be investigated.

(2) The application shall -
    (a) state that the funds of the society or branch are insufficient to meet the existing claims thereon, or that the rates of contribution fixed in the rules of the society or branch are insufficient to cover the benefits assured; and
    (b) set forth the grounds on which the insufficiency is alleged; and
    (c) request an investigation into the affairs of the society or

---

[31] Amended by Friendly Societies Act, 1908, 8 Edw. 7 c. 32, s. 8

branch with a view to the dissolution thereof.

(3) If upon the investigation it appears that the funds of the society or branch are insufficient to meet the existing claims thereon, or that the rates of contribution fixed in the rules of the society or branch are insufficient to cover the benefits assured to be given by the society or branch, the chief registrar may, if he considers it expedient so to do, award that the society or branch be dissolved, and its affairs wound up, and shall direct in what manner the assets of the society or branch shall be divided or appropriated: Provided always, that the chief registrar may suspend his award for such period as he may deem necessary to enable the society or branch to make such alterations and adjustment of contributions and benefits as will in his judgment prevent the necessity of the award of dissolution being made.

(4) A registrar proceeding under this section shall have all the same powers and authorities, enforceable by the same penalties, as in the case of a dispute referred to him under this Act.

(5) Every award under this section, whether for dissolution or distribution of funds, shall be final and conclusive on the society or branch in respect of which the award is made, and on all members of the society or branch and on all other persons having any claim on the funds of the society or branch, without appeal, and shall be enforced in the same manner as a decision on a dispute under this Act.

(6) The expenses of every investigation and award, and of publishing every notice of dissolution, shall be paid out of the funds of the society or branch before any other appropriation thereof is made.

(7) Notice of every award for dissolution shall, within twenty-one days after the award has been made, be advertised by the central office and unless, within three months from the date on which that advertisement appears, a member or person interested in or having any claim on the funds of the society or branch commences proceedings to set aside the dissolution of the society or branch consequent upon such award, and the dissolution is set aside accordingly, the society or branch shall be legally dissolved from the date of the advertisement, and the requisite consents to the application to the registrar shall be considered to have been duly obtained without proof of the signatures thereto.

81. Advertisement of notices

A notice required by this Act to be advertised shall be published in the Gazette and in some newspaper in general circulation in the neighbourhood of the registered office of the society or branch.

82. Dissolution of societies having branches

The provisions of this Act respecting the dissolution of societies shall not apply to any society having branches except with the consent of the central body of the society.

83. Notice of proceedings or order to set aside dissolution

(1) Where a person takes any proceeding to set aside the dissolution of a society or branch, he shall give notice of the proceeding to the central office not less than seven days before the proceeding is commenced.

(2) Where an order is made setting aside the dissolution of a society or branch, the society or branch shall give notice of the order to the central office within seven days after the order has been made.

Offences, Penalties, and Legal Proceedings.

84. Offences

It shall be an offence under this Act if -

(a) a registered society or branch or an officer or member thereof fails to give any notice, send any return or document, do or allow to be done any thing which the society, branch officer, or person is by this Act, or regulations under the Friendly Societies Act, 1896 to 1977[32], required to give, send, do, or allow to be done: or

(b) a registered society or branch or an officer or member thereof wilfully neglects or refuses to do any act or to furnish any information required for the purposes of this Act, by the chief or other registrar or by any other person authorised under this Act, or does anything forbidden by this Act, or regulations under the Friendly Societies Act, 1896 to 1977[32]: or

(c) a registered society or branch or an officer or member thereof makes a return or wilfully furnishes information in any respect false or insufficient: or

(d) an officer or member of a body which, having been a branch of a society, has wholly seceded or been expelled from that society, thereafter uses the name of that society or any name implying that the body is a branch of that society or the number by which that body was designated as such branch: or

(e) where a dispute is referred under this Act to the chief or other registrar, a person refuses to attend or to produce any documents, or to give evidence before the chief or other registrar: or

(f) a society or branch whether registered or unregistered pays

---

[32] Inserted by Friendly Societies (Amendment) Act, 1977 (No. 17), s. 7

money on the death of a child under ten years of age otherwise than is provided by his Act: or

(g) a parent or personal representative of a parent claiming money on the death of a child produces a certificate of the death other than is in this Act provided to the society or branch from which the money is claimed, or produces a false certificate, or one fraudulently obtained, or in any way attempts to defeat the provisions of this Act with respect to payments upon the death of children.

85. Offences by societies to be also offences by officers, &c.

Where a registered society or branch is guilty of an offence under this Act every officer of the society or branch bound by the rules thereof to fulfil any duty whereof the offence is a breach, or if there is no such officer, then every member of the committee, unless that member is proved to have been ignorant of or to have attempted to prevent the commission of the offence, shall be liable to the same penalty as if he had committed the offence.

86. Continuing offences

Every default under this Act constituting an offence, if continued, shall constitute a new offence in every week during which the default continues.

87. Punishment of fraud, false declarations and misappropriations

(1) If any person, with intent to mislead or defraud, gives to any other person a copy of any rules, laws, regulations, other documents, other than the rules of a registered society or branch, on the pretence that they are the existing rules of that society or branch, or that there are no other rules of the society or branch or gives to any person a copy of any rules on the pretence that those rules are the rules of a registered society or branch when the society or branch is not registered, the person so offending shall be guilty of a misdemeanor.

(2) If any person knowingly makes a false or fraudulent statement in any statutory declaration required by this Act, he shall be guilty of a misdemeanor.

(3) If any person obtains possession by false representation or imposition of any property of a registered society or branch, or withholds or misapplies any such property in his possession, or wilfully applies any part thereof to purposes other than those expressed or directed in the rules of the society or branch and authorised by this Act, he shall, on such complaint as is in this section mentioned, be liable on summary conviction to a fine not exceeding two hundred and fifty pounds[33], and costs, and to be order to deliver

[33] Amended by Friendly Societies (Amendment) Act, 1977 (No. 17), s. 9(1)

up all such property, or to repay all sums of money applied improperly, and in default of such delivery or repayment, or of the payment of such fine and costs as aforesaid, to be imprisoned, with or without hard labour, for any time not exceeding three months.

[34] Provided that where on such a complaint against a person of witholding or misapplying property, or applying it for unauthorised purposes, it is not proved that that person acted with any fraudulent intent, he may be ordered to deliver up all such property or to repay any sum of money applied improperly, with costs, but shall not be liable to conviction, any any such order shall be enforceable as an order for the payment of a civil debt recoverable summarily before a court of summary jurisdiction.

(4) Complaint under this section may be made -
  (a) in the case of a registered society, by the society or any member authorised by the society, or the trustees or committee of the society; or
  (b) in the case of a registered branch, by
    (i) the branch or any member authorised by the branch or the trustees or committee thereof; or
    (ii) the central body of the society of which the branch forms part; or
    (iii) any member of the society or branch authorised by the central body; or
  (c) in any case, by the chief registrar or any assistant registrar by his authority, or by any member of the society or branch authorised by the central office.

(5) Nothing in this Act shall prevent any such person from being proceeded against by way of indictment, if not previously convicted of the same offence under the provisions of this Act.

88. Fine for falsification

If any person wilfully makes, orders, or allows to be made, any entry, erasure in, or omission from a balance sheet of a registered society or branch, or a return or document required to be sent, produced, or delivered for the purposes of this Act, with intent to falsify the same, or to evade any of the provisions of this Act, he shall be liable to a fine not exceeding five hundred[35] pounds.

89. Fine for ordinary offences

A society or branch, and an officer or member of a society or branch, or other person guilty of an offence under this Act for which a fine is not expressly provided shall be liable to a fine of not more than one hundred[25] pounds.

---

[34] Inserted by Friendly Societies Act, 1908, 8 Edw. 7 c. 32, s. 9

[35] Amended: Friendly Societies (Amendment) Act, 1977 (No. 17), s. 9(2) & (3)

90. Special offences in the case of friendly societies

If an officer or person aids or abets in the amalgamation or transfer of engagements or in the dissolution of a friendly society otherwise than as in this Act provided he shall be liable on summary conviction to the fine imposed by this Act for offences thereunder, or to be imprisoned with hard labour for a term not exceeding three months.

91. Recovery of fines

(1) A fine imposed by this Act, or by any regulations thereunder, or by the rules of a registered society or branch, shall be recoverable in a court of summary jurisdiction.

(2) Any such fine shall be recoverable at the suit of the chief registrar or of any assistant registrar, or of any person aggrieved.

(3)[36] Any costs or expenses ordered or directed by the chief or other registrar to be paid by any person under this Act shall be recoverable summarily before a court of summary jurisdiction as a civil debt.

92. Jurisdiction of court of summary jurisdiction

In England and Ireland all offences and fines under this Act may be prosecuted and recovered in the manner directed by the Summary Jurisdiction Acts either -

(a) at the place where the offence was committed; or
(b) as respects a prosecution against a registered society or branch or an officer thereof, at the place where the registered office of the society or branch is situated; or
(c) as respects a prosecution against a person other than a registered society or branch or an officer thereof, at the place where the person is resident at the time of the institution of the prosecution.

93. Appeals

(1) In England or Ireland any person may appeal to quarter sessions from any order or conviction made by a court of summary jurisdiction under this Act.

(2) In Scotland any person may appeal from any order or conviction under this Act in accordance with the provisions of the Summary Jurisdiction (Scotland) Acts.

94. Legal proceedings

(1) The trustees of a registered society or branch, or any other officers authorised by the rules thereof, may bring or defend, or cause to be brought or defended, any action or other legal

---

[36] Inserted by Friendly Societies Act, 1908, 8 Edw. 7 c. 32, s. 10

proceeding in any court whatsoever, touching or concerning any property, right, or claim of the society or branch, and may sue and be sued in their proper names, without other description than the title of their office.

(2) In legal proceedings brought under this Act by a member, or person claiming through a member, a registered society or branch may also be sued in the name, as defendant, of any officer or person who receives contributions or issues policies on behalf of the society or branch within the jurisdiction of the court in which the legal proceeding is brought, with the addition of the words "on behalf of the society or branch" (naming the same).

(3) A legal proceeding shall not abate or be discontinued by the death, resignation, or removal from office of any officer, or by any act of any such officer after the commencement of the proceedings.

(4) The summons, writ, process, or other proceeding, to be issued to or against the officer or other person sued on behalf of a registered society or branch, shall be sufficiently served by personally serving that officer or other person or by leaving a true copy thereof at the registered office of the society or branch, or at any place of business of the society or branch within the jurisdiction of the court in which the proceeding is brought, or, if that office or place of business in closed, by posting the copy on the outer door of that office or place of business.

(5) In all cases where the said summons, writ, process, or other proceeding is not served by means of such personal service or by leaving a true copy thereof at the registered office of the society or branch as aforesaid, a copy thereof shall be sent in a registered letter addressed to the committee at the registered office of the society or branch, and posted at least six days before any further step is taken on the proceeding.

(6)[37] Where proceedings are taken against a society or branch for the recovery of any fine under this Act the summons or other process shall be sufficiently served by leaving a true copy thereof at the registered office of the society or branch, or at any place of business of the society or branch, within the jurisdiction of the court in which the proceeding is brought, or, if that office or place or business is closed, by posting the copy on the outer door of that office or place of business :

(7)[37] Where the person against whom the proceedings are to be taken is himself a trustee of a society or branch the proceedings may be brought by the other trustees or trustee of the society or branch

---

[37] Inserted by Friendly Societies Act, 1908, 8 Edw. 7 c. 32, s. 11

95. Remuneration of county court officers
The registrars and high bailiffs of the county courts shall be remunerated for the duties to be preformed by them under this Act in such manner as the Treasury, with the consent of the Lord Chancellor, may direct.

96. Fees[38]
(1) The Treasury may determine a scale of fees to be paid for matters to be transacted or for the inspection of documents under this Act.

(2) A fee shall not be payable on the registry of any friendly, benevolent, or cattle insurance society, or working-men's club, or of any amendment of the rules thereof.

(3) All fees which may be received by any registrar under of by virtue of this Act shall be paid into the Exchequer.

97. Fees payable to registrar of births and deaths[39]
(1) For the purpose of this Act a certificate of the birth or death of any member of or person insured or to be insured with a registered friendly society or branch shall, on application being made as in this Act provided, be given under his hand by the registrar of births or deaths for a sum not exceeding one shilling, in place of all fees or payments otherwise payable in respect thereof.

(2) Whenever application is made at one time to any such registrar for more certificates than one of the same birth or death for the purposes of and in the manner prescribed by this Act, the sum charged for every such certificate other than the first shall not exceed sixpence.

(3) Whenever the registrar is required by the person applying for any certificate of birth or death to fill up the form of application, he may demand a sum not exceeding threepence for so doing.

(4) For the purposes of this section the expression "registrar of births or deaths" shall include any person having the care of the register of births or deaths in which the birth or death is entered.

98. Forms
(1) The forms to be used for registry shall be those contained in Part I. of the Second Schedule to this Act or such other forms as are prescribed by Treasury regulations.

(2) The acknowledgment of registry of a branch and of any amendment of the rules of a branch shall be in the forms provided in

---

[38] S.I. 290/1983

[39] Altered; S. I. 46/1982, 148/1983, 359/1984

Friendly Societies Act, 1896

Part II. of the same schedule.

(3) Every annual or other return, abstract of valuation, and other document required for the purposes of this Act, shall be made in such form and shall contain such particulars as the chief registrar prescribes.

(4) A receipt under this Act endorsed upon or annexed to a mortgage or other assurance shall be in the form set forth in Part III. of the same schedule, or in any form specified in the rules of the society or branch or any schedule thereto, and a bond to be given by an officer in receipt or charge of money shall be in one of the forms set forth in the said part.

(5) Applications for certificates of birth and deaths under this Act shall be in such form and under such regulations as may be approved of by the registrar-general of births, deaths, and marriages for England, Scotland and Ireland respectively.

99. Regulations for carrying out Act[40]

(1) The Treasury may make regulations respecting registry and procedure under this Act, and the seal to be used for registry, and the duties and functions of the registrar, and the inspection of documents kept by the registrar under this Act, and generally for carrying this Act into effect.

(2) All such regulations shall forthwith be laid before both Houses of Parliament.

100. Evidence of documents

Every document bearing the seal or stamp of the central office shall be received in evidence without further proof; and every document purporting to be signed by the chief or any assistant registrar, or any inspector, or public auditor or valuer under this Act, shall, in the absence of any evidence to the contrary, be received in evidence without proof of the signature.

Application of Act

101. Application to existing societies

(1) This Act shall apply to societies and branches subsisting at the commencement of this Act which or the rules of which have been registered, enrolled, or certified, under any Act relating to friendly societies or cattle insurance societies, as if they had been registered under this Act, and the rules of those societies and branches shall, so far as they are not contrary to any express provision of this Act, continue in force until altered or rescinded.

(2) Where the contingent annual payments to which the members

---

[40] S. R.& O. 6/1987, as amended S.R. & O. 428/1897 and S.R. & O. 1/1903

304

or the nominees of the members of friendly societies or branches, established before the fifteenth day of August one thousand eight hundred and fifty, may become entitled exceed the limit fixed by this Act, the rules of those societies and branches shall continue to be valid, anything in this Act to the contrary notwithstanding.

102. Application to Scotland.

103. Application to the Isle of Man

104. Application to Channel Islands

105. Payment to representatives in Channel Islands and Isle of Man.

Supplemental

106. Definitions

In this Act, unless a contrary intention appears:

The expression "the registrar" shall mean for England the central office, and for Scotland or Ireland the assistant registrar for Scotland or Ireland:

The expression "land" shall include any interest in land:

The expression "property" shall extend to all property whether real or personal (including books and papers):

The expression "registered society" shall mean a society registered under this Act, and shall include societies subsisting at the commencement of this Act to which the provisions of this Act apply:

The expression "amendment of rule" shall include a new rule, and a resolution rescinding a rule:

The expression "branch" shall mean any number of the members of a society, under the control of a central body, having a separate fund, administered by themselves or by a committee or officers appointed by themselves, and bound to contribute to a fund under the control of a central body:

The expression "committee" shall mean the committee of management or other directing body of a society or branch:

The expression "persons claiming through a member" shall include the nominees of the member where nomination is allowed:

The expression "officer" shall include any trustee, treasurer, secretary, or member of the committee of management of a society or branch, or person appointed by the society or branch to sue and be sued on its behalf:

The expression "meeting" shall include (where the rules of a society or branch so allow) a meeting of delegates appointed by members:

The expression "gazette" shall mean the London Gazette for England, the Edinburgh Gazette for Scotland, and the Dublin Gazette[41] for Ireland:

The expression "Treasury regulations" shall mean any regulations made and approved by the Treasury and in force under this Act.

The expression "signed" in relation to a body corporate shall mean sealed.[42]

107. Repealed by Statute Law Revision Act, 1908[43]

108. Commencement and extent of Act
This Act shall ...[44] extend to the whole of the British Islands.

109. Short title
This Act may be cited as the Friendly Societies Act, 1896.

---

[41] To be construed as reference to *Iris Oifigiúil*: see Adaptation of Enactments Act, 1922 (No. 2), s. 4

[42] Inserted by Statute Law Revision Act, 1908, 8 Edw. 7. c. 49

[43] 8 Edw. 7. c. 49

[44] Deletion by Statute Law Revision Act, 1908, 8 Edw. 7. c. 49

The First Schedule

Section 9(3)

Matters to be provided for by the Rules of Society Registered under
this Act

(1) The Name and place of office of the society.

(2) The whole of the objects for which the society is to be established, the purposes for which the funds thereof shall be applicable, the terms of admission of members, the conditions under which any member may become entitled to any benefit assured thereby, and the fines and forfeitures to be imposed on any member, and the consequences of nonpayment of any subscription or fine.

(3) The mode of holding meetings and right of voting, and the manner of making, altering, or rescinding rules.

(4) The appointment and removal of a committee of management (by whatever name), of a treasurer and other officers, and of trustees, and in the case of a society with branches, the composition and powers of the central body, and the conditions under which a branch may secede from the society.

(5) The investment of the funds, the keeping of the accounts, and the audit of the same once a year at least.

(6) Annual returns to the registrar of the receipts, funds, effects, and expenditure, and numbers of members, of the society.

(7) The inspection of the books of the society by every person having an interest in the funds of the society.

(8) The manner in which disputes shall be settled.

(9) In case of dividing societies, a provision for meeting all claims upon the society existing at the time of division before any such division takes place.

And also in the case of friendly and cattle insurance societies:-

(10) The keeping separate accounts of all moneys received or paid on account of every particular fund or benefit assured for which a separate table of contributions payable shall have been adopted, and the keeping separate account of the expenses of management, and of all contributions on account thereof.

(11) (Except as to cattle insurance societies) a valuation once at least in every five years of the assets and liabilities of the society, including the estimated risks and contributions.

(12) The voluntary dissolution of the society by consent in a friendly society of not less than five sixths in value of the members, and of every person for the time being entitled to any benefit from the funds of the society, unless his claim be first satisfied or adequately provided for; and in a cattle insurance society by consent

Friendly Societies Act, 1896

of three fourths in number of the members.

(13) The right of one fifth of the total number of members or of one hundred members in the case of a society of one thousand members and not exceeding ten thousand, or of five hundred members in the case of a society of more than ten thousand members, to apply to the chief registrar, or in case of societies registered and doing business exclusively in Scotland or Ireland to the assistant registrar for Scotland or Ireland; for an investigation of the affairs of the society, or for winding up the same.

The Second Schedule

Section 98

Forms

Part I.

Acknowledgment of Registry of Society

The   Society is registered as a (friendly society, cattle insurance society, benevolent society, working-men's club, or specially authorised society) under the Friendly Societies Act, 1896, this   day of

> (Seal or stamp of central office, or signature of Assistant Registrar for Scotland or Ireland.)

Acknowledgement of registry of amendment of rules
The foregoing amendment of the rules of the   Society is registered under the Friendly Societies Act, 1896, this   day of

> (Seal or stamp of central office, or signature of Assistant Registrar for Scotland or Ireland.)

Part II.

Acknowledgment of Registry of Branch

The   is registered as a branch of the   Society (and of the   branch of the same) under the Friendly Societies Act, 1896, this   day of

> (Seal of central office, or signature of Assistant Registrar for Scotland or Ireland.)

Friendly Societies Act, 1896

Acknowledgment of Registry of Amendment of Branch Rules

The foregoing amendment of the branch rules of the
                                        is registered under the Friendly Societies
Act, 1896, this   day of

(Seal of central office or signature of Assistant
Registrar for Scotland or Ireland.)

Part III

Form of Bond

(1) - In England or Ireland

Know all men by these presents, that we, A.B. of   , one
of the officers of the   Society (or of the   branch of the
    Society) having its registered office at   , in the
county of   , and C.D. of   (as surety on
behalf of the said A.B.), are jointly and severally held and firmly
bound to E.F. of   , G.H. of   , and
I.K. of   , the trustees of the said society (or branch), in the
sum of
    to be paid to the said E.F., G.H., and I.K., as such trustees or their
successors, trustees for the time being, or their certain attorney;   for
which payment well and truly to be made we jointly and severally
bind ourselves, and each of us by himself our and each of our heirs,
executors, and administrators, firmly by these presents. Sealed with
our seals. Dated the   day of   in the year of
our Lord

Whereas the above-bounded A.B. has been duly appointed to the
office of   of the   Society (or of the
    branch of the   Society) having its registered office
situate as aforesaid, and he, together with the above bounded C.D. as
his surety, have entered into the above-written bond, subject to the
condition herein-after contained: Now therefore the condition of the
above-written bond is such, that if the said A.B. do render a just and
true account of all moneys received and paid by him on account of
the said society (or branch), at such times as the rules thereof
appoint, and do pay over all the moneys remaining in his hands, and
assign and transfer or deliver all property (including books and
papers) belonging to the said society (or branch) in his hands or
custody to such person or persons as the said society (or branch), or

309

the trustees or committee of management thereof, shall appoint, according to the rules of the said society (or branch), together with the proper and legal receipts or vouchers for such payments then the above written bond shall be void otherwise shall remain in full force.
Sealed and delivered in the presence of (two witnesses.)

...

Form of receipt to be endorsed on mortgage or further charge.

In England or Ireland

The trustees of the   Society (or the   branch of the Society) hereby acknowledge to have received all moneys intended to be secured by the within (or above) written deed.

Signed   (Signatures of Trustees.)
Trustees.
Countersigned (Signature of Secretary.)
Secretary.

The Third Schedule

Repealed by Statute Law Revision Act, 1908, 8 Edw. 7. c. 49

The Money-lenders Act, 1900
63 & 64 Victoria, chapter 51[1]

List of Sections

An Act to amend the law with respect to persons carrying on business as money-lenders.
8th August 1900

1. Re-opening of transactions of money-lenders.

(1) Where proceedings are taken in any court by a money-lender for the recovery of any money lent after the commencement of this Act, or the enforcement of any agreement or security made or taken after the commencement of this Act, in respect of money lent either before or after the commencement of this Act, and there is evidence which satisfies the court that the interest charged in respect of the sum actually lent is excessive, or that the amounts charged for expenses, inquiries, fines, bonus, premium, renewals, or any other charges, are excessive, and that, in either case, the transaction is harsh and unconscionable[2], or is otherwise such that a court of equity would give relief, the court may re-open the transaction, and take an account between the money-lender and the person sued, and may, notwithstanding any statement or settlement of account or any

---

[1] Non applic. Postal & Telecommunications Services, Act 1983 (No. 24), s. 67

[2] The Moneylenders Act, 1933 (No. 36), at section 17(1); provides that if it is found that the interest charged exceeds the rate of thirty-nine per cent. per annum, the Court shall conclusively assume, that the interest charged is excessive and that the transaction is harsh and unconscionable.

agreement purporting to close previous dealings and create a new obligation, re-open any account already taken between them, and relieve the person sued from payment of any sum in excess of the sum adjudged by the court to be fairly due in respect of such principal, interest and charges, as the court, having regard to the risk and all the circumstances, may adjudge to be reasonable; and if any such excess has been paid, or allowed in account, by the debtor, may order the creditor to repay it; and may set aside, either wholly or in part, or revise, or alter, any security given or agreement made in respect of money lent by the money-lender, and if the money-lender has parted with the security may order him to indemnify the borrower or other person sued.

(2.) Any court in which proceedings might be taken for the recovery of money lent by a money-lender shall have and may, at the instance of the borrower or surety or other person liable, exercise the like powers as may be exercised under this section, where proceedings are taken for the recovery of money lent, and the court shall have power, notwithstanding any provision or agreement to the contrary, to entertain any application under this Act by the borrower or surety, or other person liable, notwithstanding that the time for repayment of the loan, or any instalment thereof, may not have arrived.

(3.) On any application relating to the admission or amount of a proof by a money-lender in any bankruptcy proceedings, the court may exercise the like powers as may be exercised under this section when proceedings are taken for the recovery of money.

(4.) The foregoing provisions of this section shall apply to any transaction which, whatever its form may be, is substantially one of money-lending by a money-lender.

(5.) Nothing in the foregoing provisions of this section shall affect the rights of any *bona fide* assignee or holder for value without notice.

(6.) Nothing in this section shall be construed as derogating from the existing powers or jurisdiction of any court.

(7.) In the application of this Act to Scotland this section shall be read as if the words "or is otherwise such that a court of equity would give relief" were omitted therefrom.

2 & 3. Repealed: Moneylenders Act, 1933 (No. 36), s. 24(1), sch. 2

4. Penalties for false statements and representations.

If any money-lender, or any manager, agent, or clerk of a money-lender, or if any person being a director, manager, or other officer of any corporation carrying on the business of a money-lender, by any false, misleading, or deceptive statement, representation, or promise, or by any dishonest concealment of material facts, fraudulently induces or attempts to induce any person to borrow money or to agree to the terms on which money is or is to be borrowed, he shall be guilty of a misdemeanour, and shall be liable on indictment to imprisonment, with or without hard labour, for a term not exceeding two years, or to a fine not exceeding five hundred pounds, or to both.

5. Amendment of 55 & 56 Vict. c. 4. s. 2, as to presumption of knowledge of infancy.
Where in any proceedings under section two of the Betting and Loans (Infants) Act, 1892, it is proved that the person to whom the document was sent was an infant, the person charged shall be deemed to have known that the person to whom the document was sent was an infant, unless he proves that he had reasonable ground for believing the infant to be of full age.

6. Definition of money-lender.
The expression "money-lender" in this Act shall include every person whose business is that of money-lending, or who advertises or announces himself or holds himself out in any way as carrying on that business; but shall not include-
    (a)   any pawnbroker in respect of business carried on by him in accordance with the provisions of the Acts for the time being in force in relation to pawnbrokers; or
    (b)   any registered society within the meaning of the Friendly Societies Act, 1896, or any society registered or having rules certified under sections two or four of that Act, or under the Benefit Buildings Societies Acts, 1836, or the Loan Societies Act, 1840, or under the Building Societies Acts, 1874 to 1894; or
    (c)   any body corporate, incorporated or empowered by a special Act of Parliament to lend money in accordance with such special Act; or
    (d)[3]   the holder of a licence for the time being in force granted under section 9 of the Central Bank Act, 1971, or any person *bona fide* and otherwise carrying on the business of banking, or *bona fide* carrying on the business of insurance or *bona fide* carrying on any business not having for its primary object the lending of money, in the course of which and for the purposes whereof he lends money; or
    (dd)[4]   a company to which a certificate has been given by the Minister for Finance under section 39B of the Finance Act,

[3] As now amended by Central Bank Act, 1989 (No. 16), s. 136(a)(i)

[4] Inserted by Central Bank Act, 1989 (No. 16), s. 136(a)(ii)

1980 (inserted by the Finance Act, 1987), and which has not been revoked; or

(e)[5] any class or classes of body corporate in respect of which the Minister for Industry and Commerce, by order made from time to time declares that, from such date as he may specify in such order, this Act does not apply; or

(f)[6] any class or classes of industrial and provident society in respect of which the Minister for Industry, Commerce and Energy, by order made from time to time declare that, from such date as he may specify in such order[7], this Act does not apply.

6A[8]

The date specified for the purposes of an order under section 6(e) of this Act may be a date upon which the order is made if, but only if-

(a) the Minister for Finance consents to the date being specified, and

(b) such date is not a date earlier than the 1st day of September, 1971.

7 Short title

(1)[9] This Act may be cited as the Money-lenders Act, 1900

---

[5] As now substituted by the Central Bank Act, 1989 (No. 16), s. 136 (a)(iii)

[6] Ins. Industrial and Provident Societies (Amendment) Act, 1978 (No. 23), s. 37

[7] See: S. I. 344/1983, 169/1988

[8] Inserted by Central Bank Act, 1989 (No.16), s. 136(b)

[9] S. 7(2) deleted by Statute Law Revision Act, 1908

The Limited Partnership Act, 1907
7 Edward 7, chapter 24

<u>List of Sections</u>

Limited Partnership Act, 1907

An Act to establish Limited Partnerships [1]
28th August 1907

1. Short Title

This Act may be cited for all purposes as the Limited Partnerships Act, 1907.

2. Commencement of Act

This Act shall come into operation on the first day of January one thousand nine hundred and eight.

3. Interpretation of terms

In the construction of this Act the following words and expressions shall have the meanings respectively assigned to them in this section, unless there be something in the subject or context repugnant to such construction:-

"Firm," "firm name", and "business" have the same meanings as in the Partnership Act, 1890 [2] :

"General partner" shall mean any partner who is not a limited partner as defined by this Act.

4. Definition and constitution of limited partnership

(1) From and after the commencement of this Act limited partnerships may be formed in the manner and subject to the conditions by this Act provided.

(2)[3] A limited partnership shall not consist, in the case of a partnership carrying on the business of banking, of more than ten persons, and, in the case of any other partnership, of more than twenty (a) persons, and must consist of one or more persons called general partners, who shall be liable for all debts and obligations of the firm, and one or more persons to be called limited partners, who shall at the time of entering into such partnership contribute thereto a sum or sums as capital or property valued at a stated amount, and who shall not be liable for the debts or obligations of the firm beyond the amount so contributed.

(3) A limited partnership shall not during the continuance of the partnership, either directly or indirectly, drawn out or receive back any part of his contribution, and if he does so draw out or receive back any such part shall be liable for the debts and obligations of the

---

[1] Appl. S.R. & O. 1020/1907

[2] 53 & 54 Vict. c. 39

[3] Non applic. accountants and solicitors: Companies (Amendment) Act, 1982 (No. 10), ss. 13(5), 24(3)

firm up to the amount so drawn out or received back.

(4) A body corporate may be a limited partner.

5. Registration of limited partnership required[4]

Every limited partnership must be registered as such in accordance with the provisions of this Act, or in default thereof it shall be deemed to be a general partnership, and every limited partner shall be deemed to be a general partner.

6. Modifications of general law in case of limited partnerships

(1) A limited partner shall not take part in the management of the partnership business, and shall not have power to bind the firm:

Provided that a limited partner may by himself or his agent at any time inspect the books of the firm and examine into the state and prospects of the partnership business, and may advise with the partners thereon.

If a limited partner takes part in the management of the partnership business he shall be liable for all debts and obligations of the firm incurred while he so takes part in the management as though he were a general partner,

(2) A limited partnership shall not be dissolved by the death or bankruptcy[5] of a limited partner, and the lunacy of a limited partner shall not be a ground for dissolution of the partnership by the court unless the lunatic's share cannot be otherwise ascertained and realised.

(3) In the event of the dissolution of a limited partnership its affairs shall be wound up by the general partners unless the court otherwise orders.

(4) Repealed by the Companies (Consolidation) Act, 1908[6]

(5) Subject to any agreement expressed or implied between the partners-

(a) Any difference arising as to ordinary matters connected with the partnership business may be decided by a majority of the general partners;

(b) A limited partner may, with the consent of the general partners, assign his share in the partnership, and upon such an assignment the assignee shall become a limited partner with all the rights of the assignor;

(c) The other partners shall not be entitled to dissolve the

---

[4] Requirements before formation of certain companies, see: Finance Act, 1973 (No. 19), s. 69

[5] The Bankruptcy Act, 1988 (No. 27), at ss. 30 to 37 and s. 138 makes provision for the procedure in bankruptcy in partnership cases.

[6] 8 Edw. 7 c. 69, s. 286, sch. 6 pt. 1

partnership by reason of any limited partner suffering his
share to be charged for his separate debt;
(d) A person may be introduced as a partner without the consent
of the existing limited partners;
(e) A limited partner shall not be entitled to dissolve the
partnership by notice.

7. Law as to private partnerships to apply where not excluded by this Act.

Subject to the provisions of this Act, the Partnership Act, 1890, and
the rules of equity and of common law applicable to partnerships,
except so far as they are inconsistent with the express provisions of
the last-mentioned Act, shall apply to limited partnerships.

8. Manner and particulars of registration.

The registration of a limited partnership shall be effected by
sending by post or delivering to the registrar at the register office in
that part of the United Kingdom in which the principal place of
business of the limited partnership is situated or proposed to be
situated a statement signed by the partners containing the following
particulars:-
(a) The firm name;
(b) The general nature of the business;
(c) The principal place of business;
(d) The full name of each of the partners;
(e) The term, if any, for which the partnership is entered into, and
the date of its commencement;
(f) A statement that the partnership is limited, and the description
of every limited partner as such;
(g) The sum contributed by each limited partner, and whether
paid in cash or how otherwise.

9. Registration of changes in partnerships.

(1) If during the continuance of a limited partnership any change
is made or occurs in-
(a) The firm name,
(b) The general nature of the business,
(c) The principal place of business,
(d) The partners or the name of any partner,
(e) The term or character of the partnership,
(f) The sum contributed by any limited partner,
(g) The liability of any partner by reason of his becoming a
limited instead of a general partner or a general instead of a
limited partner,
a statement, signed by the firm, specifying the nature of the change

318

shall within seven days be sent by post or delivered to the registrar at the register office in that part of the United Kingdom in which the partnership is registered.

(2) If default is made in compliance with the requirements of this section each of the general partners shall on conviction under the Summary Jurisdiction Acts be liable to a fine not exceeding one pound for each day during which the default continues.

10. Advertisement in Gazette of statement of general partner becoming a limited partner and of assignment of share of limited partner.

(1) Notice of any arrangement or transaction under which any person will cease to be a general partner in any firm, and will become a limited partner in that firm, or under which the share of a limited partner in a firm will be assigned to any person, shall be forthwith advertised in the Gazette, and until notice of the arrangement or transaction is so advertised, the arrangement or transaction shall, for the purposes of this Act, be deemed to be of no effect

(2) For the purposes of this section, the expression "the Gazette" means-

....

In the case of a limited partnership registered in Ireland, *Iris Iifigiúil* [7] .

11. Repealed by Finance Act, 1973 (No. 19), s. 96, sch. 11

12. Making false returns to be misdemeanour

Every one commits a misdemeanour, and shall be liable to imprisonment with hard labour for a term not exceeding two years, who makes, signs, sends, or delivers for the purpose of registration under this Act any false statement known by him to be false.

13. Registrar to file statement and issue certificate of registration

On receiving any statement made in pursuance of this Act the registrar shall cause the same to be filed, and he shall send by post to the firm from whom such statement shall have been received a certificate of the registration thereof.

14. Register and index to be kept.

At each of the register offices hereinafter referred to the registrar shall keep, in proper books to be provided for the purpose, a register and an index of all the limited partnerships registered as aforesaid, and of all the statements registered in relation to such partnerships.

---

[7] Construction of the Dublin Gazette, Adaptation of Enactments Act,1922 (No. 2), s. 4

15. Registrar of joint stock companies to be registrar under Act.

The registrar of joint stock companies shall be the registrar of limited partnerships, and the several offices for the registration of joint stock companies in London, Edinburgh, and Dublin shall be the offices for the registration of limited partnerships carrying on business within those parts of the United Kingdom in which they are respectively situated.

16. Inspection of statements registered.

(1) Any person may inspect the statements filed by the registrar in the register offices aforesaid, and there shall be paid for such inspection such fees as may be appointed by the Board of Trade, not exceeding one shilling for each inspection; and any person may require a certificate of the registration of any limited partnership, or a copy of or extract from any registered statement, to be certified by the registrar, and there shall be paid for such certificate of registration, certified copy, or extract such fees as the Board of Trade may appoint, not exceeding two shillings for the certificate of registration, and not exceeding sixpence for each folio of seventy-two words, or in Scotland for each sheet of two hundred words.

(2) A certificate of registration, or a copy of or extract from any statement registered under this Act, if duly certified to be a true copy under the hand of the registrar or one of the assistant registrars (whom it shall not be necessary to prove to be the registrar or assistant registrar) shall, in all legal proceedings, civil or criminal, and in all cases whatsoever be received in evidence.

17. Power to Board of Trade to make rules.[1]

The *Minister for Industry and Commerce*[9] may make rules (but as to fees with the concurrence of the *Minister for Finance*[8]) concerning any of the following matters:-

(a) The fees to be paid to the registrar under this Act, so that they do not exceed in the case of the original registration of a limited partnership the sum of two pounds, and in any other case the sum of five shillings;

(b) The duties or additional duties to be performed by the registrar for the purposes of this Act;

(c) The performance by assistant registrars and other officers of acts by this Act required to be done by the registrar;

(d) The forms to be used for the purposes of this Act;

(e) Generally the conduct and regulation of registration under this Act and any matters incidental thereto.

---

[8] Construction of the "Board of Trade" and the "Treasury": Constitution (Consequential Provisions) Act, 1937 (No. 40), s. 4(1)

The Friendly Societies Act, 1908
8 Edward 7, chapter 32

An Act to amend the Friendly Societies Act, 1896
1st August 1908

Be it enacted ...

1. Amendment of section eight of the principal Act.

2. Membership of minors under the age of one year.
(1) A person of or under one year of age may be admitted as a member of a registered society or branch, and accordingly in section thirty-six of the principal Act(which relates to the membership of minors) the words "but above one year of age" shall be repealed.

(2) Where the rules of a registered friendly society or branch, in force at the commencement of this Act, provide for the admission as members of persons from the minimum age authorised by the principal Act, the rules shall be construed as providing for the admission as members of persons from birth.

3. Amendment of section forty-one of the principal Act.

4. Amendment of section forty-four (1) of the principal Act.

5. Amendment of section fifty-six of the principal Act.

6. Amendment of section sixty-eight of the principal Act.

7. Amendment of section seventy-six (4) of the principal Act.

8. Amendment of section eighty of the principal Act.

9. Amendment of section eighty-seven (3) of the principal Act.

10. Amendment of section ninety-one of the principal Act.

11. Amendment of section ninety-four of the principal Act.

12. Amendment of section one hundred and three of the principal Act.

13. Amendment of section one hundred and six of the principal Act.

14. Short title, construction, commencement and printing.

(1) This Act may be cited as the Friendly Societies Act, 1908, and the principal Act and this Act may be cited together as the Friendly Societies Acts, 1896 and 1908.

(2) This Act shall shall come in operation on the first day of January nineteen hundred and nine.

(3) Every enactment and word which is expressed to be substituted for or added to any portion of the principal Act shall form part of that Act in the place assigned to it by this Act,

The Assurance Companies Act, 1909
9 Edward 7, chapter 49

<u>List of Sections</u>

An Act to consolidate and amend and extend to other Companies carrying on Assurance or Insurance business the Law relating to Life Assurance Companies, and for other purposes connected therewith.[1,2]
3rd December 1909

Companies to which Act applies

1. Companies to which Act applies

This Act shall apply to all persons[3] or bodies of persons, whether corporate or unincorporate, not being registered under the Acts relating to friendly societies or to trade unions (which persons and bodies of persons are hereinafter referred to as assurance companies), whether established before or after the commencement of this Act and whether established within or without the *State*[4], who carry on within the *State* assurance business of all or any of the following classes[5]:-

(a) Life assurance business; that is to say, the issue of, or the undertaking of liability under, policies of assurance upon human life, or the granting of annuities upon human life;

(b) Fire insurance business; that is to say, the issue of, or the undertaking of liability under, policies of insurance against loss by or incidental to fire;

(c) Accident insurance business; that is to say, the issue of, or the undertaking of liability under, policies of insurance upon the happening of personal accidents, whether fatal or not, disease or sickness, or any class of personal accidents, disease, or sickness;

---

[1] With membership of the European Economic Community an increasing number of E.E.C. Directives have application to Insurance. These are implemented by means of statutory instrument and include: S.I.: 115/1976, 276/1976, 401/1977, 178/1978, 382/1978, 65/1983, 57, 1984, 296/1985, 297/1985, 143/1988, 144/1988, 150/1990, 211/1990, 212/1990. The advent of the Single European Market will add to these.

[2] Rstrct., Insurance (Amendment) Act, 1938 (No. 31), ss. 3(b), 12, 19(2)(b)

[3] The Insurance (Amendment) Act, 1978 (No. 30), s. 1 provides: A person shall not be regarded as having contravened any provision of the Insurance Acts, 1909 to 1971, by reason only of the fact that the person gives, enters into or accepts a bond or a contract of suretyship or guarantee to which this Act applies.

[4] Constr. of United Kingdom from Saorstát Éireann, S. R. & O. 7/1928, par. 3

[5] Appl. with mods. Insurance Act, 1936 (No. 45), ss. 54(public liability; engineering; glass; guarantee and burglary insurance business), 104(industrial assurance business).

(d) Employers' liability insurance; that is to say, the issue of, or the undertaking of liability under, policies insuring employers against liability to pay compensation or damages to workmen in their employment;

(e) Bond investment business; that is to say, the business of issuing bonds or endowment certificates by which the company, in return for subscriptions payable at periodical intervals of two months or less contract to pay the bond-holder a sum at a future date, and not being life assurance business as hereinbefore defined;

(f) mechanically propelled vehicle insurance business, that is to say, the business of effecting contracts of insurance against loss or damage to or arising out of or in connection with the use of mechanically propelled vehicles, including third party risks,[6]

A company registered under the Companies Acts which transacts assurance business of any such class as aforesaid in any part of the world shall for the purposes of this provision be deemed to be a company transacting such business within the *State*.

General

2. Deposit[7,8]

(1) Every assurance company shall deposit and keep deposited with the Paymaster-General for and on behalf of the Supreme Court the sum of twenty-thousand pounds.

(2) The sum so deposited shall be invested by the Paymaster-General in such of the securities usually accepted by the Court for the investment of funds placed under its administration as the company may select, and the interest accruing due on any such securities shall be paid to the company.

(3) The deposit may be made by the subscribers of the memorandum of association of the company, or any of them, in the name of the proposed company, and, upon the incorporation of the company, shall be deemed to have been made by, and to be part of the assets of, the company, and the registrar shall not issue a certificate of incorporation of the company until the deposit has been made.

(4) Where a company carries on, or intends to carry on, assurance business of more than one class, a separate sum of twenty thousand pounds shall be deposited and kept deposited under this section as

---

[6] Ins. Road Traffic Act, 1961 (No. 24), s. 74(1)

[7] Rstrct. on deposits, Local Authorities (Mutual Assurance) Act, 1926 (No. 34), s. 4. Deposits rules, S.R. & O. 78/1940.

[8] Appl. Insurance Act, 1936 (No. 45), s. 22(2)

respects each class of business, and the deposit made in respect of any class of business in respect of which a separate assurance fund is required to be kept shall be deemed to form part of that fund, and all interest accruing due on any such deposit or the securities in which it is for the time being invested shall be carried by the company to that fund.

(5)[9] The Paymaster-General shall not accept a deposit except on a warrant of the Board of Trade.

(6)[9] The Board of Trade may make rules with respect to applications for warrants, the payment of deposits, and the investment thereof or dealing therewith, the deposit of stocks or other securities in lieu of money, the payment of the interest or dividends from time to time accruing due on any securities in which deposits are for the time being invested, and the withdrawal and transfer of deposits, and the rules so made shall have effect as if they were enacted in this Act, and shall be laid before Parliament as soon as may be after they are made.

(7) This section shall apply to an assurance company registered or having its head office in Ireland, subject to the following modifications:-

References to the Supreme Court shall be construed as references to the Supreme Court of Judicature in Ireland, and references to the Paymaster-General shall be construed as references to the Accountant-General of the last-mentioned Court.

3. Separation of funds

(1) In the case of an assurance company transacting other business besides that of assurance of transacting more than one class of assurance business, a separate account shall be kept of all receipts in respect of the assurance business or of each class of assurance business, and the receipts in respect of the assurance business, or, in the case of a company carrying on more than one class of assurance business, of each class of business, shall be carried to and form a separate assurance fund with an appropriate name. ....[10] ..

(2) A fund of any particular class shall be as absolutely the security of the policy holders of that class as though it belonged to a company carrying on no other business than assurance business of that class, and shall not be liable for any contracts of the company for which it would not have been liable had the business of the company been only that of assurance of that class, and shall not be applied, directly or indirectly, for any purposes other than those of the class of business to which the fund is applicable.

---

[9] Appl. Insurance Act, 1936 (No. 45), s. 23(4). Deposit rules, S.R. & O. 140/1933.

[10] Repealed by Insurance Act, 1936 (No. 45), s. 7(3)

Assurance Companies Act, 1909

4. Accounts and balance sheets.[11]

(1) Every assurance company shall, at the expiration of each financial year of the company, prepare-

(a) A revenue account for the year in the form or forms set forth in the First Schedule to this Act and applicable to the class or classes of assurance business carried on by the company;

(b) A profit and loss account in the form set forth in the Second Schedule to this Act, except where the company carries on assurance business of one class only and no other business;

(c) A balance sheet in the form set forth in the Third Schedule to this Act.

5. Actuarial report and abstract.[12]

(1) Every assurance company shall, once in every five years, or at such shorter intervals as may be prescribed by the instrument constituting the company, or by its regulations or byelaws, cause an investigation to be made into its financial condition, including a valuation of its liabilities, by an actuary, and shall cause an abstract of the report of such actuary to be made in the form or forms set forth in the Fourth Schedule to this Act and applicable to the class or classes of assurance business carried on by the company.

(2) The foregoing provisions of this section shall also apply whenever at any other time an investigation into the financial condition of an assurance company is made with a view to the distribution of profits, or the results of which are made public.

6. Statement of assurance business.[13]

Every assurance company shall prepare a statement of its assurance business at the date to which the accounts of the company are made up for the purposes of any such investigation as aforesaid in the form or forms set forth in the Fifth Schedule[14] to this Act and applicable to the class or classes of assurance business carried on by the company: Provided that, if the investigation is made annually by any company, the company may prepare such a statement at any time, so that it be made at lease once in every five years.

---

[11] Am.: Insurance Act, 1936 (No. 45), ss. 97(foreign companies), 99(syndicates) & S. I. 401/1977, reg. 4.

[12] Restricted by Insurance Act, 1936 (No. 45), s. 58

[13] Ext. Insurance Act, 1936 (No. 45), s. 102(1)

[14] Fifth Schedule amended by Insurance Act, 1936 (No. 45), s. 95

328

Assurance Companies Act, 1909

7. Deposits of accounts, &c. with Board of Trade.[15,16]

(1)[17] Every account, balance sheet, abstract, or statement hereinbefore required to be made shall be printed, and four copies thereof, one of which shall be signed by the chairman and two directors of the company and by the principal officer of the company and, if the company has a managing director, by the managing director, shall be deposited at the Board of Trade within six months after the close of the period to which the account, balance sheet, abstract, or statement relates: Provided that, if in any case it is made to appear to the Board of Trade that the circumstances are such that a longer period than six months should be allowed, the Board may extend that period by such period not exceeding three months as they think fit.

(2) The Board of Trade shall consider the accounts, balance sheets, abstracts, and statements so deposited, and if any such account, balance sheet, abstract, or statement appears to the Board to be inaccurate or incomplete in any respect, the Board shall communicate with the company with a view to the correction of any such inaccuracies and the supply of deficiencies.

(3) There shall be deposited with every revenue account and balance sheet of a company any report on the affairs of the company submitted to the shareholders or policy holders of the company in respect of the financial year to which the account and balance sheet relates.

(4) Where an assurance company registered under the Companies Acts in any year deposits its accounts and balance sheet in accordance with the provisions of this section, the company may, at the same time, send to the registrar a copy of such accounts and balance sheet; and, where such copy is so sent, it shall not be necessary for the company to send to the registrar a statement in the form of a balance sheet as required by subsection (3) of section twenty-six of the Companies (Consolidation) Act, 1908[18] , and the copy of the accounts and balance sheet so sent shall be dealt with in all respects as if it were a statement sent in accordance with that subsection.

8. Right of shareholders, &c. to copies of accounts, &c.

A printed copy of the last-deposited accounts, balance sheet, abstract or statement, shall on the application of any shareholder or

---

[15] Am. Insurance Act, 1936 (No. 45), ss.100, 101

[16] Appl. Insurance Act, 1936 (No. 45), s.102(2)

[17] Appl. Insurance Act, 1936 (No. 45), s. 103(2)

[18] To be construed as Companies Acts, 1963 to 1990, see Interpretation Act, 1889, 52 & 53 Vict. c. 63, s. 38(1)

policy holder of the company be forwarded to him by the company by post or otherwise.

9. Audit of accounts.

Where the accounts of an assurance company are not subject to audit in accordance with the provisions of the Companies (Consolidation) Act, 1908[18], or the Companies Clauses Consolidation Act, 1845, relating to audit, the accounts of the company shall be audited annually in such manner as the Board of Trade may prescribe, and the regulations made for the purpose may apply to any such company the provisions of the Companies (Consolidation) Act 1908, relating to audit, subject to such adaptations and modifications as may appear necessary or expedient.

10. List of Shareholders

Every assurance company which is not registered under the Companies Acts, or which has not incorporated in its deed of settlement section ten of the Companies Clauses Consolidation Act, 1845, shall keep a "Shareholders Address Book," in accordance with the provisions of that section, and shall, on the application of any shareholder or policy holder of the company, furnish to him a copy of such book, on payment of a sum not exceeding sixpence for every hundred works required to be copied.

11. Deed of Settlement.

Every assurance company which is not registered under the Companies Acts shall cause a sufficient number of copies of its deed of settlement or other instrument constituting the company to be printed, and shall, on the application of any shareholder or policy holder of the company, furnish to him a copy of such deed of settlement or other instrument on payment of a sum not exceeding one shilling.

12. Publication of authorised, subscribed, and paid-up capital.

Where any notice, advertisement, or other official publication of an assurance company contains a statement of the amount of the authorised capital of the company, the publication shall also contain a statement of the amount of the capital which has been subscribed and the amount paid up.

13. Amalgamation or transfer.[19]

(1) Where it is intended to amalgamate two or more assurance companies, or to transfer the assurance business of any class from one assurance company to another company, the directors of any

---

[19] Rstrct., Insurance (Amendment) Act, 1938 (No. 31), ss. 7(3), 14(3)

one or more of such companies may apply to the Court, by petition, to sanction the proposed arrangement.

(2) The Court, after hearing the directors and other persons whom it considers entitled to be heard upon the petition, may sanction the arrangement if it is satisfied that no sufficient objection to the arrangement has been established.

(3) Before any such application is made to the Court-

(a) notice of the intention to make the application shall be published in the Gazette; and

(b) a statement of the nature of the amalgamation or transfer, as the case may be, together with an abstract containing the material facts embodied in the agreement or deed under which the amalgamation or transfer is proposed to be effected, and copies of the actuarial or other reports upon which the agreement or deed is founded, including a report by an independent actuary, shall, unless the Court otherwise directs, be transmitted to each policy holder of each company in manner provided by section one hundred and thirty-six of the Companies Clauses Consolidation Act, 1845, for the transmission to shareholders of notices not requiring to be served personally:

Provided that it shall not be necessary to transmit such statement and other documents to policy holders other than life, endowment, sinking fund, or bond investment policy holders, nor in the case of a transfer to such policy holders if the business transferred is not life assurance business or bond investment business; and

(c) the agreement or deed under which the amalgamation or transfer is effected shall be open for the inspection of the policy holders and shareholders at the offices of the companies for a period of fifteen days after the publication of the notice in the Gazette.

(4) No assurance company shall amalgamate with another, or transfer its business to another, unless the amalgamation or transfer is sanctioned by the Court in accordance with this section.

14. Statements in case of amalgamation or transfer.

(1) Where an amalgamation takes place between any assurance companies, or where any assurance business of one such company is transferred to another company, the combined company or the purchasing company, as the case may be, shall, within ten days from the date of the completion of the amalgamation or transfer, deposit with the Board of Trade-

(a) certified copies of statements of the assets and liabilities of the companies concerned in such amalgamation or transfer, together with a statement of the nature and terms of the amalgamation or transfer; and

(b) a certified copy of the agreement or deed under which the amalgamation or transfer is effected; and

(c) certified copies of the actuarial or other reports upon which that agreement or deed is founded; and

(d) a declaration under the hand of the chairman of each company, and the principal officer of each company, that to the best of their belief every payment made or to be made to any person whatsoever on account of the amalgamation or transfer is therein fully set forth, and that no other payments beyond those set forth have been made or are to be made either in money, policies, bonds, valuable securities, or other property by or with the knowledge of any parties to the amalgamation or transfer.

15. Special provisions as to winding up of assurance companies.

The Court may order the winding up of an assurance company, in accordance with Companies (Consolidation) Act[18], 1908, and the provisions of that Act shall apply accordingly, subject, however, to the following modification:-

The company may be ordered to be wound up on the petition of ten or more policy holders owning policies of an aggregate value of not less than ten thousand pounds:

Provided that such a petition shall not be presented except by the leave of the Court, and leave shall not be granted until a *prima facie* case has been established to the satisfaction of the Court and until security for costs for such amount as the Court may think reasonable has been given.

16. Winding up of subsidiary companies.

(1) Where the assurance business or any part of the assurance business of an assurance company has been transferred to another company under an arrangement in pursuance of which the first-mentioned company (in this section called the subsidiary company) or the creditors thereof has or have claims against the company to which such transfer was made (in this section called the principal company), then, if the principal company is being wound up by or under the supervision of the Court, the Court shall (subject as hereinafter mentioned) order the subsidiary company to be would up in conjunction with the principal company, and may by the same or any subsequent order appoint the same person to be liquidator for the two companies, and make provision for such other matters as may seem to the Court necessary, with a view to the companies being wound up as if they were one company.

(2) The commencement of the winding up of the principal company shall, save as otherwise ordered by the Court, be the commencement of the winding up of the subsidiary company.

(3) In adjusting the rights and liabilities of the members of the several companies between themselves, the Court shall have regard to the constitution of the companies, and to the arrangements entered into between the companies, in the same manner as the court has regard to the rights and liabilities of different classes of contributories in the case of the winding up of a single company, or as near thereto as circumstances admit.

(4) Where any company alleged to be subsidiary is not in process of being wound up at the same time as the principal company to which it is subsidiary, the Court shall not direct the subsidiary company to be wound up unless, after hearing all objections (if any) that may be urged by or on behalf of the company against its being wound up, the Court is of the opinion that the company is subsidiary to the principal company, and that the winding up of the company in conjunction with the principal company is just and equitable.

(5) An application may be made in relation to the winding up of any subsidiary company in conjunction with a principal company by any creditor of, or person interested in, the principal or subsidiary company.

(6) Where a company stands in the relation of a principal company to one company, and in the relation of a subsidiary company to some other company, or where there are several companies standing in the relation of subsidiary companies to one principal company, the Court may deal with any number of such companies together or in separate groups, as it thinks most expedient, upon the principles laid down in this section.

17. Valuation of annuities and policies.

(1) Where an assurance company is being wound up by the Court, or subject to the supervision of the Court, or voluntarily, the value of a policy of any class or of a liability under such a policy requiring to be valued in such winding up shall be estimated in manner applicable to policies and liabilities of that class provided by the Sixth Schedule to this Act.

(2) The rules in the Sixth and Seventh Schedules to this Act shall be of the same force, and may be repealed, altered, or amended, as if they were rules made in pursuance of section two hundred and thirty-eight of the Companies (Consolidation) Act, 1908, and rules may be made under that section for the purpose of carrying into effect the provisions of this Act with respect to the winding up of assurance companies.

18. Power to Court to reduce contracts

The Court, in the case of an assurance company which has been proved to be unable to pay its debts, may, if it thinks fit, reduce the amount of the contracts of the company upon such terms and subject to such conditions as the Court thinks just, in place of making a winding-up order.

19. Extension of 8 Edw. 7. c. 69, s. 274 to all assurance companies established outside the United Kingdom.

Section two hundred and seventy-four of the Companies (Consolidation) Act, 1908[18] (which contains provisions as to companies incorporated outside the *State*), shall apply to every assurance company constituted outside the *State*[4] which carries on assurance business within the *State*, whether incorporated or not.

20. Custody and inspection of documents deposited with Board of Trade.

The Board of Trade may direct any documents deposited with them under this Act, or certified copies thereof, to be kept by the registrar or by any other officer of the Board of Trade; and any such documents and copies shall be open to inspection, and copies thereof may be procured by any person on payment of such fees as the Board of Trade may direct.

21. Evidence of documents.

(1) Every document deposited under this Act with the Board of Trade, and certified by the registrar or by any person appointed in that behalf by the President of the Board of Trade to be a document so deposited, shall be deemed to be a document so deposited.

(2) Every document purporting to be certified by the registrar, or by any person appointed in that behalf by the President of the Board of Trade, to be a copy of a document so deposited shall be deemed to be a copy of that document, and shall be received in evidence as if it were the original document, unless some variation between it and the original document be proved.

22. Alteration of forms.

The Board of Trade may, on the application or with the consent of an assurance company, alter the forms contained in the schedules to this Act as respects that company, for the purpose of adapting them to the circumstances of that company.

23. Repealed by Insurance Act, 1989 (No. 3), s. 9, sch. 1

24. Penalty for falsifying statements, etc.

If any account, balance sheet, abstract, statement, or other document required by this Act is false in any particular to the knowledge of any person who signs it, that person shall be guilty of a misdemeanour and shall be liable on conviction on indictment to fine and imprisonment, on summary conviction to a fine not exceeding fifty pounds.

25. Recovery and application of penalties.

Every penalty imposed by this Act shall be recovered and applied in the same manner as penalties imposed by the Companies (Consolidation) Act, 1908[18] , are recoverable and applicable.

26. Service of notices

Any notice which is by this Act required to be sent to any policy holder may be addressed and sent to the person to whom notices respecting such policy are usually sent, and any notice so addressed and sent shall be deemed and taken to be notice to the holder of such policy:

Provided that where any person claiming to be interested in a policy has given to the company notice in writing of his interest, any notice which is by this Act required to be sent to policy holders shall also be sent to such person at the address specified by him in his notice.

27. Accounts, &c. to be laid before Parliament.

The Board of Trade shall lay annually before Parliament the accounts, balance sheets, abstracts, statements, and other documents under this Act, or purporting to be under this Act, deposited with them during the preceding year, except reports on the affairs of assurance companies submitted to the shareholders or policy holders thereof, and may append to such accounts, balance sheets, abstracts, statements, or other documents any note of the Board of Trade thereon, and any correspondence in relation thereto.

28. Savings.

(1) This Act shall not affect the National Debt Commissioners or the Postmaster-General, acting under the authorities vested in them respectively by the Government Annuities Acts, 1829 to 1888, and the Post Office Savings Bank Acts, 1861 to 1908.

(2) This Act shall not apply to a member of Lloyd's, or of any other association of underwriters approved by the Board of Trade, who carries on assurance business of any class, provided that he complies with the requirements set forth in the eight schedule to this Act, and applicable to business of that class.

(3) Save as otherwise expressly provided by this Act, nothing in this Act shall apply to assurance business of any class other than one of the classes specified in section one of this Act, and a policy shall not be deemed to be a policy of fire insurance by reason only that loss by fire is one of the various risks covered by the policy.

29. Interpretation.

In this Act, unless the context otherwise requires,-

The expression "chairman" means the person for the time being presiding over the board of directors or other governing body of the assurance company;

The expression "annuities on human life" does not include superannuation allowances an annuities payable out of any fund applicable solely to the relief and maintenance of person engaged or who have been engaged in any particular profession, trade, or employment, or of the dependants of such persons;

The expression "policy holder" means the person who for the time being is the legal holder of the policy for securing the contract with the assurance company;

The expression "underwriter" includes any person named in a policy or other contract of insurance as liable to pay or contribute towards the payment of the sum secured by such policy or contract;

The expression "financial year" means each period of twelve months at the end of which the balance of the accounts of the assurance company is struck, or, if no such balance is struck, then the calender year;

The expression "Court" means the High Court of Justice in England, except that in the case of an assurance company registered or having its head office in Ireland it means, in the provisions of this Act, the High Court of Justice in Ireland, and in the case of an assurance company registered or having its head office in Scotland it means, in the provisions of this Act other than those relating to deposits, the Court of Session, in either division thereof;

The expression "Companies Acts" includes the Companies (Consolidation) Act, 1908 and any enactment repealed by that Act;

The expression "registrar" means the Registrar of Joint Stock Companies;

The expression "actuary" means an actuary possessing such qualifications as may be prescribed by rules made by the Board of Trade;

The expression "Gazette" means the London, Edinburgh, or Dublin Gazette[20], as the case may be.

---

[20] To be construed as reference to *Iris Oifigiúil*; Adaptation of Enactments Act, 1922 (No. 2), s. 4

30. Application to life assurance companies.

Where a company carries on life assurance business, this Act shall apply with respect to that business, subject to the following modifications:-

(a) "Policy on human life" shall mean any instrument by which the payment of money is assured on death (except death by accident only) or the happening of any contingency dependent of human life, or any instrument evidencing a contract which is subject to payment of premiums for a term dependent on human life;

(b) Where the company grant annuities upon human life, "policy" shall include the instrument evidencing the contract to pay such an annuity, and "policy holder" includes annuitant;

(c) The obligation to deposit and keep deposited the sum of twenty thousand pounds shall apply notwithstanding that the company has previously made and withdrawn its deposit, or been exempted from making any deposit under any enactment hereby repealed;

(d) Where the company intends to amalgamate with or to transfer its life assurance business to another assurance company, the Court shall not sanction the amalgamation or transfer in any case in which it appears to the Court that the life policy holders representing one-tenth or more of the total amount assured in the company dissent from the amalgamation or transfer;

(e) Nothing in this Act providing that the life assurance fund shall not be liable for any contracts for which it would not have been liable had the business of the company been only that of life assurance shall affect the liability of that fund, in the case of a company established before the ninth day of August eighteen hundred and seventy, for contracts entered into by the company before that date;

(f) In the case of a company carrying on life assurance business and established before the ninth day of August eighteen hundred and seventy, by the terms of whose deed of settlement the whole of the profits of all the business carried on by the company are paid exclusively to the life policy holders, and on the face of whose life policies the liability of the life assurance fund in respect of the other business distinctly appears, such of the provisions of this Act as require the separation of funds, and exempt the life assurance fund from liability for contracts to which it would not have been liable had the business of the company been only that of life assurance, shall not apply;

(g) Any business carried on by an assurance company which under the provisions of any special Act relating to that company is to be treated as life assurance business shall continue to be so treated, and

337

shall not be deemed to be other business or a separate class of assurance business within the meaning of this Act;

(h) In the case of a mutual company whose profits are allocated to members wholly or mainly by annual abatements of premium, the abstract of the report of the actuary on the financial condition of the company, prepared in accordance with the Fourth Schedule to the Act, may, notwithstanding anything in section five of this Act, be made and returned at intervals not exceeding five years, provided that, where such return is not made annually, it shall include particulars as to the rates of abatement of premiums applicable to different classes or series of assurances allowed in each year during the period which has elapsed since the previous return under the Fourth Schedule.

31. Application to fire insurance companies

Where a company carries on fire insurance business, this Act shall apply with respect to that business, subject to the following modifications:-

(a) It shall not be necessary for the company to prepare any statement of its fire insurance business in accordance with the Fourth and Fifth Schedules to this Act:

(b), (c), (d) Repealed: Insurance Act, 1936 (No. 45), s. 7(1)

(e) So much of this Act as requires an assurance company transacting other business besides assurance business, or more than one class of assurance business, to keep separate funds into which all receipts in respect of the assurance business or of each class of assurance business are to be paid shall not apply as respects fire insurance business:

(f) Repealed by Insurance Act, 1989 (No. 3), s. 9, sch. 1

32. Application to accident insurance companies.[21]

Where a company carries on accident insurance business, this Act shall apply with respect to that business, subject to the following modifications:-

(a) In lieu of the provisions of sections five and six of this Act the following provisions shall be substituted:-

"The company shall annually prepare a statement of its accident insurance business in the form set forth in the Fourth Schedule to this Act and applicable to accident insurance business, and the statement shall be printed, signed, and deposited at the Board of Trade in accordance with section seven of this Act":

(b), (c) repealed by Insurance Act, 1936 (No. 45), s. 7(1)

(d) So much of this Act as requires an assurance company

---

[21] S-s. (d), (f) & (g), appl. with mod, Insurance Act, 1936 (No. 45), s. 104(c) and Road Traffic Act, 1961 (No.24), s. 74(2)

transacting other business besides assurance business, or more than one class of assurance business, to keep separate funds into which all receipts in respect of the assurance business or of each class of assurance business are to be paid shall not apply as respects accident insurance business.

(e) Repealed by Insurance Act, 1989 (No. 3), s. 9, sch 1

(f) The expression "policy" includes any policy under which there is for the time being an existing liability already accrued, or under which a liability may accrue:

(g) Where a sum is due, or a weekly or other periodical payment is payable, under any policy, the expression "policy holder" includes the person to whom the sum is due or the weekly or other periodical payment payable.

33. Application to employers' liability insurance companies.

(1) Where a company carries on employers' liability insurance business, this Act shall apply with respect to that business, subject to the following modifications:-

(a) Repealed by Insurance Act, 1936 (No. 45), s. 7(1)

(b) This Act shall not apply where the company carries on the employers' liability insurance business as incidental only to the business of marine insurance by issuing marine policies, or policies in the form of marine policies covering liability to pay compensation or damages to workmen as well as losses incident to marine adventure or adventure analogous thereto :

(c) In lieu of the provisions of sections five and six of this Act the following provisions shall be substituted:-

"The Company shall annually prepare a statement of its employers' liability insurance business in the form set forth in the Fourth Schedule to this Act and applicable to employers' liability insurance business, and shall cause an investigation of its estimated liabilities to be made by an actuary to far as may be necessary to enable the provisions of that form to be complied with, and the statement shall be printed, signed, and deposited at the Board of Trade in accordance with section seven of this Act":

(d) & (e), Repealed by Insurance Act, 1936 (No. 45), s. 7(1)

(f) Where money is paid into a county court under the provisions of the Eight Schedule to this Act, the court shall (unless the court for special reason sees fit to direct otherwise) order the lump sum to be invested or applied in the purchase of an annuity or otherwise, in such manner that the duration of the benefit thereof may, as far as possible correspond with the probable duration of the incapacity:

(g) the expression "policy" includes any policy under which there is for the time being an existing liability already accrued, or under which any liability may accrue;

(h) Where any sum is due, or a weekly payment is payable, under any policy, the expression "policy holder" includes the person to whom the sum is due or the weekly payment payable:

(i) Repealed by Insurance Act, 1989 (No. 3), s. 9, sch. 1

(2) In the application of this section to Scotland the expression "county court" means sheriff court.

34. Application to bond investment companies.

Where a company carries on bond investment business, this Act shall apply with respect to that business, subject to the following modifications:-

(a) the expression "policy" includes any bond, certificate, receipt, or other instrument evidencing the contract with the company, and the expression "policy holder" means the person who for the time being is the legal holder of such instrument:

(b) & (c) Repealed by Insurance Act, 1936 (No. 45), s. 7(1)

(d) The first statement of the bond investment business of the company shall be deposited at the Board of Trade on or before the thirtieth day of June nineteen hundred and eleven:

(e) The company shall not give the holder of any policy issued after the passing of this Act any advantage dependent on lot or chance, but this provision shall not be construed as in anywise prejudicing any questions as to the application to any such transaction, whether in respect of a policy issued before or after the passing of this Act, of the law relating to lotteries.

35. Power of Board of Trade to exempt unregistered trade unions and friendly societies.

The Board of Trade may, on the application of any unregistered trade union .....[22] . extend to the trade union the exemption conferred by this Act on registered trade unions, and may on the application of an unregistered friendly society extend to the society the exemption conferred by this Act on registered friendly societies if if appears to the Board, after consulting the Chief Registrar of Friendly Societies, that the society is one to which it is inexpedient that the provisions of this Act should apply.

36. Repealed by Insurance Act, 1936 (No. 45), s. 7(2)

---

[22] Deletion by Insurance Act, 1936 (No. 45), s. 7

37. Repeal
The enactments mentioned in the Ninth Schedule to this Act are hereby repealed to the extent specified in the third column of that schedule: Provided that nothing in this repeal shall affect any investigation made, or any statement, abstract, or other document deposited, under any enactment hereby repealed, but every such investigation shall be deemed to have been made and every such document prepared and deposited under this Act.

38. Short title.
(1) This Act may be cited as the Assurance Companies Act, 1909.
(2) This Act shall come into operation on the first day of July nineteen hundred and ten, except that as respects section thirty-six it shall come into operation on the passing thereof.

Schedules[23]

---

[23] Insurance Act, 1936 (No. 45) s. 96(1), provides that Minister may ...... alter all schedules other than eight or ninth. For further power to alter see below.

First Schedule

Section 4

N.B.- Where marine insurance business or sinking fund or capital redemption insurance business is carried on, the income and expenditure thereof to be stated in like manner in separate accounts. Any additional businesses (including employers' liability insurance business transacted out of the State*) to be shown in a separate inclusive general account.

(A) Form applicable to Life Assurance Business

Revenue Account of the   in respect of Life Assurance Business

for the Year ending

	Business within the State*	Business out of the State*	Total
	£	£	£
Amount of life assurance fund at the beginning of the year			
Premiums			
Consideration for annuities granted			
Interest, dividends, and rents £			
Less income tax thereon			
Other receipts (accounts to be specified)			
	£		

	Business within the State*	Business out of the State*	Total
	£	£	£
Claims under policies paid and outstanding			
By death			
By maturity			
Surrenders, including surrenders of bonus			
Annuities			
Bonuses in cash			
Bonuses in reduction of premiums			
Commission			
Expenses of management			
Other payments (accounts to be specified)			
Amount of life assurance fund at the end of the year, as per Third Schedule			
			£

Note 1. Companies having separate accounts for annuities to return the particulars of their annuity business in a separate statement.
Note 2. Companies having both Ordinary and Industrial branches to return the particulars of the business in each department separately.
Note 3. Items in this Account to be net amounts after deduction of the amounts paid and received in respect of re-assurances of the Company's risks.
Note 4. If any sum has been deducted from the expenses of management account, and taken credit for in the Balance Sheet as an asset, the sum so deducted to be separately shown in the above Account.
Note 5. Particulars of the new life assurances effected during the year of account to be appended to the above Account showing separately, as respects business within and business out of the State*, the number of policies, the total sums assured, the amount received by way of single premiums, and the amount of the yearly renewal premium income, the items to be net amount after deduction of the amounts paid and received in respect of re-assurances of the company's risks. The particulars as to yearly renewal premium income need not be furnished in respect of Industrial business.
Note 6. The columns headed "Business out of the State*," in the case of companies having their head office in the State*, apply only to business secured through Branch Offices or Agencies out of the State*.

* Construction of United Kingdom, Constitution (Consequential Provisions) Act, 1937 (No. 40), s. 4(1)

(B). Form applicable to Five Insurance Business

Revenue Account of the   for the Year ending   19   in respect of Fire Insurance Business.

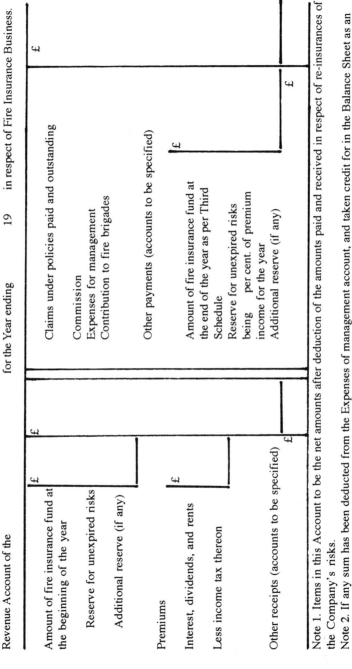

	£	£		£	£
Amount of fire insurance fund at the beginning of the year			Claims under policies paid and outstanding		
Reserve for unexpired risks			Commission		
Additional reserve (if any)			Expenses for management		
			Contribution to fire brigades		
Premiums			Other payments (accounts to be specified)		
Interest, dividends, and rents			Amount of fire insurance fund at the end of the year as per Third Schedule		
Less income tax thereon			Reserve for unexpired risks being per cent. of premium income for the year		
Other receipts (accounts to be specified)			Additional reserve (if any)		

Note 1. Items in this Account to be the net amounts after deduction of the amounts paid and received in respect of re-insurances of the Company's risks.

Note 2. If any sum has been deducted from the Expenses of management account, and taken credit for in the Balance Sheet as an asset the sum so deducted to be separately shown in the above Account.

Section 4

Second Schedule

Profit and Loss Account of the   for the Year ending   19

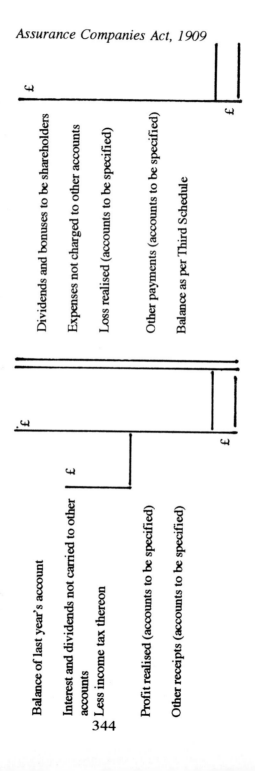

£	£
Balance of last year's account	
Interest and dividends not carried to other accounts	£
Less income tax thereon	
Profit realised (accounts to be specified)	
Other receipts (accounts to be specified)	
	£

£	£
Dividends and bonuses to be shareholders	
Expenses not charged to other accounts	
Loss realised (accounts to be specified)	
Other payments (accounts to be specified)	
Balance as per Third Schedule	
	£

344

Third Schedule

Section 4
Balance Sheet of the .... on the 19

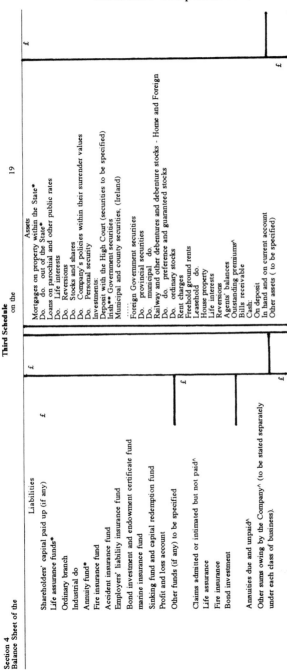

Liabilities	£	£	Assets	£	£
Shareholders' capital paid up (if any)			Mortgages on property within the State*		
Life assurance funds*			Do. do. out of the State*		
Ordinary branch			Loans on parochial and other public rates		
Industrial do			Do. Life interests		
Annuity fund*			Do. Reversions		
Fire insurance fund			Do. Stocks and shares		
Accident insurance fund			Do. Company's policies within their surrender values		
Employers' liability insurance fund			Do. Personal security		
Bond investment and endowment certificate fund			Investments:		
marine insurance fund			Deposit with the High Court (securities to be specified)		
Sinking fund and capital redemption fund			Irish** Government securities		
Profit and loss account			Municipal and county securities, (Ireland)		
Other funds (if any) to be specified			......		
			Foreign Government securities		
			Do. provincial securities		
Claims admitted or intimated but not paid^			Do. municipal do.		
Life assurance			Railway and other debentures and debenture stocks - Home and Foreign		
Fire insurance			Do. do. preference and guaranteed stocks		
Bond investment			Do. ordinary stocks		
			Rent charges		
Annuities due and unpaid^			Freehold ground rents		
Other sums owing by the Company^ (to be stated separately under each class of business).			Leasehold do.		
			House property		
			Life interests		
			Reversions		
			Agents' balances		
			Outstanding premiums^		
			Bills receivable		
			Cash:		
			On deposit		
			In hand and on current account		
			Other assets (to be specified)		

* Life companies having separate annuity fund to show amount thereof separately.

^ These items are or have been included in the corresponding items in the First Schedule.

Note 1. When part of the assets of the company are specifically deposited, under local laws, in various places out of the State*, as security to holders of policies there issued, each such place and the amount compulsorily lodged therein must be specified in respect of each class of business, except that in the case of fire, accident, or employers' liability insurance business, it shall be sufficient to state the fact that a part of the assets has been so deposited.

Note 2. A Balance Sheet in the above form must be rendered in respect of each separate fund for which separate investments are made.

Note 3. The Balance Sheet must state how the values of the Stock Exchange securities are arrived at, and a certificate must be appended, signed by the same persons as sign the Balance Sheet, to the effect that in their belief the assets set forth in the Balance Sheet are in the aggregate fully of the value stated therein, less any investment reserve fund taken into account. In the case of a company transacting life assurance business or bond investment business, this certificate is to be given on the occasions only when a statement respecting valuation under the Fourth Schedule is made.

Note 4. In the case of a company required to keep separate funds under section 3 of this Act, a certificate must be appended, signed by the same persons as signed the Balance Sheet and by the auditor, to the effect that no part of any such fund has been applied, directly or indirectly, for any purpose other than the class of business to which it is applicable.

* Constr., S.R.&O. 7/1928, par. 5 and Constitution (Consequential Provisions) Act, 1937 (No. 40), s. 4(1). ** Const., E.C.O. 5/1923, pt. 2, par. 1.

Assurance Companies Act, 1909
Fourth Schedule

Sections 5, 30, 32 & 33.

N.B. Where sinking fund or capital redemption insurance business is carried on, a separate statement signed by the actuary must be furnished, showing the total number of policies valued, the total sums assured, and the total office yearly premiums, and also showing the total net liability in respect of such business and the basis on which such liability is calculated.

(A.) - Form applicable to Life Assurance Business

STATEMENT respecting the VALUATION of the LIABILITIES under LIFE POLICIES and ANNUITIES of the
, to be
made and signed by the ACTUARY.

(The answers should be numbered to accord with the numbers of the corresponding questions.)

1. The date up to which the valuation is made.
2. The general principles adopted in the valuation, and the method followed in the valuation of particular classes of assurances, including a statement of the method by which the net premiums have been arrived at, and whether these principles were determined by the instrument constituting the company, or by its regulations or byelaws, or how otherwise; together with a statement of the manner in which policies on under average lives are dealt with.
3. The table or tables of mortality used in the valuation. In cases where the tables employed are not published, specimen policy values are to be given, at the rate of interest employed in the valuation, in respect of whole-life assurance policies effected at the respective ages of 20, 30, 40, and 50, and having been respectively in force for five years, ten years, and upwards at intervals of five years respectively; with similar specimen policy values in respect of endowment assurance policies, according to age at entry, original term of policy, and duration.
4. The rate or rates of interest assumed in the calculations.
5. The actual proportion of the annual premium income, if any, reserved as a provision for future expenses and profits, separately specified in respect of assurances with immediate profits, with deferred profits, and without profits. (If none, state how this provision is made.)
6. The consolidated revenue account since the last valuation, or, in

case of a company which has made no valuation, since the commencement of the business. (This return should be made in the form annexed. No return under this heading will be required where a statement under this schedule is deposited annually.)

7. The liabilities of the company under life policies and annuities at the date of the valuation, showing the number of policies, the amount assured,and the amount of premiums payable annually under each class of policies, both with and without participation in profits; and also the net liabilities and assets of the company, with the amount of surplus or deficiency. (These returns to be made in the forms annexed.)

8. The principles upon which the distribution of profits among the shareholders and policy holders is made, and whether these principles were determined by the instrument constituting the company or by its regulations or byelaws or how otherwise, and the number of years' premiums to be paid before a bonus (a) is allotted, and (b) vests.

9. The results of the valuation, showing -

(1) The total amount of profit made by the company, allocated as follows :-

    (a) Among the policy holders with immediate participation, and the number and amount of the policies which participated;

    (b) Among policy holders with deferred participation, and the number and amount of the policies which participated;

    (c) Among the shareholders;

    (d) To reserve funds, or other accounts;

    (e) Carried forward unappropriated.

(2) Specimens of bonuses allotted to whole-life assurance policies for £100 effected at the respective ages of 20, 30, 40, and 50, and having been respectively in force for five years, ten years, and upwards at intervals of five years respectively, together with the amounts apportioned under the various modes in which the bonus might be received, with similar specimen bonuses and particulars in respect of endowment assurance policies, according to age at entry, original term of policy, and duration.

Note.- Separate statements to be furnished throughout in respect of Ordinary and Industrial business respectively, the basis of the division being stated.

(Form referred to under Heading No. 6 in Fourth Schedule (A).)

Consolidated Revenue Account of the _____ for _____ years
commencing _____ and ending _____

	£		£
Amount of life assurance fund at the beginning of the period		Claims under policies paid and outstanding	
		By death £	
	£	By maturity	
Premiums			
Consideration for annuities granted		Surrenders	
		Annuities	
Interest, dividends, and rents		Bonuses in cash	
Less income tax thereon		reduction of premiums	
Other receipts (accounts to be specified)		Commission	
		Expenses of management	
		Other payments (accounts to be specified)	
		Amount of life assurance fund at the end of the period, as per Third Schedule	
	£		£

Note - If any sum has been deducted from the expenses of management account and taken credit for in the Balance Sheet as an asset, the sum so deducted to be separately shown in the above Statement.

(Form referred to under Heading No. 7 in Fourth Schedule(A).)

Summary and valuation of the policies of the   as at   19

Description of Transactions.	Particulars of the Policies for Valuation				Valuation				
					Value by the Table, Interest per cent				
	Number of Policies	Sums assured and Bonuses	Office yearly Premiums	Net Yearly Premiums	Sums assured and Bonuses	Office Yearly Premiums	Net Yearly Premiums	Net Liability
ASSURANCES								
1.–With immediate participation in profits								
For whole term of life								
Other classes (to be speified)								
Extra premiums payable								
Total assurance with profits								
II. With deferred participation in profits.								
For whole term of life								
Other classes (to be specified)								
Extra premiums payable								
Total assurances with profits								
III. Without participation in profits								
For whole term of life								
Other classes (to be specified)								
Extra premiums payable								
Total assurances without profits								
Total assurances								
Deduct re-assurances								
(to be specified according to class in a separate statement)								
Net amount of assurances								
Adjustments, if any (to be separately specified)								
ANNUITIES ON LIVES								
Immediate								
Other classes (to be specified)								
Total of the results								

Note 1. The term "extra premium" in this Act shall be taken to mean the charge for any risk not provided for in the minimum contract premium. If policies are issued in or for any country at rates of premium deduced from tables other than the European mortality tables adopted by the company, separate schedules similar in form to the above must be furnished.

Note 2. Separate returns and valuation results must be furnished in respect of classes of policies valued by different tables of mortality, or at different rates of interest, also for business at other than European rates.

Note 3. In cases also where separate valuations of any portion of the business are required under local laws in places outside the State*, a summary statement must be furnished in respect of the business so valued in each such place showing the total number of policies, the total sums assured and bonuses, the total office yearly premiums, and the total net liability on the bases as to mortality and interest adopted in each such place, with a statement as to such bases respectively.

Assurance Companies Act, 1909

(Form referred to under Heading No. 7 in Fourth Schedule (A).)

Valuation Balance Sheet of   as at   19

Dr.	£	Cr.	£
To net liability under Life Assurance and Annuity transactions (as per summary statement provided in Fourth Schedule (A))		By Life Assurance and Annuity funds (as per balance sheet under Schedule 3)	
To surplus, if any		By deficiency, if any	

350

Section 6

N.B. - Where sinking fund or capital redemption business is carried on, a separate statement, signed by the actuary, must be furnished showing the total sums assured maturing in each calendar year and the corresponding office premiums.

(A). - Form applicable to Life Assurance Business.

STATEMENT of the LIFE ASSURANCE and ANNUITY BUSINESS of the
   on the 19 , to be signed
by the Actuary.

(The answers should be numbered to accord with the numbers of the corresponding questions. Statements of re-assurances corresponding to the statements in respect of assurances are to be given throughout.)
Separate statements are to be furnished in the replies to all the headings under this schedule for business at other than European rates.
Separate statements are to be also furnished throughout in respect of ordinary and industrial business respectively.

1. The published table or tables of premiums for assurance for the whole term of life and for endowment assurances which are in use at the date above mentioned.
2. The total amount assured on lives for the whole term of life which are in existence at the date above mentioned, distinguishing the portions assured with immediate profits, with deferred profits, and without profits, stating separately the total reversionary bonuses and specifying the sums assured for each year of life from the youngest to the oldest ages, the basis of division as to immediate and deferred profits being stated.
3. The amount of premiums receivable annually for each year of life, after deducting the abatements made by the application of bonuses, in respect of the respective assurances mentioned under Heading No. 2, distinguishing ordinary from extra premiums. A separate statement is to be given of premiums payable for a limited number of years, classified according to the number of years' payments remaining to be made.
4. The total amount assured under endowment assurances, specifying sums assured and office premiums separately in respect of

each year in which such assurances will mature for payment. The reversionary bonuses must also be separately specified, and the sums assured with immediate profits, with deferred profits, and without profits, separately returned.

4A[24] The total amount assured under endowments, specifying sums assured and office premiums separately in respect of each year in which such assurances will mature for payment. The reversionary bonuses must also be separately specified, and the sum assured with immediate profits, with deferred profits, and without profits, separately returned.

5. The total amount assured under classes of assurance business, other than assurances dealt with under Questions 2 and 4, distinguishing the sums assured under each class, and stating separately the amount assured with immediate profits, with deferred profits, and without profits, and the total amount of reversionary bonuses.

6. The amount of premiums receivable annually in respect of each such special class of assurances mentioned under Heading No. 5, distinguishing ordinary from extra premiums.

8.[25] The total amount of immediate annuities on lives, distinguishing the amount for each year of life, and distinguishing male and female lives.

9. The amount of all annuities on lives other than those specified under Heading No. 8, distinguishing the amount of annuities payable under each class, and the amount of premiums annually receivable.

10. The average rate of interest yielded by the assets, whether invested or uninvested, constituting the life assurance fund of the company, calculated upon the mean fund of each year during the period since the last investigation, without deduction of income tax.

It must be stated whether or not the mean fund upon which the average rate of interest is calculated includes reversionary investments.

11. A table of minimum values, if any, allowed for the surrender of policies for the whole term of life and for endowments and endowment assurances, or a statement of the method pursued in calculating such surrender values, with instances of the application of such method to policies of different standing and taken out at various interval ages from the youngest to the oldest. In the case of industrial policies, where free or paid up policies are granted in lieu of surrender values, the conditions under which such policies are granted must be stated, with specimens as prescribed for surrender values.

---

[24] Inserted by Insurance Act, 1936 (No. 45), s. 95(a)

[25] Note 7 deleted by Insurance Act, 1936 (No. 45), s. 95(b)

Section 17

Rules for valuing policies and liabilities

(A) - As respects life policies and annuities.

Rule for valuing an annuity.

An annuity shall be valued according to the tables used by the company which granted such annuity at the time of granting the same, and, where such tables cannot be ascertained or adopted to the satisfaction of the court, then according to such rate of interest and table of mortality as the court may direct.

Rule for valuing a policy

The value of the policy is to be the difference between the present value of the reversion in the sum assured according to the contingency upon which it is payable, including any bonus or addition thereto made before the commencement of the winding up, and the present value of the future annual premiums.

In calculating such present values interest is to be assumed at such rate, and the rate of mortality according to such tables, as the court may direct.

The premium to be calculated is to be such premium as according to the said rate of interest and rate of mortality is sufficient to provide for the risk incurred by the office in issuing the policy, exclusive of any addition thereto for office expenses and other charges.

(B) - as respect fire policies

Rule for valuing a policy

The value of a current policy shall be such portion of the last premium paid as as is proportionate to the unexpired portion of the period in respect of which the premium was paid.

(c) - as respects Accident policies

Rule for valuing a periodical payment

The present value of a periodical payment shall, in the case of total permanent incapacity, be such an amount as would, if invested in the purchase of a life annuity from the National Debt Commissioners through the Post Office Savings Bank, purchase an annuity equal to seventy-five per centum of the annual value of the periodical payment, and, in any other case, shall be such proportion of such amount as may, under the circumstances of the case, be proper.

Rule for valuing a policy

The value of a current policy shall be such portion of the last premium paid as as is proportionate to the unexpired portion of the period in respect of which the premium was paid.

(D) - As respects Employers' Liability Policies

Rule for valuing a weekly payment

The present value of a weekly payment shall, if the incapacity of the workman in respect of which it is payable is total permanent incapacity, be such an amount as would, if invested in the purchase of an immediate life annuity from the National Debt Commissioners through the Post Office Savings Bank, purchase an annuity for the workman equal to seventy-five per cent. of the annual value of the weekly payment, and in any other case, shall be such proportion of such amount as may, under the circumstances of the case, be proper.

Rule for valuing a policy

The value of a current policy shall be such portion of the last premium paid as is proportionate to the unexpired portion of the period in respect of which the premium was paid, together with, in the case of a policy under which any weekly payment is payable, the present value of that weekly payment.

(E)- as respect Bonds or Certificates

Rule for valuing a policy or certificate

The value of a policy or certificate is to be the difference between the present value of the sum assured according to the date at which it is payable, including any bonus or addition thereto made before the commencement of the winding up, and the present value of the future annual premiums.

In calculating such present values, interest is to be assumed at such rate as the court may direct.

The premium to be calculated is to be such premium as, according to the said rate of interest, is sufficient to provide for the sum assured by the policy or certificate, exclusive of any addition thereto for office expenses and other charges.

Seventh Schedule

Section 17

Where an assurance company is being wound up by the court or subject to the supervision of the court, the liquidator, in the case of all persons appearing by the books of the company to be entitled to or interested in policies granted by such company, is to ascertain the value of the liability of the company to each such person, and give notice of such value to such persons in such manner as the court may direct, and any person to whom notice is so given shall be bound by the value so ascertained unless he gives notice of his intention to dispute such value in manner and within a time to be prescribed by a rule or order of the court.

Eight Schedule

Sections 28 & 33

Requirements to be complied with by underwriters being member's of Lloyd's or of any other association of underwriters approved by the Board of Trade

(A) - As respect life assurance business.

1. Every underwriter shall deposit and keep deposited in such manner as the board of Trade may direct a sum of two thousand pounds. The Board of Trade may make rules as to the payment, repayment, investment of, and dealing with, a deposit, the payment of interest and dividends from any such investment, and for any other matters in respect of which they may make rules under section 2(6) of this Act in relation to deposits made by assurance companies. The sum so deposited shall, so long as any liability under any policy issued by the underwriter remains unsatisfied, be available solely to meet claims under such policies.
2. The underwriter shall furnish every year to the Board of Trade a statement in such form as may be prescribed by the Board showing the extent and character of the life assurance business effected by him.

(B) and (C) - As respects fire and accident insurance business.

1. Expect as hereinafter provided, every underwriter shall comply with the following requirements : -
(a) He shall deposit and keep deposited in such manner as the

Board of Trade may direct a sum of two thousand pounds in respect of each class of business. The Board of Trade may make rules as to the payment, repayment, investment of, and dealing with, a deposit, the payment of interest and dividends from any such investment, and for any other matters in respect of which they may make rules under section 2(6) of this Act in relation to deposits made by assurance companies. The sum so deposited shall, so long as any liability under any policy issued by the underwriter remains unsatisfied, be available solely to meet claims under such policies.

(b) He shall furnish every year to the Board of Trade a statement in such form as may be prescribed by the Board showing the extent and character of the fire or accident insurance business effected by him.

2. An underwriter who carries on fire insurance or accident insurance business may, in lieu of complying with the above requirements, elect to comply with the under mentioned conditions :

(a) All premiums received by or on behalf of the underwriter in respect of fire and accident insurance or re-insurance business carried on by him, either alone or in conjunction with any other insurance business for which special requirements are not laid down in this schedule, shall without any apportionment be placed in a trust fund in accordance with the provisions of a trust deed approved by the Board of Trade:

(b) He shall also furnish security to the satisfaction of the Board of Trade (or, if the Board so direct, to the satisfaction of the committee of the association), which shall be available solely to meet claims under policies issued by him in connexion with fire and accident insurance and any other non-marine business carried on by him for which special requirements are not laid down in this schedule.

The security may be furnished in the form of either a depositor or a guarantee, or partly in the one form and partly in the other.

The amount of the security to be furnished shall never be less than the aggregate of the premiums received or receivable by the underwriter in the last preceding year in connexion with such fire and accident and other non-marine business :

(c) The accounts of every underwriter shall be audited annually by an accountant approved by the committee of the association, who shall furnish a certificate to the committee of the association and to the Board of Trade in a form prescribed by the Board of Trade :

(d) For the purposes of these requirements "non-marine

insurance business" means the business of issuing policies upon subject-matters of insurance other than the following, namely: -

Vessels of any description, including barges and dredgers, cargoes, freights, and other interests which may be legally insured by, in, or in relation to vessels, cargoes, and frights, goods, wares, merchandise, and property of whatever description.

(D) - As respects employers' liability insurance business

1. Every underwriter shall deposit and keep deposited in such manner as the board of Trade may direct a sum of two thousand pounds. The Board of Trade may make rules as to the payment, repayment, investment of, and dealing with, a deposit, the payment of interest and dividends from any such investment, and for any other matters in respect of which they may make rules under this Act in relation to deposits made by assurance companies. The sum so deposited shall, so long as any liability under any policy issued by the underwriter remains unsatisfied, be available solely to meet claims under such policies.

2. Where the person insured by any policy issued by an underwriter is liable to make a weekly payment to any workman during the incapacity of the workman, and the weekly payment has continued for more than six months, the liability therefor shall before the expiration of twelve months from the commencement of the incapacity be redeemed by the payment of a lump sum in accordance with paragraph (17) of the First Schedule to the Workmen's Compensation Act, 1906, and the underwriter shall pay the lump sum into the county court, and shall inform the court that the redemption has been effected in pursuance of the provisions of this schedule.

3. The underwriter shall furnish every year to the Board of Trade a statement in such form as may be prescribed by the Board showing the extent and character of the employers' liability business effected by him.

4. For the purpose of this schedule "policy" means a policy insuring any employer against liability to pay compensation or damages to workmen in his employment.

(E) - As respects bond investment business

1. Every underwriter shall deposit and keep deposited in such manner as the Board of Trade may direct a sum of two thousand pounds. The Board of Trade may make rules as to the payment, repayment, investment of, and dealing with, a deposit, the payment of interest and dividends from any such investment, and for any other matters in respect of which they may make rules under section 2(6) of this Act in relation to deposits made by assurance companies. The sum so deposited shall, so long as any liability under any policy issued by the underwriter remains unsatisfied, be available solely to meet claims under such policies.

2. The underwriter shall furnish every year to the Board of Trade a statement in such form as may be prescribed by the Board showing the extent and character of the bond investment business effected by him.

Ninth Schedule

Enactments repealed

Session & chapter	Act	Extent of repeal
33 & 34 Vict. c. 61	The Life Assurance Companies Act, 1870	The whole Act
34 & 35 Vict. c. 58	The Life Assurance Companies Act, 1871	The whole Act
35 & 36 Vict. c. 41	The Life Assurance Companies Act, 1872	The whole Act
39 & 40 Vict. c. 22	The Trade Union Act Amendment Act, 1876	Section 7
7 Edw. 7 c. 46	The Employers' Liability Insurance Companies Act, 1907	The whole Act

An Act to amend section sixteen of the Merchandise Marks Act, 1887
16th December 1911

1. Power to require information in respect of imported goods bearing fraudulent marks.

(1) Where any goods which, if sold, would be liable to forfeiture under the Merchandise Marks Act, 1887, are imported into the *State*[1], and the goods bear any name or trade mark being or purporting to be the name or trade mark of any manufacturer, dealer, or trader in the *State*, and the *Revenue Commissioners*[2] are, upon representations made to them, satisfied that the use of the name or trade mark is fraudulent, the proper officer of *the Revenue Commissioners* may require the importer of the goods, or his agent, to produce any documents in his possession relating to the goods, and to furnish information as to the name and address of the person by whom the goods were consigned to the *State* and the name and address of the person to whom the goods were sent in the *State*; and, if the importer or his agent fails within fourteen days to comply with any such requirement, he shall, for each offence, forfeit the sum of one hundred pounds.

(2) Any information obtained from the importer of the goods or his agent under this section, or from any other source, may be communicated by the Commissioners to any person whose name or trade mark is alleged to have been used or infringed.

(3) This section shall have effect as if it were part of section sixteen of the Merchandise Marks Act, 1887.

2. Short title

This Act may be cited as the Merchandise Marks Act, 1911, and the Merchandise Marks Acts, 1887 to 1894, and this Act may be cited together as the Merchandise Marks Act, 1887 to 1911.

---

[1] From construction of United Kingdom as Saorstát Eireann, Merchandise Marks Act, 1931 (No. 48), s. 29(1)

[2] Constr., of Commissioners of Customs and Excise, Merchandise Marks Act, 1931 (No. 48), s. 29(8)

The Industrial and Provident Societies (Amendment) Act, 1913
3 & 4 George 5, chapter 31

List of Sections

An Act to amend the Industrial and Provident Societies Act, 1893.
5th August 1913

1. Registration of society consisting of two or more other societies

A society consisting solely of two or more registered societies may, notwithstanding anything contained in section five of the Industrial and Provident Societies Act, 1893 (in this Act referred to as the principal Act), be registered if the application to register the society is signed by two members of the committee and the secretary of each of the constituent societies, and is accompanied by two printed copies of the rules of each such society.

2. Audit of accounts

(1) Every registered society shall once in every year submit its accounts for audit to one or more of the public auditors appointed under the provisions of the principal Act.

(2) An auditor shall not hold any other office in connexion with the society.

3. Annual return

(1) For paragraph (c) of subsection (2) of section fourteen of the Principal Act (which relates to the date to which annual returns are to be made up) the following paragraph shall be substituted: -
see: 56 & 57 Vict. c. 39, page 163 ante

(2) A registered society shall, together with the annual return, send to the Registrar a copy of the report of the auditors and a copy of each balance sheet made during the period included in the return.

4. Triennial returns of shareholders

A registered society shall, once at least in every three years, make out and send to the Registrar, together with the annual return for the year, a special return signed by the auditor or auditors showing the holding of each person in the society (whether in shares or loans) at the date to which the said annual return is made out:

Provided that, where such person are in the list of members kept by the society distinguished by numbers, it shall be sufficient if they are distinguished in the special return by such numbers, and in that case it shall not be necessary to specify their names.

5. Amendment of principal Act as to nominations

(1) The principal Act shall as respect nominations made after the commencement of this Act have effect as if the following provisions were substituted for section twenty-five of the principal Act : -
see: 56 & 57 Vict. c. 39, page 166 ante

(2) The principal Act shall as respect nominators dying after the commencement of this Act have effect as if the following provisions were substituted for subsection (1) of section twenty-six of the principal Act : -
see: 56 & 57 Vict. c. 39, page 167 ante

6. Substitutes section 28 of the principal Act (subsequently repealed).

7. Amendment of section 29 of the principal Act

8. Dissolution and transfer of engagements

On dissolution or transfer of engagements, as provided for in sections fifty-eight and fifty-three of the principal Act, the society shall not be dissolved and registration of the society shall not be cancelled until a certificate signed by the liquidator or by the secretary or some other officer of the society approved by the Registrar has been lodged with the Registrar that all property vested in the society has been duly conveyed or transferred by the society to the persons entitled.

9. Amends section 50(4), of the principal Act

10. Substitutes section 62, of the principal Act

11. Addition of subsections (3)&(4), of section 69 of the principal Act

12. Short title and construction

(1) This Act may be cited as the Industrial and Provident Societies (Amendment) Act, 1913, and the Industrial and Provident Societies Act, 1893 to 1895, and this Act may be cited together as the Industrial and Provident Societies Acts, 1893 to 1913.

(2) This Act shall be construed as one with the Industrial and Provident Societies Act, 1893, and shall come into operation on the first day of January nineteen hundred and fourteen.

(3) The Principal Act is hereby repealed to the extent specified in the third column of the Schedule to this Act.

Schedule
Amends the principal Act

Statutes Revised

on

Commercial Law
1695 - 1913

Is available from:
Sean E. Quinn, 15 Rathclaren, Bray, Co. Wicklow, Ireland.
Telephone : -353-1-286 7206